Elfhame's Children

The Covenant of Witch and Faery

Veronica Cummer

Pendraig Publishing, Inc

ISBN: 978-1-936922-91-8

Editing by Raven Womack
Book illustrations by Veronica Cummer
Front cover image and Cover design by Helga Hedgewalker
Lyrics "The Fires of Samhain Eve" used by permission from Beth Hansen
Book design by Raven Womack

Printed and bound in the USA

Published by:
Pendraig Publishing, Inc
PO Box 8427
Green Valley Lake, CA 92341
www.pendraigpublishing.com

...shade has communicated with shade
in moments of common memory
that recur like the figures of a dance
in terror or in joy,
but now they run together like to like,
and their covens and fleets
have rhythm and pattern...

-William Butler Yeats The Celtic Twilight 1893

It is as if I were in a trance during the rites;
I can scarcely remember what happened;
something seems to brush against my soul
and I ever think of it with excitement--
the old secrets of joy and terror
quicken my blood.

-Gerald B Gardner Witchcraft Today 1954

∼ Faery Queen Messages ∼

Truth is written in the soul
—but must be written in the Blood

What you love is the brightest star
—follow it

All roads taken, lead to yourself
—and all not taken

Beware fears made flesh
—who holds the power

To lose yourself is the only way to be lost
—remember

All dreams are the same dream
—awaken

Laughter and joy are the greatest weapons
—use them

Sing and shout to change the world
—start within

Dedication

This dedication is an easy one to make.

Of course, I must acknowledge the Muse, for by Her blessing, with the touch of Her hand, inspiration comes, and creation can finally begin in earnest. As mother to what some call the *Unseelie Court*, She knows all about spinning, about the thread which is woven into the All.

I must also acknowledge the bond between myself and my own Fey-other, indeed, between myself and the whole of Faery. Without that bond, I don't know if I would be a witch today. Faery and Fey have guided me, guarded me, and sustained me through many a trial, ordeal, and hardship, even the dangerous turning of a path that once threatened my health and even my life.

I know now that they have been with me since the beginning and never forgot me, even when I couldn't always remember them. When that dread black coach comes again, I shall know it and make my decision as I have made it before, without fear and without hesitation. For when you know and love those from the other side, you have no doubt that you are known and loved there and will be accepted back with open arms to the family, to your Fey brothers and sisters.

As for those here in the world of the living with me, I must dedicate this work to all who encouraged me to "write a book about Faery." After hearing it time and time again from friends, and also from those I had just barely met and who didn't even know me or my history with Faery, well...I got the picture.

I would also like to say thank you to Peter Paddon, who took a chance on my first book and was always friendly and encouraging and inspiring. His dedication to the Craft was honest and true, and he will be sorely missed. I wish this book had been finished in time for Peter to see it, as I always appreciated his insights and thoughts. Sadly, though, that was not to be.

Life and death have a habit of distracting us with their endings and beginnings. The last three years have also seen the passing of one of my parents, the death of a devoted craft-sister of many years, the conclusion of a Pagan gather I've been involved with for two decades, the start of a new job, the loss and betrayal of old friends and the discovery and kindness of new ones. Through it all, my connection to the realm of Faery has endured, and my Fey-other has been there for me, for theirs is a love which never dies.

～ *Legend* ～

The folk who fill the floating air
Come and go through moon swept doors
Set upon the turning edge of time
Their eyes black as dusk and starred divine
For within their souls we come to know
We are such, and thus
By love entwined.

For to see the other side
Is to brave the face within the mirror
The kiss, the tear, the clasp, the touch
Of wrist to wrist and heart to heart
Across two worlds
In promise made, no fear
When you hear the whispered words
We are here
We are here.

A pillared hall to catch the winds
Four and one,
And so the tower sings
Made of crystal, blood and breath
It waits for those who pass the test
And who, in knowing daring come to be
To will themselves beyond themselves
Through the gates
Of ecstasy and need.

The lord of fire and the ghosts of air
Of old, they met and in conspire joined
This place no place
This time no time
Below, afar, within, above
But yet more real than what we see
The ripple of the circle's stone
Raised by laughter

No world alone.

Invisible powers let to fly
Carried on the back of the dragon's storm
First white, then black
Then white once more
Five points of fire, a pentacle
A swan, a mirror, a dove
She lifts her arms to welcome him
Who once
The witches loved, adored.

Incense rises, drifts and spins
Forms shapes upon the air
The God of old his face renewed
By the morning star arose
The illumined field
Where roses, lilies, hawthorn and rue
Grow up where mystery
Fell and pled.

By a circle drawn, by a name reborn
By the eternal pledge of air and flame
It's kept sacred the day
When the stars bowed down
When fire first fell to the land
Burning flesh and burning bone
No pain too great to bear
For choice, for time, forlorn.

For when those who watched
First saw and knew
The earthly daughters of man, beauty truth
And so captured flesh
The starry skies swept down
And clothed the lord of light
The lady in splendid green.

Table of Contents

Introduction

The Gate of Joy and Terror

The fog was cold and rose up from the ground as if called by restless spirits, the breath of the earth. Other spirits shone in the eyes of those pressed close around the fire, those of us yet instilled in flesh, but who had been called back to the service of the Gods, the service of the realms of spirit.

There was no music, no words, just a silent understanding that passed from one to the next. A knowledge that it was time. One by one, we acted upon that knowledge. One by one, we faded into the night, to meet up again in an old place, a ruin, with torches already lit to guide the four quarters to the center. We shivered with anticipation and nervousness, with the chill in the air as if the gates to the Otherworld stood open already. All Hallows, and how could it be otherwise than this? How could so many have forgotten for so very long?

A plate, a cup, a feast promised and surrendered to the night...beginnings and endings. We kiss each other over the ashes of a dying fire, over the last red glow of the most precious embers. Cold outside, but warm within. Warm in the way of all families when they are gathered together. Of such passions and shared joys are shattered chains forged anew and broken stitches mended. We take hands, we touch and know each other as of old. As if no time had passed at all.

Like a plate and a cup left upon an altar of stone. Like candles lit to guard the night. A fire to call and the mists to rise...

It is a spell, wordless and true. A spell of the family, a spell of the blood, a spell to summon them all back again.

To start with, I must admit that I have generally used the term "Fey" in this book when talking about the entities of the realm of Faery, as it has been our experience that they really don't like being called "Fairies," but will tolerate "Fey." This dislike of the name Faery can be seen in a poem written by Robert Chambers, published in the book "*Popular Rhymes of Scotland*" from 1870, a work which tells us that they don't much like the name elf or imp either:

> *Gin ye ca' me imp or elf,*
> *I rede ye look weel to yourself;*
> *Gin ye ca' me fairy,*
> *I'll work ye muckle tarrie;*
> *Gin guid neibour ye ca' me,*
> *Then guid neibour I will be;*
> *But gin ye ca' me seelie wicht,*
> *I'll be your friend baith day and nicht*

The term *wicht* or *wight* is Germanic for "being," while the word *seelie* means happy or blessed, hence "happy beings." Definitely, we'd like to call the Fey happy as we'd prefer they remain that way in their dealings with us if at all possible. No sane person would prefer the Fey to be *unseelie wichts*, non-blessed or unhappy beings, especially if it's us they are unhappy with. Other terms such as the *Gentry*, the *Shining Ones*, the *Good Neighbors*, the *Kindly* or *Gude Folk* and so on are generally more acceptable to them since they are titles and euphemisms rather than being seen as names. Not only that, by using the terms *Good Neighbors* and *Kindly Folk*, we are calling upon their better nature in relationship with us. To be honest, we cannot pronounce their real names since their language is completely inhuman, sounding more like trilling or buzzing or humming or murmuring than anything else.

Down through history, the Fey have been described in a multitude of ways, including being tall or small in stature, beautiful and graceful beyond measure or dreadful, ugly, and utterly terrifying. But the recent vision of them as cute creatures with acorn or flower-blossom hats, striped tights, and butterfly-like sparkling wings owes rather more to Victorian sensibilities and children's stories and modern interpretations than anything else. It is a recent permutation that we have placed upon them and they might play it our way...or not.

They feel that we tend to reduce them in size and equate them with pretty things in order to try and make them less frightening. This doesn't mean that they *can't* appear in such a fashion—for they are shapeshifters—but, if they do, it would be more as a joke or to prove some kind of point for they are, ever and always, tricksy in nature.

In reality, visions of the Fey are beyond easy acceptance or understanding, and they can take on many forms, or no form at all. They can be a whirl of leaves passing by, a swirl of dark water, a tiny dancing light in the dark woods, strange thin creatures appearing in your bedroom in the middle of the night, or even a very elf-like figure peering around the trunk of a tree through mist and moonlight. They can appear as dark figures, walking past a lit window moving shadows beyond the reach of a campfire, a glimpse of a face outside a window. Or they can remain unseen but present all the same.

I never saw them in any particular form beyond that of shifting shadows and unseen presences when I was young, but now I know that the Fey have always been with me. I had no name for them as a child, as I had no name for the rituals and beliefs that I held. They simply were there, my companions of the shadows, of twilight, of the woodlands I played in and of my most precious dreams. I ran with them. I *flew* with them. I just *knew* things. I worked magick and built an altar with a huge old rock and a pig's skull. I roamed with the cats through the brush and grass and felt at one with the Earth. Out there, in the night, roaming through the trees of the apple orchard or sitting on the swing set to listen to the rustling of the corn leaves, I somehow sensed I wasn't really alone.

All of this was natural to me and to my life, but I didn't talk about it with anyone else. It seemed far removed from what I was being taught about God, about religion, about how the world should work. Looking back now, I realize that I knew nothing about Paganism when I was young, except what I believed was Pagan. All I knew consciously of witches and Faery was what I read in books and saw in movies and on television, but I practiced the Craft and interacted with the Fey purely and instinctively. I just didn't have a name for it, for what I believed and what I did.

No one in my family taught me these things. The knowledge came naturally, subtly, creeping in as though it just belonged in my life. Even as I tried and tried to make myself a good little Catholic girl and failed miserably, I worshiped the night and the moon and fancied myself a creature of the wilds and of magick. I lived in two worlds that seemed to have nothing to do with each other. One was what I should believe—or so I was being told by my parents, teachers, nuns, and priests—and one was what I really believed and no explanation or argument seemed necessary.

And so I looked up at the night sky and prayed to the moon, calling her *Mother Moon, Mother Moon, Mother Moon*...just as, now, I call Her *Ama Luna, Ama Luna, Ama Luna*. To me, she was my secret mother. At the same time, the darkness was my secret home, never frightening but mysterious and welcoming. I would stand outside, craning my head back as far as I could, staring out into the stars, and each of those distant lights symbolized my kindred of the spirit, my brothers, my sisters. I longed for them. I longed to be with them. I would be filled with deep wonder and sadness; two feelings wrapped tightly around each other, feelings that no one else seemed to have but me.

My secret nights molded me as much as my daylight life. Yet the disconnect between the two worlds grew bigger as I grew up, as I had no context in which to make the two work as one. So, in time, I forgot my secret night-time life and friends. Until, years later, I ran into people who called themselves witches and pagans. I was immediately drawn to all of it with an air of...oh, there you are. Here's a name for what I've always done and thought and felt and didn't think anybody else could ever understand. After that, I tried out both eclectic and traditional groups until I was trained and initiated into a coven whose main goal was to rediscover what had been lost from the Craft we'd inherited, which included the ancient relationship between witch and Faery.

In that coven, we talked about our experiences with strange beings that we suspected were the Fey and, one Beltane, we did a ritual outdoors at the edge of a woods. Those of us on the east side of the circle grew colder and colder as the ritual went on—while everyone else was fine—and we kept hearing these sounds out in the darkness, the snapping of twigs as though someone was creeping around our circle. At first, we tried to convince ourselves that it was just branches falling, but eventually, it became obvious that we weren't alone. Later that night, some of us had disturbing dreams, and we decided to do some hypnosis work to get to the heart of what happened that night. The commonality between what was discovered and those "dreams" was much too perfect to be mere coincidence, including the remembrance of exact words.

It was after this that we decided to do a ritual to make direct contact with the Fey. We hung a mask to the east of the circle and we "sang," using free-form toning, and sent out our wish for the Fey to talk to us. This was the very first time that I had the experience of channeling or being possessed. The Fey came and spoke through me and, after that ritual, it was a rare event that one of them—or they as a collective spirit—didn't come through in our circles. We were told that this was how it was supposed to be—that the Fey had been waiting a long, long time for us to remember and renew our bond with them. That they had never forgotten...but that, to their great sorrow and pain, we had forgotten for such a long time.

After this, the Fey, as well as the gods, took an active part in helping us in our journey of rediscovery of what had been lost. If connecting to the Craft had been familiar, a homecoming of sorts, then communing with Faery was the same a thousand-fold. They were there with us in every circle. They appeared to us in meditation work and in our bedrooms in the middle of the night, when we would wake in a strange state of trance that was heralded by a feeling of absolute fear...before we realized who was there in the shadows with us and all we had to do was open up and accept the experience for that fear to turn to joy. They stood with us and within us and linked their magick to our own.

It was beautiful and terrifying in turn, a wild ride, as we forged a new connection to them. As we began to remember what we had long forgotten, and Faery opened its gateway to us. For that's what keeps us from Faery, from being able to cross over the veil and come back with magick and knowledge of all kinds—a curse of forgetfulness. A forgetting of not just the Fey, but a forgetting of who and what we are.

Through this, I realized that they had been the ones who were with me when I was a child. That they were why I had never felt alone in the darkness. They were who I'd longed for when I stared up at the stars in the night sky until my neck ached. They were the ones I was writing poems about. They were part of the "home" that I missed and dreamed of, what

I finally realized was the realm of Faery, the realm where witches and the Fey dance together under the spinning stars.

As Faery doesn't forget us, neither does Faery ever leave us. There are many fantasy and folklore stories about the passing of the elves, the closing of the gates of Faery, yet this is a metaphor really for something that we did ourselves. We chose to forget Faery and so the elves "left" and the gates "closed." We eventually came to think the veil between the worlds an almost insurmountable barrier, that there was life and death and a wall between them, yet we have always had it within us to reach across that boundary.

For even as we saw that land become misty and distant, even as some of us went so far as to deny it, it was never any further than an indrawn breath, the silence between moments, a circle created in a place that is not a place, in a time that is not a time. For the circle lies, as we've always heard tell of, *between the worlds*. We can see this in-betweenness when we experience the Fey sneaking peeks at us from around a corner that simply can't exist, from the depths of a bright doorway that has opened up in the middle of nowhere, a rip in the fabric of what we learned to call reality, when it is but a pale shade of true reality.

Elfhame is an old word for the land of Faery, a twilight world ruled by the beautiful and dangerous moon-pale Queen of Elfhame and by a *Lord of Shadows* sometimes known simply as the Horned One. Elfhame means *Elf-Home* and is one of the names for the land of Faery. What we tend to know about Faery we get from folklore, from stories that go back into the mists of the unknown, but we also know about Faery because many of us have been there. Our conscious minds may not remember all of the time or only recall bits and pieces—even things that may seem shockingly nonsensical—but some part of us knows.

The child within each of us remembers Faery, is eternally enraptured by it and by those who dwell there. When we can see like that child, we can see the Fey and dwell in Faery. To be a hedgewitch or cunning one, we *have* to see and know in both worlds, to walk that edge, one foot here and one foot there, half in joy and half in terror.

We may grow up and away from Faery, becoming distracted by the concerns of this world, trusting in the religion of science and rationalism, all that would deny what it can't see, scorning the world of spirits, of the gods, of the Fey, and the world that lies wrapped closely with our own as two lovers, skin to skin, two hearts beating as one. But we can go back, reclaim, remember, for the Fey never went away, they cannot and will not ever leave us. We are a part of them, just as they are a part of us, evolving together, even as some of us live in the seen and others in the unseen. For what binds us together is love; love of family and love of other, and there is no greater power.

But there are problems when discussing Faery and the Fey, especially in such a concrete language as English. So much of Faery is mutable, both at the whim and need and desire of the Fey themselves and by our own expectations, fancies, and necessities. One might say that Faery is half what we would see and half what they would have us see, and any and all of that is likely to change. It also tends to be a mask for a greater, more mysterious, truths that can't otherwise be told or known save in poetry, art, songs, dreams, and visions.

This book will primarily concentrate on those of the Fey we have histories of interacting with the most—those of the light and those of the dark, what some call the Seelie and the Unseelie. In forming relationships with both the light and the dark Fey, the form this communication and interaction takes is different for how they see things and what makes them tick are very different, from us and from each other. In order to interact with them, we must understand those differences as best we can and especially try not to place human thought processes on them. For the Fey are not human. They are infinitely familiar, but not human.

We know, deep down, the face of our Fey-lover, our Fey-husband, our Fey-wife...our most beloved Fey-other. Companion, guardian, advisor, brother, and sister in magick, the one who knows us best, the one who loves us dearly. The one that, once we remember them, we remember ourselves, and will never be truly alone again. It can be said then; there are no witches who are ever really alone, for each of us has our Fey-other with us and, with them, we can journey to their land, to Faery.

Those who become aware of the spirit that resides within may call it forth and send it to other realms, other lands, other worlds. For all things, physical have immortal spirits. The outer form may change with belief and knowledge and will, but the spirit within is eternal. It springs from the source and returns to it once again, and yet is never parted from it. The spirit can journey, with Fey knowledge, across all of time, knowing that linear time is an illusion, that separation is an illusion. For the concept we hold of time springs from a belief about time and as we believe and know in greater ways, so time is altered and the idea of past and future fall away.

Still, in the embrace of linear time, we experience loss and death, life and rebirth. We participate in the story that springs forth from the paradox, the promise that is the *source*. Yet when we learn to see as the Fey see, this change of perception changes everything and nothing at the same time. We can see both the passage of time and the eternity of that which lies hidden. This is true knowledge, neither learned nor earned, but just known as Faery just knows.

Through our desire and our efforts years ago, the *Gates of Faery* opened to our coven, and we each walked willingly through that gate and never looked back. We couldn't. Because once you've walked through that door willingly and consciously, you can't ever go back for it is a true initiation, a death to your old life and a birth to your new one. That would be the biggest warning I have regarding dealing with the Fey—that once you start down this path with them, you will never be the same again. You will not be able to go back to how you looked at the world before you made the choice to honor this ancient covenant, to reclaim it, to make it part of you, blood and breath and bone.

∾ *The Little Ones* ∾

Sweet fresh milk and pancakes
Yellow as the sun
Left upon a hillside
Where the shadows run
The little ones of twilight
On those who give them least

They shall have the final fun
They shall make their feast.

Oh watch out they're coming
To take you for a ride
As horse or or man or golden straw
Trisksey their delight
Name them at your own risk
They shall mock your pride
The Picktree Brag, the Dunnie, and the Hedley Kow.

From laughter in the deep wells
Howling on the moors
Ghostly haunts at sunset
Scratching at the doors
Prayer cannot protect you
Their games are old as time
Cold as graven darkness
Wild as berry wine.

Oh watch out they're coming
To take you for a ride
As horse or man or golden straw
Trisksey their delight
Name them at your own risk
They shall mock your pride
The Picktree Brag, the Dunnie, and the Hedley Kow.

Should you see straw a dancing
A horse as black as soot
Preying on the good folk
Turning their good luck
When empty lies the hearth place
And from its depths they peer

Know that death is merry
When ye have naught to fear.

Chapter 1

Never What They Seem

"You say we are glamour, but what do you know of glamour?
We hold what is true and you clothe it in what you believe is true.
You make what you believe as truth and we, as kin to you and to your
dream, see what you dream become as reality. We hold all as reality,
all as truth. We will believe as you believe for you are masters of the
art. But you must believe strong and utterly and honestly and without
fear. Otherwise, your fears will color what is and make monsters out
of the drift of shadows.

We exist in shadow. We drift on the winds and change and change
again, but we do not forget what lies behind all change. You call this by
many names, and some of them are Her, though she is not a she. Fate
has no gender, no face, no name. Fate is beyond all shadow and all
light. Even those of the North do not entirely understand Her, though
they know better than most. When you are as old as they, perhaps you
will see more clearly...if that be your destiny.

Through all we know, all we have seen, all we have hoped, this is our
brightest and best hope. For though we know, we do not know, what
will be when knowledge ends, and hope is all that remains."

-The Fey

Wheels in the sky. Circles in the grain. Little green men. Little grey men.
Aliens. Leprechauns. Flying saucers. Pretty butterfly-winged figures.
Squat little men with pointed red hats and long beards. White ladies
like ghosts in the night. Sorrowful figures washing bloody clothes in
a rushing stream. Black horses with laughing, dreadful eyes. Shadowy
hooded figures with skeletal fingers. Work-a-day builders of shoes and
tricksy weavers of horse's manes and tails. A shining court riding by in a
jangle of bells. Tall and small, elegant, earthy, ethereal, shining and dark,
floating, rushing, spinning, flying, terrible and mysterious, no one can
pin the Fey down to be just one thing.

Some of their euphemisms include the *Gentry*, the *Good Folk*, the *Guld
Neighbors*, the *Grey Neighbors*, the *People of Peace*, the *Little Ones*, the
Hill Folk, the *Wee Folk*, the *Rushing Horde*, the *Shining Ones*. Their
names are also numerous, as numerous as they are odd and whimsical,
strange and scary. Some express where they are said to reside and some,
what they do, both the good and the bad. Some attempt to capture their
incredible beauty and some serve to warn of their inhuman cruelty.

Like their names, the descriptions of the Fey are also changeable and
diverse. They are as diverse as the many cultures that have existed across
the world and down through time for they are known on every continent
and have co-existed with us back into the unknown and nameless darkness that lies at the heart of history and of mystery. Sometimes, they are
viewed as kindly and friendly and sometimes as angry and even wicked.
They can be helpful and harmful in equal measure, and always dangerous to cross.

The Fey can be caught drifting upon the wayward swirl of the air or
riding and roaring upon the wings of a storm. They can be seen drifting
in the secret currents and tangled water weeds of some stream or in the
white foam of a churning river. They can be found in the dark caverns
and mines of the earth, keepers of jewels and hidden knowledge, brothers and sisters to the great dragons of old. They can ride out on tall and
pale horses, with their own ghost-white and blood-red hounds at their
call, moving to the sound of bells and secret songs that, once heard, you
can never quite remember and never quite forget. Or they can be found
dancing and feasting in great gleaming courts below the hills or in soft

meadows lit by the moon, leaving behind Faery rings of mushrooms or circles of dark grass hidden in the heart of a woods.

The Fey can appear as dancing lights in the distance that might lead you deep into the moors or into a swamp. As a shock of straw laying by the roadside that, if you pick it up, would grow heavier and heavier until you are forced to put it down, at which point it would jump up and laugh at you. They could take the seeming of a black horse and, once you climbed on their back, you couldn't get unstuck again, not even once the "horse" rushed into a lake or stream and attempted to drown you. They can appear as small homely people deep in the mines, puttering around your home or barn, even making those ever-fabled shoes. Or they can hide under rocks, only emerging to drink down the offerings of milk left for them or to eat an oaten cake made by someone who wanted their favor.

The Fey might choose to look like inhumanly tall beings with painfully thin limbs and impossibly pointed faces peering around the edge of nowhere, as beautiful women with the faces of foxes, shape-shifting seal people, as fanged creatures with a taste for human flesh. Or they can show up as handsome men who seduce unwary women so that they literally die for love of him. They can be called to attend to the birth of a child in order to bestow blessings, to name the fate of the new baby. They can be found combing out their hair by the river, washing the clothing of the soon to be dead at the ford, or stealing away children—the more lovely and golden-haired the child the better to make a Fey-bride—and leaving behind the famed fussy changeling.

But Fey encounters don't just belong to the stories of the past. Over the years, quite a few of us have seen the Fey while attending a gather in a secluded area or when doing a ritual outside or even while camping or hiking or staying at a cabin in a park. After the initial reaction of astonishment and even disbelief, of fear and uncertainty, we acknowledge and honor them, and so our experiences have been positive for the most part. We have a context to place them in because of our Pagan beliefs and so can more readily accept that what we have seen and experienced is real.

A friend of mine once saw one of the Fey in the forest. He was fishing in a river and sensed he was not alone. When he turned to look behind him, he saw a little nut-brown man with a gnarled face standing by the edge of the woods. He glanced back at the river, then at the woods again, but the little man had vanished. Another friend has seen the Fey for years. Generally, she sees one who is tall and very thin that she has long called "skinny man," while the other ones, the little Fey who tend to scurry around, she calls "Charlie Brown heads." I have seen both of these types. Quite often, I have been woken up in the middle of the night to find tall, pale figures standing around me and, when I reach out to them, feel their fingers close round my own.

It doesn't help that there is a lot of confusion these days over what a "Faery" is, even over how to spell it. Faery. Fairy. Fey. Fae. Fee. Not to mention, all of the fantastical names for various types of Fey. One fabulous English list has always been my favorite and can be found in *The Denham Tracts* by Michael Denham published in 1892 and 1895, with some of the names previously having appeared in *The Discovery of Witchcraft* by Reginald Scot. Not all of the creatures appearing on this list are considered to be Fey, but a goodly portion of them are.

...when the whole earth was so overrun with ghosts, boggles, bloody-bones, spirits, demons, ignis fatui, brownies, bug-bears, black dogs, spectres, shellycoats, scarecrows, witches, wizards, barguests, Rob-in-Goodfellows, hags, night-bats, scrags, breaknecks, fantasms, hob-goblins, hobhoulards, boggy-boes, dobbies, hob-thrusts, fetches, kelpies, warlocks, mock-beggers, mum-pokers, Jemmy-burties, urchins, satyrs, pans, fauns, sirens, tritons, centaurs, calcars, nymphs, imps, incubasses, spoorns, men-in-the-oak, hell-wains, fire-drakes, kit-a-can-sticks, Tom-tumblers, melch-dicks, larrs, kitty-witches, hobby-lanthorns, Dick-a-Tuesdays, Elf-fires, Gyl-burnt-tails, knockers, elves, raw-heads, Meg-with-the-wads, old-shocks, ouphs, pad-foois, pixies, pictrees, giants, dwarfs, Tom-pokers, tutgots, snapdragons, sprets, spunks, conjurers, thurses, spurns, tantarrabobs, swaithes, tints, tod-low-ries, Jack-in-the-Wads, mormos, changelings, redcaps, yeth-hounds, colt-pixies, Tom-thumbs, black-bugs, boggarts, scar-bugs, shag-foals, hodge-pochers, hob-thrushes, bugs, bull-beggers, bygorns, bolls, caddies, bomen, brags, wraithes, waffs, flay-boggarts, fiends, gallytrots, imps, gytrashes, patches, hob-and-lanthorns, gringes, boguests, bonelesses, Peg-powlers, pucks, fays, kidnappers, gally-beggers, hudskins, nickers, nacks (necks), waiths, miffies, buckies, gholes, sylphs, guests, swarths,

freiths, freits, gy-carlins (gyre-carling), pigmies, chittifaces, nixies, Jinny-burnt-tails, dudmen, hell-hounds, dopple-gangers, boggleboes, bogies, redmen, portunes, grants, hobbits, hobgoblins, brown-men, cowies, dunnies, wirrikows, alholdes, mannikins, follets, korreds, puckles, korigans, sylvans, succubuses, black-men, shadows, banshees, lianhanshees, clappernappers, Gabriel-hounds, mawkins, doubles, corpse lights or candles, scrats, mahounds, trows, gnomes, sprites, fates, fiends, sybils, nick-nevins, whitewomen, fairies, thrummy-caps, cutties, and nisses...

It's quite telling that some of the beings on this list are generally considered evil spirits such as the *incubus* and the *succubus*. *Hag* would also fall under that same grouping as a creature once said to lay on top of you at night and suck the life out of you, a being also known as the night-hag or nightmare. Hag is also related to the word *heagtesse* and *heag*, meaning hedge-rider or hedge and equates not just to the Fey but to those witches who interact with both the human community and supernatural beings of all sorts. The hedge, of course, represents the boundary between worlds, that which a hedgewitch or hedge-rider traverses.

Others on this list are magickal people like *witches* and *wizards* and *conjurers* and *sybils*. Some are Greek creatures such as *nymphs, satyrs, sirens,* and *centaurs*. *Nick-nevins* is obviously related to the Scottish goddess of the Wild Hunt, Nicknevin, once related to the Fey and later said to keep company with demons. Along the same line, *pans* are clearly from the Greek god, Pan. *Gy-carlin* or *gyre-carling* also are associated with Nicknevin, especially since *carlin* is another name for a witch. This can be found in the words from an old reel of the 1600's equated to the Witches of North Berwick:

Cummer, go ye before
Cummer, go ye
If ye willna go before,
Cummer let me.
Ring-a-ring a-widdershins,
Linkin' lithely widdershins,
Cummer, carlin, crone and queen,
Roun' go we.

Fire-drakes are not dragons, but Fey who are attached to the male of the household. He honors the drake, and the drake brings luck and plenty to the home and family. Other names for this type of Fey include *Dracs* or *Drachen* and their association with fire is because they look like a flame when they fly around.

Some names are different spellings of the same sort of creature such as with *pixies* and *pictrees* (one variation missing from this already vast list is *piskies*). They could also be called *urchins* for their liking to change themselves into the shape of hedgehogs. *Gabriel-hounds* or *yeth-hounds* are the creatures who travel with the Wild Hunt or the Old Horned God. While *gholes* we might better know today as "ghouls." *Hobbits* were made famous by the works of J.R.R. Tolkien, while we can also recognize a few other names from the recent popular Harry Potter books by J.K. Rowling, most especially *dobbies, pad-fooits,* and *boggarts.*

Hobs and *hobgoblins* and *hobthrusts* are mainly human-friendly, tricksy in nature, yet still helpful to people. Of course, in recent times, the name *hobgoblin* and *goblin* has taken on a much more sinister note, partially from their depiction through the writings of Tolkien, various movies, and stories, as well as via gaming. Like the original *hobgoblins, portunes* are also friendly, lucky, and helpful Fey, with some similarities to the household brownies. They were said to be tiny folk, much akin to *Tom Thumbs,* one of the Fey who inspired the fairytale by the same name.

A few other interesting names on this list include *kidnappers* and *black-men,* especially in light of the UFO-alien abduction mythos of flying saucers and little green (or grey) men from "out there," a form that the Fey have transformed into for some who interact with them that is based on modern sensibilities and fears. For, as of old, the unwary who encounter the Fey or who foolishly sleep on a *Faery Hill* might wake to find themselves in another world, just as people today are abducted from their beds or from their cars on a lonely road somewhere—losing time and experiencing terror or wonder or both. While, not only are the *Men In Black* famous in UFO conspiracy circles these days, but also have ties back to witchcraft in the *Black Man* who would appear at the sabbats, sometimes also described as a "Moor" or a "Moorish man."

Waffs or *waiths* or *wraiths* are similar to *doubles* and *dopple-gangers.*

They are all names for co-walkers, a figure that can be seen by those with the "Second Sight" and who looks exactly like the man or woman they accompany or foreshadow. Sometimes this figure would appear before the person shows up and sometimes they would appear after they left, almost like an echo.

Black dogs are still known to appear to some and are sometimes called *hell-hounds* or *Faery dogs*, but sometimes Faery dogs are also described as being white with red ears, and there are also, even fairly recently, people in England who claim to have seen giant black cats, the famous *cait-sidhe*. A vision of the black dog was often seen as a forewarning or a death-omen, so it's not surprising that they also became equated with hellhounds. There are also stories about Faery cats being representative of death.

Shag-foals, brags, grants, boggles, barguests, and *bogies* are somewhat sinister Fey who generally like to shape-shift into black shaggy horses or dogs. They range from the merely mischievous to the truly terrifying. Another form of *boggle,* more on the mischievous side is the *shellycoat,* a Fey who lives near the water and is covered with shells, hence the name. The *barguest,* on the other hand, is a black dog with huge red eyes and a definite foreshadowing of impending death. A *mumpoker* is another kind of dangerous bogie, one often used to scare children into good behavior.

Corpse-lights, corpse candles, hobby-lanthorns or *hob-and-lanthorns, ignis fatui, spunks,* and *Elf-fires* are other names for the *Will O' the Wisp,* the Fey lights that appear in the night, often to lead the unwary astray into a bog or marsh. *Lanthorn* is an old word for the lantern, while a *wad* is a torch and a *hob* is part of the hearth. It was these Faery lights that gave birth to the modern Jack O' Lanterns that you see around Hallow-een. Some claim that these lights are the souls of those being taken away by the Fey to the Otherworld. Jack O'Lanthorn was King of the Pixes in Cornish mythology and matched to Joan the Wad, the Queen of the Pixies. Jack and Joan were the names used to indicate gender in the past (as well as Jack and Gill, from which we get the famous Jack and Jill who went up the hill), the same as when we use John or Jane today.

Korreds are underworld Fey, living in caves or beneath standing stones. They are said to have great magickal power, including the gift of foretelling the future. They are one of the Fey about which you are warned not to join in their dances lest you end up dancing yourself to death. Much more immediately frightening, though, are the Fey who haunt deep pits or pools, such as *rawheads* and *bloody-bones,* Fey who are said to grab unwary children and drag them down to the depths.

Other dangerous Fey include *Peg Powler,* a name for a particular water Fey who would drown you if she gets half a chance, just like her fellows, *Nellie Long-Arms* and *Jenny Greenteeth.* The Fey of ponds and lakes and rivers were supposed to be especially notorious for their dangerous qualities and predilections. This held true, as well, for the supernatural ocean Fey such as *mermaids* and *selkies,* not to forget the *sirens* whose beautiful singing would draw sailors to run their ships right up on the rocks.

Redcaps are also considered quite dangerous for the "red" of their caps is said to be colored by blood. Though, it's also possible that the term refers to the red caps of the traditional Faery mushroom, the *amanita muscaria* with its red cap and white spots. We probably have all seen images of tiny Fey figurines depicted with actual red and white mushroom caps or sitting on a large red and white mushroom. They may look cute, but this Faery mushroom has a long association with shamanistic practice, particularly with undertaking the risky, sometimes even deadly, trance journey to the Otherworld.

These are but a few names and types of Fey, for creatures like the Fey can be found throughout the world. In fact, you could fill entire books with stories and descriptions of them as they are depicted down through the centuries, as well as from land to land and people to people. For example, the Middle Eastern version of Elfhame is known as *Jinnestan,* the otherworldly home to light and dark Fey known as *deevs* and *peries.* There is also the *djinn,* from which we get the modern idea of genies. Like the Fey of other lands, the Middle Eastern Fey are shape-shifters that are older than humankind; some considered friendly to us and some dangerous. Like the Fey we know from Europe, they are said to be able to travel in the whirlwind and, if they have children with people, those sons and daughters have magickal powers. We would call them shamans or witches.

Middle Eastern Fey were demonized under Islam, just as the Fey of

Europe were demonized under Christianity. So, it's hardly surprising that some old depictions of so-called "demons" looks amazingly akin to how the Fey were once imagined to appear, especially in some surviving woodcuts. Doubtless, this relates to the Christian-influenced myth that says the Fey are those angels who fell from heaven and were not good enough to return above but were not evil enough to be condemned to the below. Or you could go with the other story that says that God was so concerned that all of the angels were leaving with Lucifer that He slammed the gates of both heaven and hell shut and those who were somewhere between ended up taking residence in the earth, sky, and waters. Clearly, there is a kernel of truth behind these stories, especially since the Fey are so closely linked to nature and the Elements.

Today, many people who do not have a context that includes interaction with Faery can experience the Fey as "aliens." Where once people saw a crew of "little men in green" who took them away beneath the fabulous hollow hills, some now see a crew of "little green men" (or grey) who take them away to a fabulous UFO or flying saucer. Where some once saw the Seelie Court and the Unseelie Court, others now see the "Nordics" and the "Greys," and believe they are experimenting on us or that we are unwittingly caught up in a war between the two alien races.

At the same time, we are fed the idea that Faery isn't real. The tall shining elves in white robes, the ax-wielding rustic dwarves, the butterfly-winged petite Fey with flower petal dresses and a sprinkling of sparkly magick dust fill our children's stories but do not give rise to an adult view and version of the Fey once we grow up. Only in fantasy stories do we some- times see a more complex version of the Fey meant for adult consump- tion. Still, even this is labeled as "escape" fiction because, of course, the land of Faery and the Fey aren't real.

It's human blindness, ego blindness, that leads us to believe that we are alone on this planet. Not only do we share it with countless numbers of living beings, plants, fish, birds, animals, and other creatures so tiny we can't see them without the aid of modern technology, but we also share it with spiritual beings that are even more difficult to see. To learn to see, we must seek out and seduce our inner talents and sensibilities, ones that many of our ancestors once knew and made good use of. We must trust our instincts and break free of the limitations that the modern world of science and reason has placed on our vision.

Children are said to have an easier time seeing the Fey than the majority of adults. All of those "rational" filters haven't snapped into place yet, and the world is still a place where anything can happen, a place of continual discovery and enchantment. Children also still have the power of belief behind them. They can more easily slip into that place of magick and the fantastical, of whimsy and wonder, that the Fey also inhabit.

When we grow up, most of us tend to lose that essential sense of enchantment and wonder, and the veil comes down over our eyes, over our minds, and we doubt what our spiritual senses tell us about Faery. We don't believe, and so we don't see. We are indoctrinated into thinking that something must be proven by scientific and rational means in order to actually exist. Our belief is based on only that which can be proven by those same means, and we tend to discount our personal experiences that contradict the reality created by the majority viewpoint.

Which doesn't mean, of course, that we have to turn our backs on the world that science and reason have created. We must expand it, take back what has been lost of the knowledge and insights of the past, and go forward with something that partakes of the best of both. In so doing, not only will we be able to see Faery again but see in Faery what we need to see to continue to explore and expand the boundaries of understanding of this world and of the universe.

How we see influences what we see, and Faery is very changeable in part because of that. Yes, the Fey are very tricksy and inclined to be fluid, but each of us and our cultural viewpoint, our cultural "filters" helps shape how Faery appears as a "place" and how the Fey we interact with seem to look like. Faery is both how and is not we perceive it to be. There is something continuous about Faery and the Fey, but this appearance transforms according to the time, the place, the culture, expectation, and need. Hence, the variety we have in descriptions of the land of Faery and of the Fey depends, in part, on us, on our imaginations, but we are only putting a mask on something that is otherwise incomprehensible.

Faery transforms as our world transforms. The Fey change as we change.

Both our needs and the needs of Faery come together to form the basis for our experiences of the Fey and form a foundation for an even greater need—the transformation of the Earth and the evolution of all who live here, both physically and spiritually. We are all in this together, even though the Fey have actually been here long before we appeared on the scene. The Fey are, after all, the *First Children*, the *Elder Children*. We are the younger ones, brighter and more vibrant in some ways, as volatile and potentially as destructive as we are creative.

Yet, just as we must remain true to our deepest selves, so they remain true to theirs. The masks that they wear are always in flux. They are like the shimmer of moonlight on the water, the play of sunlight on leaves, and the dance and drift of the distant stars. But there remains something stern and real and vital behind all of that—their essential nature. But knowing all this, what precisely, is that nature?

As they are so mutable, can we ever truly understand them? And what do personal accounts and folklore tell us about them? Is it all just our imagination playing tricks on us, or is there something more to it, something that only our imaginations can help us see?

What is essentially true is that the Fey, like the gods and other spirits, often work with the images and understandings of our unconscious minds. They appear clothed by our imagination, by our expectations, by what is necessary for us to comprehend them. This doesn't mean that we imagine the Fey, only that how they appear to us is influenced by the power of our creativity and imagination. The Fey are not imaginary, but they can take on the form of what is imaginary in order to be able to interact with us.

The Fey *are* real and here and with us. They are tied up with us in mutual need and affection. Our fates are intertwined, just as our worlds are intertwined. They are our *Elder-brothers* and *Elder-sisters*, and the world that they inhabit is the *Elder-land*. It's the metaphysical pattern from which our world takes its physical form, as a projection of the spiritual realm beyond normal vision, the "place" we call the otherworld or Faery.

The way we see the Fey is how they project into our world, into our means of perception—be it from the five mundane senses or those considered more extraordinary that some are naturally born with or that others cultivate in their spiritual quests. So their true form remains ever strange to us, even as we court each other, as we grow in acceptance and understanding of our essential kinship. Still, some deep part of us knows them no matter their guise.

Sometimes this deep, unconscious recognition can take the form of faith in beneficial plant spirits, luck spirits, even in angels, and sometimes it sparks deep-rooted fears, rousing a paranoia to see demonic beings as the cause for every bit of bad luck or illness. The gist of all of this is that some part of us just *knows* that we are not alone here. The way that this manifests is dependent upon cultural and religious expectations and inner desires and fears, in particular how we deal with the unknown, with the mysterious.

Which isn't to say that there aren't angelic beings or even demonic ones, but that the whole thing can easily become muddled. Where one person might see a guardian angel, another might see their Fey-other looking out for them. Where one might see the Wild Hunt passing by being led by a faery or witch goddess or an ancient king, another might see hellhounds and Satan himself on some red-eyed, fire-breathing black horse. Where some see an elf peering out at them from a brilliant door of light, others might see an alien intending to kidnap them for some unpleasant medical experimentation. This results in confusion not only for those involved but those seriously trying to have a discussion about the Fey.

Faery glamour reveals the Fey to us and conceals them at the same time. We and they decide how they will be perceived. We find ourselves looking at it, seeming to seek clues as to not just their nature, but our own. Why do they appear like fantasy elves to some and like aliens from space to another? Why do some find the experience enlightening and others, frightening?

The truth is that the doors to Faery lie through joy or through terror, through extremes of emotional reaction that opens us up to vision. We have the power to choose which gate we will use. If we don't make that choice consciously, our unconscious self will choose for us. Our cultural expectations will choose for us. The Fey will make use of either gate, so the choice really is up to us.

For example, despite years of interacting with them, sometimes I find myself waking up abruptly in the wee hours of the night—for some reason, they tend to show up at around 4 am—and find that I'm not alone. I can still feel scared half to death, frozen, my heart racing, hardly able to breathe as I see the figures standing in my bedroom, moving closer to me, leaning over me. The feeling is intense, overwhelming, instinctual, as you are filled with the fear of the unknown, of the inexplicable. It takes an absolute act of will and trust to push past that, to reach out to those figures, to say to them "yes...I'm listening...yes..."

It takes the courage of a witch.

Once you manage that, accept it, make that leap, the state of absolute fear snaps. It disappears and is replaced with wonder instead. Where there was terror, there is now joy. The gate to Faery is transformed as our experience of the Fey transform, as they become not invaders but welcome guests, deeply familiar no matter their form. For the form only matters in so far as it opens that door.

Meditation to Meet Your Fey-other

Love creates spirits, including the Fey.
Not physical love...
which creates a body for the spirit to enter into this world,
but the love between two spirits.
Spirits are created from love.
The Fey are created from love.
Like the light of dawn breaking over the horizon.
Like a child's laughter breaking into a million pieces
which became the Fey.

You can either have someone read the following meditation or record it to play back for your own individual work.

Start by making yourself as comfortable as possible. Sit or lie

down in a comfortable position and begin to pay attention to your breathing.

Breathe in and out slowly, allowing your body to relax further with each breath. Feel only your breathing—long, slow, calm, gentle. Relax further with each breath. Relax. Relax. Relax.

Picture a full moon. A great pale moon in the middle of a deep black sky filled with stars near and far

Let the moon's light fill your vision until all you see is its ghostly pale light. Let it get inside you, a gentle soft touch. Let it fill your body, your veins. A cool, calming touch.

See only that pale glow. Hear only my voice. Feel only your breathing making you lighter and lighter. Making you feel calm and peaceful. Nothing else matters. Not here. Not now.

With each breath in and out, the moon glow flows through your blood, making you feel light, making you feel as through you are drifting. The weight of your body falling away, the weight of the earth no longer holding you.

A shape begins to form in the silver light, a shape round like the moon. It flattens and sharpens into a large mirror. An old mirror. An ancient mirror, tarnished around the edges.

You look at the surface of the mirror, but it is empty, blank, devoid of any reflection.

Stare into the mirror and know it is more than a mirror, more than just a flat surface.

As you look deeply into it, the tarnish around the edges of the mirror begin to move, to shift, to drift. It turns into a mist, into smoke and shadows that twist and move almost like living things, forming ever-changing shapes.

Something begins to move within the depths of the mirror, some-thing beyond the mist.

You reach out to the mirror and there is no longer a hard surface there. You fingers pass beyond the edge. You feel the mists curl and twine around your fingers, cool and soft, silky and comforting.

Then you feel another touch upon the very tips of your fingers. A small electric feeling as long fingers carefully slide along your own. As they intertwine with your own.

A hand grips your hand and you know this touch. You know

this feeling. You know who this is. You've always known. Just as they have always known.

The mists swirl and part and you see a face looking back at you. You know this face. You know the eyes staring deeply into your own. Just as they know you.

This is your Fey-other. Your Fey-match. Your guardian and your protector. Th eone who knows you best. Who will love you for ever.

Look into the eyes of your Fey-other as they look into you.

See the message in their eyes. Hear the message in your mind. Feel the message in your heart.

(remain silent for a time)

It's time to return. Time to withdraw. To leave the embrace of Faery.

Yet, even as you must leave, know the Faery and your Fey-other yet lies within you and will never leave you. That your Fey-other is always with you, just a whisper, just a breath, just a finger-tip away.

Before you leave, ask your Fey-other for a name, a sign, a symbol, a song, a phrase-whatever means they wish you to use to contact them. This is for you and your fey-other alone, your secret compact.

Take a deep breath and let it out slowly. Loosen your grip on upir Fey-other and feel their fingers quietly slip from your own. Watch as the face of your Fey-other drifts back, back beyond the mists.

As you pull your hand back, the mists slow and stop, turning back into tarnish. The mirror becomes blank and flat and empty. Just a mirror again.

Take another breath and let it out slowly. A silver glow begins to come fro the mirror. A silver glow fills your vision and ever so gently pulls back to reveal the moon once again.

A great pale moon in a black sky filled with stars near and far.

You can do this meditation with or without drawing a circle or performing a ritual. It might be best, at first, to undertake it after drawing a circle, perhaps as part of a Full Moon rite. It can be done by yourself or in a group. If in a group, then each person can take a turn reading the meditation for the others.

If possible, keep a journal of your impressions, thoughts, and feelings. Don't be surprised, though, if some of what you experience can't easily be written down. If so, don't worry about it, but just write it down as best you can recall and, quite often, it can make more sense at a later time. Much of what we experience with the Fey we don't have words for. Some of it takes the form of riddles and some of seems paradoxical, even silly or impossible. Like dreams, Fey encounters do have their own logic, even if, to our waking minds, to our mundane sensibilities, it no longer makes sense like it did when we were actually in the midst of the experience.

Ritual to See Yourself Through the Eyes of Your Fey-other

Beyond all space and beyond all time
There I see you looking back at me
My hands and yours
My heart your door
Do not fear

We are together once more

For this ritual you will need:

- Altar
- Altar cloth
- Candle holder with red candle
- Candle holder with white candle
- Mirror
- Blue-green ribbon or yarn or cord

- A token or image or symbol you use or a picture of yourself
- A token or image of your Fey-other
- Taper or lighting candle
- Incense (if desired)

Place a cloth on your altar. Conversely, for the sake of comfort, you can also place a cloth on a low coffee table, anything you can sit before comfortably.

To the right, set a candle holder with a red candle. To the left, a candle holder with a white candle.

Directly in front of you, place a mirror, either one with a stand or one that you can prop up. You need to be able to see into the mirror.

You can choose, at this point, to draw a circle in whatever fashion you normally use.

Take a blue-green piece of ribbon or yarn or cord and lay it straight across between both candle holders. Take another piece and lay it cross ways over the first ribbon so that it starts at the mirror and ends right before where you will be facing the altar or table.

Set your Fey token or image right before the mirror, at one end of the cord or ribbon and your own token or image at the other end, in front of you.

If desired, you can set an incense holder at the point where the two ribbons meet. You can use a bowl with a charcoal and loose incense if desired, perhaps the incense from this book or any other incense that helps get you into the proper meditative, trance mode. You can also use a stick incense holder.

Take the taper or lighting candle and light the red candle, and then move it directly towards the white candle and light it, saying:

Blood to blood

Move the lit taper or candle from the white candle to the red candle, saying:

> *Spirit to spirit*

Hold up the taper or candle between the two, saying:

> *Become as one*
> *Become as one*
> *Across worlds*
> *Across time*
> *What the heart knows*
> *Cannot ever be forgotten*
> *What is sung in shadow*
> *Ever knows the light*

Gently blow out the taper or candle and set it aside.

Close your eyes and do whatever breathing or technique you normally do to get into a proper trance state.

Then use your mantra, your visualization, a name or symbol that you have developed with your Fey-other to connect to them.

When you feel your Fey-other is near, invite them to move close to you, to step into the same space as you. In particular, you need to feel them about your face and your eyes. As though your sense of self had slipped back, and a mask had been placed upon your face, a living mask, the face of your Fey-other.

When your sense of this becomes very strong, very powerful, gaze at the reflection in the mirror.

Once you have received any sensation or message or idea from this connection, to end close your eyes and quicken your breathing. Ground any excess energy into the Earth or shake it out of your hands. If you still feel jazzed up with too much energy, having something right away to eat can help settle things down. Fey energy is often a "buzzy" feeling and, if you're not used to it, can make you feel nervous and jumpy.

Write down any thoughts or impressions as soon as possible. Again, what we get from the Fey can be confusing and may take months, or even years, to figure out. At other times, we might well get strong impressions that make perfect sense at the time, but then become strange or confusing once we've returned to ourselves and regular consciousness. That doesn't mean that what we understand in conjunction with our Fey-other isn't real, only that it's not an understanding that our logical mind can recognize or appreciate.

It takes practice, but our Fey-other is there to work with us and they desire this communion as much as we do...if not more. They will reach out to us in ways that best suit us, that will get through to us. By exploring the visions and messages that they give us, we can not only learn how to be closer to them but come to a better understanding of who we are.

Finding and Charging Your Tokens

"We wait. We watch. We have always watched, just out of view, just out of touch. Those who see us, who hear us, they know our touch. They are born knowing our touch and so vision comes. What the heart knows, none may gainsay, for in the heart Truth resides."

-The Fey

Many people place statues or emblems of their gods and goddesses upon the altar—touch points for the gods and symbolic representation of their presence in the circle. So we can create our own touch points, our own symbols. Generally, these tokens are related to our own internal flame, our spirits, though some people tend to pick something that reminds them of their totem spirit. There is no right or wrong type of token to pick, so long as it feels like you to you. And so long as you charge up the item with some of your personal energy.

We place our token objects, objects imbued with our personal energy and that have meaning to us, upon the altar as representing our presence and focus on becoming as one within the circle. Some paths and covens use token objects on their altars, in order to represent members when they are absent from ritual and also as part of ritual. Generally, we store all of the coven tokens together in a bag or box so that they are together even when we ourselves might not be together, at least physically. As a part of starting ritual, then, each person can take their token and place it upon the altar, either by where they are sitting or around the central candle or candles or around any statute of the God or Goddess.

Which isn't to say that, should you work alone, you can't also use a token object. When you place that object on the altar along with your ritual tools, your representations of your Gods, the Ancestors, your spirit familiars or totems, you are placing a symbol of yourself among your spiritual landscape. You are taking your place among your allies, kin-dred, and other spirits and powers.

For much the same reason, we can also use a token to represent our Fey-other, thus symbolizing our relationship and serving as a focus for the work we intend to do together. If you already have, or plan to get a token to represent yourself for coven work, you can either use the same one for yourself or get a second one that will be used specifically for Fey rituals. Though, if your entire group is focused on involving the Fey in rituals and magick, then it might be best to use your regular tokens in order to strengthen all of those bonds.

If you do decide to use two tokens, they can be slightly different repre-sentations of the same symbol. For example, if you pick a feather for your token, you can have a real feather for the coven and a silver feather for your Fey interaction. One token could be a small wooden carving of a wolf and one could be a wolf made of stone.

Of course, they can also represent different aspects of yourself and so need not be the same image at all. For instance, your coven token might be a compass and represent your role in the group of being there to help point out the direction that the coven needs to go in or serve to help find things that are needed. Your Fey token then could be a raven, for example, and symbolize another aspect of yourself, this time your attraction to shiny new ideas and your role as being a messenger of the divine. Both are aspects that are related to each other but symbolize a deeper truth in slightly different ways.

It should be what "speaks" to you, no matter what form it takes, though the object chosen must be practical. Tokens should be small enough to not take up too much space when placed on an altar or to be kept near you if need be, such as while dancing or traveling or running through the woods in the middle of the night.

When it comes to choosing your token, you can certainly go looking for a specific item—a small silver or gold charm in the shape of a snake or rose or dragonfly or crescent moon, for example. You can use a favorite earring or a ring you inherited. You can choose a shell from a trip you took to the sea, a stone from a stream you used to play in as a kid, or you might see a piece of fossilized wood in a nature store and have it feel just right when you pick it up for a closer look.

You can also decide to go out looking without a notion of what exactly your token will end up being. Which is, by the way, how you should go looking for a token to represent your Fey-other. In both cases, you might be surprised at how your token or your Fey-token—or both—might just come to you without you actively looking for them. Sometimes, it might appear as a gift from someone who has no clue that it might mean something special to you. This is how one token came to me. A rose quartz stone with a crow engraved on it was given to me as a birthday gift by a relative, unknowing of my connection to crows. A mere coincidence? Unlikely. It was my altar token for years.

My Fey-token came to me, fittingly enough, under even more mysterious circumstances. I was working in the basement of a building for a small company when a fellow employee walked into the office I was managing and handed me a small metal object. They said, "this must be yours." I had never seen it before in my life, but immediately felt the significance as it was a little figure of a pointy-eared naked pixie—or a "piskie" as was imprinted on the bottom of the figure—with a loop on top so you could wear it on a cord or chain. I told the person that it wasn't mine and I hadn't lost it, but they just shrugged and said, "well, it is now," and that was that.

They had apparently found the object in the parking lot and immediately thought of me, even though we had never even discussed the idea of Faery or Paganism. I put the pixie on a gold-colored chain and wore it in circle for years. When I'm not wearing it, it sits on a pottery piece I made on the headboard overlooking my bed, along with a small statute of a beautiful Fey girl with a rose, a small collection of stones, and a turtle carved of bone that was given to me by my grandmother when I was young. This constitutes my little private Fey altar. My "piskie," roses, stones, and bone, the turtle shape being linked to one of the Native emblems of America.

All of this shows that your token or the token for your Fey-other can just "wander" into your life. But you can also take the conscious step of opening yourself up to such a possibility by doing a ritual to that effect.

Of course, you can also do a little chant each time you go out to the mall or some antique store or craft show or flea market or a Pagan festival. A chant such as: *"Seek and find what form be mine,"* or *"Seek and find what form be thine."*

Or you can perform the following ritual, keeping in mind what you need.

For this ritual you will need:

- A bowl of consecrated water
- Sea salt
- White taper candle
- Candle holder
- Scented oil
- A small bag or wooden box or a plain chain or cord
- Incense

The scented oil should preferably one that has frankincense in it or

patchouli, though you can also use an oil that is meant to draw something to you. You can also pick an oil that is made up of some of the
same ingredients as the incense you intend to burn.

Whether you get a bag or box or chain or cord depends on how you
intend to keep your token. Of course, once the item is found it may work
one way or the other, but in this case it is the intent of having a place for
it that is important.

For this ritual, you can choose to draw a basic circle or do it as part of a
larger ritual.

Mix the salt and water together by putting three small pinches of salt
in the bowl of water and stirring it around three times clockwise,
whispering:

> *To be*
> *To dare*
> *Thee I bless*
> *Sacred earth*
> *The water's kiss*

Take the white candle and cleanse it with the water, saying:

> *Purify this candle*
> *With salt*
> *Purify this candle*
> *With water*
> *Purify this candle*
> *For the good*
> *That it may best*
> *Serve my purpose*

Dry the candle and anoint it with the scented oil by taking some of the
oil on your fingers and rubbing it along the candle, beginning in the
middle and going out to one end first and then the other.

Hold the candle in the smoke of the incense or pass it through the smoke three times.

Breathe on the candle three times.

Hold up the candle, concentrating on the purpose of finding a token to represent you, saying:

> *Breath to breath*
> *Bone to bone*
> *Seek and find*
> *What form be mine*
> *In name*
> *In heart*
> *In dream*
> *In home*
> *What will to be*
> *What form be known*

Set the candle into the candle holder and coil the chain or cord around it or set the empty box or bag next to it. If the box is big enough, you can set the candle holder down inside the box itself.

Light the candle and concentrate on the flame, concentrate on your intent, repeating:

> *Seek and find*
> *Seek and find*
> *Seek and find*
> *What form be mine*

Let the candle burn for at least an hour. Light it again each night until it is gone or nearly gone. If there is any of the candle left, you can take it and throw it into running water.

When you are doing this ritual to find a token for your Fey Other, then follow the same steps but change the words while holding up the candle to:

Breath to breath
Bone to bone
Seek and find
What form be thine
In name
In heart
In dream
In home
Where knowledge dwells
Thy form be known

And repeat instead while concentrating on the candle flame:

Seek and find
Seek and find
Seek and find
What form be thine

After doing this ritual, keep your eye out for what comes to you for either your token or your Fey token at flea markets or antique stores or gift shops or arts and crafts shows or garage sales or Pagan events. Do what you normally do, go out shopping for what you normally would buy, attend what events you would normally attend and just keep your need for a token at the back of your mind. What you are looking for will appear eventually and it will feel right to you.

As for the Fey token, that will most likely show up when you least expect it to, given the nature of the Fey.

Who knows, you might just find the perfect token in the gift shop of an airport or discover it lying along a hiking trail or even buy a jacket at thrift store and find it hidden in the pocket. Or a friend or relative could give it to you as a holiday or birthday gift, unaware that it is just what you've been looking for.

Once you find your own token, you should purify it before charging it with your energy and using it. Most likely, it has been in other people's hands, unless you find it in the woods somewhere, and will have remnants of their energy. You will want to start with a clean slate.

However, before cleansing it, you should take into account what it's made of first. If your token is metal or stone, you will find that most stones can be cleansed in salt and water—though, there are some stones that should not be immersed—but you definitely wouldn't want to do that with a feather. Some metallic objects also can be badly effected by salt water, so have a towel ready to dry the object right after and, in the case of metal, you might want to wipe it with plain water before drying it in order to get the salt off.

For this, you will need:

- Two bowls (you can usual your regular ritual salt and water bowls)
- Sea salt
- Consecrated water
- Incense
- Candle

You can do this after drawing a basic circle or as part of a regular ritual.

Place the candle on the middle of your altar, with the bowl of salt to one side and bowl of water to the other side.

Place the token to be purified before the candle.

Light the candle and hold out the palms of your hands towards it, saying:

> *Be thou pure*
> *In order to purify*

Hold up the incense or hold your hands over it, palms toward it, saying:

> *Be thou pure*
> *In order to purify*

Light the incense with the flame from the candle, saying:

> *Star fire*
> *Elf fire*
> *Witch fire*
> *Be thou a sacred flame*
> *Of joy and truth*
> *A bright flame of destiny*

Hold up the bowl filled with salt and say:

> *Be thou pure*
> *In order to purify*

Hold up the bowl filled with water and say:

> *Be thou pure*
> *In order to purify*

Take three pinches of salt, one at a time, and put it into the water. Use your fingers and stir, clockwise, three times, saying:

> *To dare*
> *To be*
> *Thee I bless*
> *Sacred waters*
> *Eternal bliss*

Hold the object in one hand and dip your fingers into the water and cover the object with the blessed salt water. As you do, concentrate on the object being made pure, with no outside energies remaining in it.

Take the object then and pass it through the smoke from the incense three times as you continue to concentrate on it being cleansed.

If you cannot use salt water to purify the item, just pass the object three times through the incense smoke alone.

Hold the object and close your eyes and charge it with your personal energy. You will know it has been done when the object feels at home in your hands, when it feels very much like yourself, part of you.

Wrap the object up—preferably in silk, as silk helps keep out other energies—and put it someplace safe or place it on your altar if you prefer, so long as no one else touches the object. It would also be a good idea to keep the token next to you for those three days; if you can't keep it on a chain or cord or put it on your pocket, then keep it by your bed.

For your Fey-token, you can also pass it through incense smoke and/or salt water if practical, before asking your Fey-other to invest it with some of their energy.

On the other hand, it might be that your Fey-token will appear and already feel charged up, in which case you won't want to purify it. One way of testing this is, once your Fey token appears, hold it in your hand and try to sense the energies within it. If you feel the presence of your Fey, then the token is fine already. If it feels blank or your sense other sorts of energies, it would be best to purify it.

If the Fey token needs to be purified first, then afterwards have your Fey-other communicate with you any directions they would like you to follow to have them charge it. If such communication doesn't come, then there are several choices. If you have a Faery altar or Faery tree set up, put the token item into a small glass jar that can be sealed and leave the jar on the altar or hidden by the tree for three nights. These should be the night before the full moon, the night of the full moon, and the night after. If your Fey tree or altar is in a place where no one else but you might go, you can place the jar with the token out in plain sight. You might also want to suspend the jar from a cord off of one of the branches of your Faery tree.

When you set out the Fey token to be charged, it is also a good idea to put out an offering of cream at the same time. If you are unable to leave out your Fey token, you can set it on your altar within your home, also with a bowl or goblet of cream along with three Faery cakes if desired. You can put the bowl and the cakes on a platter or large plate and also put the token on the plate. This should also be done for three nights around the full moon.

Once both tokens are charged, take them and bind them together with a piece of red thread or cord or yarn and place them between one red and one white candle, both having been purified and anointed with scented oil.

Burn the candles while you concentrate on your relationship with your Fey-other. Do this three nights in a row and then unbind the objects.

The rest of the candles can be used on your or your Fey altar for future rituals. The red thread or yarn or cord can be tied on a branch of your Faery tree or laid out on your Faery altar. It can also be woven into the braid you create for use to travel to Faery.

～ *Willow* ～

Nine pale maidens in a row
Danced beneath the moon so slow
Turning thoughts of moss and stone
To the ancient mill
None could bear the terror found
In the mouth which makes no sound
Earth rose up and wrapped their round
So they dream there still.

Green-eyed willow why
Bend thee to the well-side
Red and yellow ribbons tied
For the luck that's there
Grey-fingered willow knows
Seek the way the waters go
Cast a charm and will it so
But only if you dare.

Horses in the river wild
Bow their heads and bid to ride
Black of eye, a whirling tide
Of the dark below
Those that in the water bide
Twill change all that would survive
What is death to those alive
One must die to know.

Hear the music neath the hill
No holy writ can make it still
To listen long will bind your will
To the open door
Folk like jewels upon the air

Teach the soul such beauty pure
Stripped from flesh the bone is bare
Some cannot let go.

Pretty little withy glow
Lightly flickers high and low
Beckons for the brave to go
Deep into the mist
There such treasures lie within
Pleasures of immortal kin
Some see naught but where they've been
So are ever lost.

Green-eyed willow why
Bend thee to the well-side
Red and yellow ribbons tied
For the luck that's there
Grey-fingered willow knows
Seek the way the waters go
Cast a charm and will it do
But only if you dare.

Chapter 2

Of Earth and Air and Water

"Once upon a time; long, long ago...for that is how you begin your stories, is it not? Yet, for us, it is not the same. There is no time, no long ago, no past, no future, only the now that is eternal. We know, we are the knowing ones, and what we know is the now. What is...is. We do not judge. We do not choose, for that is not our place. We see, and we know, and through our eyes, you may well see and know. In order to choose, in order to choose the good and proper road, you see and know and do and dare.

This is hinted at in your Four Quarters—to see, to be, to know as we know, to do, to act, to choose, and finally to dare, to risk, full of heart and bright of hope. Thus, the circle returns to being, to seeing what is and the eternal now. If you may but master this round, you master both self and the world, and know they are as one."

-The Fey

Several magical traditions use particular names and attributes for the Fey beings of the different directions or Elements. The names that you generally see is that of Sylphs for the East/Air, Undines for the West/ Water, Gnomes for the North/Earth, and Salamanders for the South/Fire.

These names for the elemental beings are said to stem from the occult writings of Paracelsus in the 1600's. Whether this work was based upon earlier beliefs is unknown, but it formed the basis for Hermetic practice and the early explorations and workings of science. However, it may or may not have much relation to the Faery Faith of the past.

Where the word "gnome" comes from is disputed—some believe it stems from a word meaning dweller of the earth and some from a word meaning knowledge or *gnosis*—but certainly they are not meant to be the red or blue capped little creatures that exist on people's lawns today, a figure that descends from German depictions of them. Gnomes definitely would come across as closer to what we call dwarves today for their tendency to live deep within the earth and collect and protect their treasure.

The name "sylph" relates to an old word for butterfly and, certainly, could have had a hand in the Victorian belief that the Fey can appear as tiny little flying creatures who enjoy hanging out with flowers. It certainly alludes to their close connection to the natural world, yet also makes them little fancies that have little of danger about them. Still, it's true that some believe that spirits can appear as butterflies, especially when someone leaves their body to spirit travel or upon death, so there is a definite link to Air.

"Undine" stems from a word for waves and clearly shows an association with water, whether of river, lake, or the sea. They are said to be beautiful, yet a water Fey never really loses their element of danger. There are far too many fairy tales that relate how the Fey of the rivers or pools with their green hair and long arms hunger to take children down to the depths and eat them. Stories of how the sirens lure ships to destruction on the rocks and mermaids who seduce sailors and take them under the waves to drown them.

The common association of the Element of Fire with "salamander" seems to stem from an old belief that salamanders could exist in the middle of flames without being burnt, that they actually stop fires. In actuality, a real salamander is not proof against fire and it seems strange to equate the mythological salamander with flames when they are said to put them out. It makes much more sense that the elemental salamander is really what is better named a "dragon," a winged serpent associated with the fiery currents of the Earth, the dragon lines, the ley lines. In fact, how these salamanders of fire were portrayed in the past actually looked far more like dragons than salamanders.

Unfortunately, though, when it comes to modern ideas of the elemental entities, some simplify it a bit too much. They state that Air elementals are creatures of pure thought and Water elementals are all feelings and Earth elementals are just silence. But consciousness is not so simple nor so easily defined and even the names and associations of gnome, sylph, undine and salamander are just a means of trying to grasp something that is beyond easy definition.

In the Shetland Islands, the *Trows* were said to be of land or of water, to dress in green and ride around on rushes, were heavily into drinking and dancing, and had the ability to cure or to make someone ill. In the Baltic region, the Fey could be divided into three types that related to the colors of white, brown, and black. The white Fey were lovely and gentle, tended to appear in the form of birds, and loved to dance. The brown Fey were also still beautiful and good, danced a lot at night, and could shapeshift. But the black Fey were considered to be ugly and malicious and generally liked to hang out near elder trees.

In Eastern Europe, there are Fey of each of the Elements named the *Zracne Vila*, spirits of the Air, the *Pozemne Vila*, spirits of the Earth, and the *Povodne Vila*, spirits of the Water. Accordingly, the Fey belonged to every Element save Fire for, traditionally, the power of Fire is linked to the practice of witchcraft and to smithcraft; both sacred and secret paths. The fire in the blood of a witch is that which makes us, "of the blood," granting the inner knowing of the Second Sight that gives each witch their power and link to the forces of divine, including Faery.

The Fey of the Elements are the conscious entities of the Elements, of the forces of that Element and, also, of what that Element represents. The material aspect of each Element is but one part of it—the one that is most easily seen as it exists here in the material world. But there are spiritual and mystical and mythological aspects to each Element and much more than that, things that we haven't even thought of or experienced yet. For each Element shares in mystery and so there is always something greater, something unknowable at the heart of each, and together, the four Elements come together to make an even greater mystery.

Which doesn't mean that we can't explore the Elements and form relationships with their conscious spirits, the Fey of the Elements. Some of this will come easily, and some will be more difficult, for we do have ancient holdings with the different Fey, old bargains that can be called upon and new ones we can forge. Some of these relationships simply need to be acknowledged and renewed, remade for this time and this place. Others will take the work of a lifetime, of many lifetimes, even of many generations. Some we just aren't ready for yet.

When it comes to the Fey of the Elements, this especially holds true for the Fey of the Earth. They are the oldest, the most unknowable to us. They are not just spirits of silence, but of essences, of life itself. The Fey of Earth sprang to being when life first began on the planet. Their power is that of eternal creation.

After them came the Fey of Water, of daring and of death. Earth and Water knew the world long before there were humans of any kind. Together, they are life and death, creation and destruction, beginnings and endings. Things come together, they make order. Things fall apart, chaos ensues. Both are right and necessary and part of each other.

Where the Fey of Earth and Water mingle lie the sacred landscapes of the bogs, the swamps, the secret depths and currents of Mother Earth. There is the power of the caves, the dark places where all things can be remade. Where healing or death can occur. Where people used to go to be initiated and born again. Theirs, also, is the clay that can be molded and fired into objects such as bowls, pots, figurines of gods and spirits, one of the first Elements that humans used to create after using stone and antler and bone. We are all born of clay; our bodies are formed of clay and infused and enlivened with breath and fire. Once that breath and fire leave, then our bodies go back from whence it came, back to the clay, back to Earth and Water.

The Fey of Earth and the Fey of Water are about what is needful—not what is considered right or necessary by human standards of morality, but what is necessary by divine right, divine necessity, a power older even than the gods. We have a place in that, but we do not rule it any more than we can rule the Fey of Earth and of Water. We can only persuade, honor, hope, and dream. Earth and Water will go as they will, and we must act in accord with that. We must acknowledge that, though we are a great power in our own right, we are not the only great power.

After the Fey of Water, come the Fey of Air, of knowledge, of understanding and clarity. In fact, the Gaelic name for the Fey, "sidhe," also means wind and they are said to travel in the whirlwind. The Fey of Air are close enough to witches to be numbered as our brothers and sisters, our elder kindred. We were of the Air before we were of the Fire. Realization and thought come, and action is born out of that; what happens in this world has its beginnings in the otherworld, in the realm of Faery, for the material world is an extension of the spiritual.

The Fey of Air are far more attuned to the needs of humankind. Their purpose is bound to our purpose, to the purpose of witches. Our destiny and theirs are woven together. The Fey of Air know and can see possibilities, potentials, permutations. Their view might not be as long as that of those of the Earth and of the Water, but they can see further than us. They don't see just one past, one future, but all that could be, should be, and might be. To the Fey of Air, the past is as mutable as the future. They can see that change as it radiates out in all directions, not just one. The Fey of Air not only know that time is not linear but exist in non-linear time. This is part of why they can see in so many ways. Yet, despite this power of vision—or, perhaps, because of it—theirs is not the power of choice.

For that, we have the Fey of Fire, the witches. We are all about choice, and it's our very nature to act, to do, to learn, to teach, to be points of possibility in the material world. We have the fire within us, the desire to seek, to create, to become, and even to destroy. We have the power to curse as much as to cure, to dance for life or to dance for death. Like the Fey of Air, we go back and forth between worlds, between forms of being, and know both sides of the veil. Also, by coming to Fire, we circle back around again to the beginning—to the star fire, the fire of creation, the spark that began all things and that resides within all things. The fire that came before the Earth and that began the Earth; that began all things. The same fire that is in the blood of witches.

We witches, and smiths, and magicians are creatures of elemental Fire. We are inherently neither good nor evil...just natural. Of course, we can put our magick to doing good or ill, for magick is neither black nor white, but a force that can be turned to the use the mind and will put it to. The word "good" didn't use to mean what it does today, but good as in what is right, what is honorable, what is pure to what it is meant to be. Just as the word, "nice" used to mean what is proper. To be good and nice as witches then, as creatures of flame, is to be true to your best nature. Just as the Fey are meant to be true to their best nature.

The Fey of Fire and the Fey of Air make the dance that pierces between worlds, that stitches together possibility with choice. When witches work magick with the Fey of Air, we can directly touch and affect the bright sparks upon the Web of Wyrd, the points of transformation. From those points, what we do ripples out across time and space. We are filled with the force of divine prophecy, of possibility, of divine purpose. Our hearts burn with desire for more, to reach, to make, to seek, to create, and we know what to seek for, what to create, by hearing the voices of those of the Air, our closest kindred. For our power and their power are meant to work together, to complement each other, just as the Fey of Earth and of Water complement each other. But whereas, theirs is the landscape of the eternal; ours is of time.

The many manifestations of the Fey are tied to the land, to nature, and to the Elements. The Fey are conscious aspects of nature. We and they are a part of this world, as guardians and guides. In this, we are meant to work together—not to just protect the land and keep the energies of Mother Earth flowing and healthy, but to protect the human community that relies on that land and on the waters in order to live. We are meant to try and keep the balance.

Without water, without air, without the fruitful bounty of the earth, without the magnetic field that protects the Earth...we would all suffer and die. People seem to forget this in their pursuit of another god, that of profit and greed and dominion when they use and abuse the Earth, and so endanger the future of all creatures on this planet, including their own children. The visible world is only part of the picture, so when the earth is ruined, its spiritual aspect is also hurt. Faery reflects this and, understandably, it is deeply of concern to the elemental Fey who are charged with protecting the Earth.

The veins of Mother Earth are currents of energy, what some call ley lines, and they are often marked out by sacred sites. These sacred sites tend to be on the nodes, places where the lines of power meet, the cross-roads. Like any currents that have power flowing in and out of them, these nodes can become blocked or tangled and thus adversely affect the vitality and fertility of the land they are part of. Part of the job of the Fey and of witches is to help keep these nodes and currents in good health, to keep them flowing freely and naturally. Obviously, it's no coincidence that the sacred crossroads are the places where witches and the Fey meet and dance and work magick.

The Fey and witches and the gods play a vital role in bestowing fertility upon the fields and pastures and orchards...or in taking it away. Hence, the belief and accusations that witches could make women and animals barren and, even worse to some, steal the favorite private parts of men who crossed them and hide them away, generally in bird's nests. As silly as this sounds, it has a basis in acknowledging that witches have author-ity over the regenerative forces, the same as the gods or the Fey can bless or curse your fields or household if pleased or crossed. In much the same way, the passage of the Wild Hunt can bless or blast the fields.

We are part of the Elements that come together to form the framework of Earth and Fire, Air and Water. Powers that manifest both here and in the realm of Faery, each affecting the other. What happens in Faery transforms what happens here and what happens here changes what happens in Faery, and both are based on the interlocking forces of nature, of creation and destruction. Of course, we each have, within us, all the Elements, but how that power manifests itself can take on differ-ent forms depending on our current nature. When we are with the Fey, when we are in the otherworld, then the manifestation is that of Air, and when we are here, in the physical world, the manifestation is that of Fire. This means that to be a witch, is to be a conscious aspect of Fire and so witches, as beings of the Elements, cannot be properly judged by human standards, not entirely.

For it's no coincidence there are four Elements as four is the basis, the building blocks of creation. We find this in science—the most notable being DNA—and in mythology. Besides the four Elements and the four Quarters, there are the four seasons, the four rivers said to spring from Paradise or from Asgard, the four winds, the four directions of the heart in Buddhist belief, the four cardinal virtues in Christianity, even the four Horsemen of the Apocalypse. Of course, there are also the four powers of the magus, familiar to the witch as, "to will, to dare, to know, and to keep silent." There are also have four pillars or giants or dwarves or guardians or angels who stand at the four quarters and the crown of Fate Herself is said to have four sides.

Four stems from the oneness that is the all, what some name the ultimate divine or the godhead or just God. From the center comes the four powers, the four winds, the four Elements, the four roads that form the crossroads. When all the Fey of the Elements come together, we echo that source. We make the crossroads of both time and eternity. We become the beginning point. It's from that point, the true crossroads, that lies betwixt and between, that great magicks can be worked, magick that ripples out across time, across many worlds. This crossroads is the witches' sabbat, the otherworldly sabbat.

Earth, Water, Air, and Fire, from the eldest to the youngest, the Fey of the Elements are complex, mysterious, beautiful and frightening, familiar in some ways and strange in others. The Elements are all around us. They are a part of us. By seeking to come to an understanding of them, we can come to greater understanding of ourselves, of where we come from and where we are meant to go, what we are meant to become. We have our foundation in the Elements, and we are the ones who are destined to build upon that, to go beyond.

When we, as witches, call quarters, summoning the Elements, we are creating and drawing upon not just Earth, Air, Fire, and Water, but the consciousness of the Elements, and as one of those Elements, we are also calling upon the shared power and knowledge of all witches, the *Hidden Company*. Whenever we draw a circle or lay a compass, we are acknowledging the sacred landscape of the Elements and activating this crossroads. Of course, it's even better if this can be done on one of the actual nodes where the currents of the Earth cross, where many rituals have taken place.

When the elemental Fey come together, the place where we meet is formed by the union of Water and Earth—the material sacred place with its wellspring or holy well or lake or river or the cosmic tree with its well of memory. Dancing there, Air and Fire interweaved, we raise that first fire, the fire of creation, the *Witch Fire*, the *Star Fire*. We dance the crossroads of infinite possibility.

This makes it easier to tap into that power, the power of the dragon. This dragon power exists in all of the Elements and has its beginnings in the divine fire of the stars. It's in the blood of the Fey, of the witches, and in the claims of divine blood and the authority of kings, the lore that talks about the king and the land being as one. To awaken the dragon is to come to consciousness, to the understanding of the connection of all things in the Web of Wyrd, the dragon lines of the universe.

Faery Offerings-Seelie and Unseelie

"Be sure what you offer is what you mean to offer. Do not offer in jest or unknowing. This is a bond, a bargain, a pledge. A promise. Those you name Unseelie, the dark ones, those who scurry and rush and whirl and spin, do not take such lightly. They will hold to what you have asked, whether you want the end or no. Do not make the deal of blood and bone and flesh unknowing of what you ask, let alone what you shall receive. They are only demons if you make them so. An honest bond makes them your best helpmeets. A broken word unleashes forces better kept.

Neither shall you break any bond with those you name Seelie, for they also do not accept such lightly. They are not as mine, they who will hold to the bargain no matter what, but their honor and their bond are perfect, and so they expect perfection in turn. Their wrath may be turned by love, but better still to not invoke their wrath at all. Do not break with them. Do not offer without such love as perfection may wish for, do not muddy your own name and your own honor, for that is what you truly honor them with."

-Goddess of the Unseelie Fey

Some religions teach that we make offerings to curry favor with beings more powerful than us to try and make sure that they won't be angry with us. Yet offerings are much more than that. They are a means of connection—as any gift is—along which energies can flow. That is why we should always give of the best and not be stinting in them. Better still, if the offering is something that you've a hand in creating, such as making the drink or baking the cakes. But, as this is not always possible, then always pick something that you would enjoy yourself or that the Fey have indicated to you that they enjoy. This message may come in a dream or a vision or just a strong feeling that they much preferred that thick cookie filled with fruit you offered last time over the thin crispy peanut butter one you gave them this time.

When it comes to making liquid offerings to the Fey, milk is a good choice, but cream is much, much better. Folklore is filled with stories about how much the Fey enjoy their cream. Today, we can buy heavy whipping cream at the store and offer that, as most of us do not have access to whole milk that still contains cream. Half and half will do in a pinch or even regular milk, but when I am going to work magick with the Fey and want their attention and good will, I make sure to have heavy whipping cream around and offer all of it. Don't keep any back for yourself, as an offering should be given wholeheartedly. No food or drink destined for an offering to the Fey should be a leftover. You should always try to give of your best.

Wine is also a good choice, but it should be red wine, red like the blood it is meant to represent. The blood of the vine. When making an offering of wine its best to be given after midnight.

Red wine mixed with heavy whipping cream is also a good offering, but one of the best offerings of all is cream mixed with a few drops of your own blood if that is an acceptable part of your practice. But only give of your own blood if this is comfortable for you and if you are fully aware of the bond that it can create. Blood is a connection, and blood magick is old and strong and must be respected. This is especially true for the Unseelie, for whom the bargain is all.

Also, never eat of the cakes you are making as an offering once you have separated them from the rest of the cakes. If you are baking the cakes, set aside the ones you are going to use as an offering as soon as possible and it's best if they are the nicest cakes in the batch. If you are buying cakes for offerings, pick ones that you enjoy yourself and set aside the offering cakes as soon as you open the package. Don't pick the cheapest cakes in the store, unless those are the ones you actually like, as this cheapens the offering. Cakes made with fewer chemicals are the best, the more natural and organic the better.

If you plan on making regular offerings to the Fey, it would be best to pick out a cup or bowl that will only be used for that purpose. You can keep this bowl or cup on your Fey altar or in a safe place so that no one will use it accidentally. The choice of cup or bowl is up to you, but it can be made of metal or glass or pottery or wood. It can be as simple or as fancy as you like. But the best bowl or cup is one that you make yourself. The next best is one that just comes to you as a gift or that you find and just know immediately as you see it that this is the one the Fey would like for you to use.

In a pinch, you can use your regular libation bowl if you have one, but it would be a good idea to eventually have one dedicated to Fey offerings alone. You can, of course, have one bowl or cup for the Seelie and one for the Unseelie. Your regular circle libation bowl can then serve for the Fey of the North, while your coven cup or goblet is, of course, the one that serves for the Fey of Fire, the witches.

For offerings of cakes, having a particular plate is also a good idea. Again, you can have one plate for all your Fey offerings or have four, each designated for the Fey of North, South, East, and West. If you do have such designated plates, then the plate used for the Fire Quarter should also be the plate you use in your own rites. The plates can also be made up of metal or glass or wood or pottery. You can have them be of different colors, ones that you equate to the Elements or quarters, even have them match the cups or bowls that you use.

My own Fey offering bowl is of green Depression glass or I use a clear, green, glass goblet that was given to me as a gift by a family member. If I am making an offering of cream or wine, I tend to use the goblet, and if I am making an offering of cream or wine and cakes, then I tend to use the bowl, so I can put the two together. When I set them on the altar, I sometimes place them on a hammered copper plate or, in a group, I use the plate to carry around the cakes so that everyone can take one to use for their offering.

The reason I picked out green was because of the long association of the Fey with that color. Though, of course, the Fey have also been associated with red and with black or white. You could even have one cup or bowl of each color—in which case, I would associate the green with the Fey of the East, the red with the Fey of the West, the black with the Fey of the North and the white with the Fey of the South. Of course, different paths and different groups and different cultures have their own color association with the Elements and with the Fey. I could also make an argument that the Fey of the South should have red because of its tie to our blood and the white should be with the Fey of the East because their blood is that color.

Basically, whatever works best for you or your group and brings to mind that direction or Element would be a good choice. Though, of course, if you get one cup or plate and then it gets broken time and again or you keep losing it, it might be a good idea to revisit that choice. The Fey may well have their own ideas about what they want you to present offerings in.

If you are going to make offerings to both the Seelie and Unseelie, it would be best to have separate items for each of them for the relationships between us and them is different. This is why you can use your normal ritual items for the Seelie, who are part of the same family we belong to but should not use them for the Unseelie because they are not part of that family.

Whatever you get, though, you should cleanse it first before using it. Wash it thoroughly, if possible in blessed spring or moon water mixed with salt, then censed thoroughly with incense smoke. This can be done outside of ritual, but it would be better to do it within a ritual context. If the cup or bowl or plate ends up being used for mundane reasons at some point accidentally, be sure to repeat this step and consecrate it to its chosen purpose again.

If you don't have a dedicated Fey altar to keep the objects on, it might be a good idea to wrap them up in silk when not in use and keep them in a safe place. If you have space inside your altar that would be a good choice, otherwise you can get a nice wooden box, marking or decorating it as you like. If you end up finding a container at a store or sale, then you should also cleanse it before using it.

Ritual Offering to the Seelie

"Good, good, good...what do you see as good? That, that is what we desire. We hunger for the sunlight world, for the taste and touch of the summer's day. We, we who dance in moon glow, we know not the sun the way you know the sun. We are no longer children of the day. But once we were. Once we will be again. But as the moon is our mother, we dance by her song, shadows to her light. Just as we would dance to thee..."

-The Fey

Offerings to the Seelie, our kindred, can be done at any time and on a regular basis. It can be part of your regular ritual practice or on special occasions, though they definitely should be given an offering at All Hallow's Eve if at no other time. The offering can be made inside, in your normal circle space, or outside. It can take place at your Faery altar or beneath your Faery tree (check inside this book for the creation of a Faery altar or dedication of a Faery tree).

For this ritual you will need:

- A carton or small bottle of heavy whipping cream (half and half or regular milk can also be used, but cream is best)
- Offering plate
- Offering cup or goblet

Place the offering plate and cup or goblet on the altar or beneath your Faery tree. Hold up your hands and say:

By the ancient covenant, I call you
My brothers and sisters
Breath of my breath
From now until forever
Through rushing wind
Through whirling fire
Be here
Be mine
As I am thine

Kneel down, if possible, and pour the cream or milk into the cup or goblet. Place three cakes onto the offering plate.

Hold your hands over the offerings and concentrate on putting your personal energy into them.

Hold up the cup or goblet, saying:

This I offer to thee
Freely and from my heart
That joy and laughter
That luck and love
That all that is good and proper
Shall be thine
And all that is good and proper
Be returned

Hold up the plate of cakes, repeating the same words.

If you do have a particular need at this time, simply state it out loud and make any promise as to how you will make offerings in exchange for the fulfillment of this need. It doesn't have to just take the form of offerings of cream and cakes, but can also be by writing a poem, creating a song, leading a ritual, doing charity work, helping to clean up a park or a roadway, so long as it honors the Fey in some way and the balance between the land and the community, between this world and the otherworld.

If you do not have a need at this time, just finish with:

We are kindred all
In service to the work
Children of the Gods
Of Elfhame
Of the Earth and of the Starry Heavens

The web of Mother Fate

If you are outside, you can pour out the milk or cream and place each cake down one at a time in the offering place.

If you are inside and in the middle of ritual, you can go and set the offerings to the East of the circle until you can libate them. Any libation should, if at all possible, be done on the same night as the offering or ritual.

Ritual Offering to the Unseelie

"We are the bread of the land. We are the fruit of the harvest. As you reap, so we sow. We are the gnawers of the dead. We take what must be taken. It is ever so. Many deny us. They deny what may not be denied. Few serve us, for we are frightful. Yet is not loyalty rewarded. Some prefer a darker coin. We shake, we stir, we spin, we weave, we build, we wind ourselves in every thread. We may not be denied. Our breath is cold. You know it. Our hands are small. You know them.

*We cradle the universe, born of the Great Abyss you know as space, as Void, yet is it not full of wonders and joyful promise. Learn **our** riddle, and you learn the secrets of the graveyard and beyond. All come to us. So it must be. Embrace us or not, we will be. Between the indrawn breath, between the narrow spaces, between light and dark—we run. Fear us, do not fear us, it is all one."*

-Unseelie message as given through the Seelie

An offering to the Unseelie Fey should be made as part of an on-going bargain. When we give them offerings, we must eventually ask for something in return. Otherwise, if we do not ask and only give, there is a lack of balance and the Unseelie might even do something that they consider is needful in keeping up their end of that balance, rather than something we want to ask for.

As they do not think as we do, their idea of a need to be fulfilled might be very different than what we consider a need or even something we would ever have wanted in our lives or at a particular time in our lives. This isn't to say that they would bring about something bad, but it might be something we aren't quite ready for or aren't geared up to handle or would have liked to consider for a while first. The Unseelie just aren't as understanding of such things as the limitations of time and physical needs as the Seelie are.

If you do decide to seal a bargain with the Unseelie, consider it deeply and honestly before undertaking it. Is it really necessary? Is it truly a need or simply a desire? Is it really for the good? Are your motives just and pure and have you considered the consequences and the responsibility you will bear for whatever does or doesn't happen as a result? Be very precise, as precise and clear as possible. The Unseelie can be very literal.

If, in the end, you decide to strike a bargain, pick a length of time during which you will make your offerings. Three is a good, traditional number, so you can do it for three months at the dark of the moon. You could also choose to do it once a month for a year or from All Hallows to Beltane.

Pick out a bowl and a cup or goblet that will be reserved for making your offerings to the Unseelie. When not in use, you can wrap the objects in black or grey silk and keep them near your Faery altar at home. You do not need to consecrate these objects, but you should cleanse them with consecrated salt or moon water and incense smoke before using them.

The offering can be made as part of a normal ritual or by itself. If outside, a tree stump or by the roots of a tree are good places to make the offering or the flat of a large stone. If you own the land, you can also make a simple offering place by laying out a small ring of stones and place any offerings in the middle of them.

For the offering, you will need:

- A carton or small bottle of heavy whipping cream (half and half or regular milk can also be used, but cream is best)
- Offering plate
- Offering cup or goblet

Pour some of the cream or milk into the bowl or goblet and put it in the offering place. Put three Faery cakes on the plate and set that in the offering place. If any cream or milk is left over, you can draw a Circle around the tree or rock or ring of stones with it.

Put your hands out over the offerings and fill them up with your personal energy.

Kneel or stand by the offering place and lift up your hands, saying:

Old One
Horned One
Lord of Shadows
Lady of Dreams
Mistress of Night
Summon ye
Summon ye
Call your children
The deal to make
This gift accept

Make your request out loud as well as your promise of what you will do in return, whether a future series of cream and cake offerings or some form of service. Never make a promise that you are not sure you can keep.

Take up the cup or goblet of cream or milk and pour it out on the ground or on the tree or rock. Take up the plate and, one at a time, lay each cake in the same spot.

When you return to make additional offerings, provide more cream or milk and cakes or even a portion of your evening meal. Put it in the offering place and state:

> *This gift accept*
> *The bargain kept*

If you are doing a service, once completed you should go back to the place where you set the bargain and say:

> *This gift accept*
> *The bargain kept*

If you are making the offering inside your home instead of outside, place the cup of cream or milk and the plate of Faery cakes on your regular or Faery altar. Again, kneel or stand and hold up your hands, saying:

> *Old One*
> *Horned One*
> *Lord of Shadows*
> *Lady of Dreams*
> *Mistress of Night*
> *Summon ye*
> *Summon ye*
> *Call your children*
> *The deal to make*
> *This gift accept*

State your need and the manner of your future offerings.

If you are doing this as part of ritual, take the plate and cup or goblet to the West of the circle and keep it there until you have concluded. Then take the milk and cream and Faery cakes out to your Faery tree or stone outside or the place where you normally libate offerings and pour the milk and cream there and lay down the Faery cakes in the same spot. It's okay to make the offering in the same place where you make your offerings to the gods or spirits after ritual, but keep the offerings separate otherwise.

When you make your future offerings, if in ritual inside, you can again set the offering to the West of the Circle until ritual is concluded and you can libate it later.

When you go outside to pour out the cream or milk and lay down the cakes, again, say:

This gift accept
The bargain kept

Once the time period you have bargained for is concluded, then wash the plate and cup or goblet you have been using three times and cleanse them consecrated moon or salt water and pass them three times through incense smoke. This marks the conclusion of that particular bargain so that any future bargain set will be fresh and new.

Faery Circle Quarter Calls

"You are part of the Three and of the Four. Fire is yours, the gift of the Gods. Not the flickering flames of the hearth, of the wildfire, of the sun, but the fire of what you name Will, though tis better to call it choice. By choice are you known, by choice must you claim your rightful heritage. If you give up choice, you give up who you are. You are lost. The Four you know best as such Powers of Being, Knowing, Will and Daring, but they are only symbols of truth. Name them Foundation, for so they are. They are the thread upon which Great Mother Fate spins and which none of us can wholly understand.

The Three you name are the knots that bind the threads together. Mothers of Earth, Air and Water, of the Past, Present, and Future, of Life, Death, and Rebirth, and so the world is made. Fire runs between, fire runs within, the most hidden and most precious power of the Gods, but even not of them if truth be known, for They too are but a part of it. You are of the Four—of the Will for which you are famed and feared and loved and despised—and you are of the Three, the hidden face, the hidden power of the stars, that which you name Witchblood,

Witchfire, the Thread, the Flow, the flame of love that is the heart of all things and without which naught would be. This is what calls you to your rites and unites your kindred. If you know not this, this One thing, then you do not know anything.

The Three and the Four that are Seven and the Seven that are One."

-The Goddess of Riddles

These Quarter calls can be used as part of a Faery ritual that you create or for one of the other Faery rituals contained in this book. Feel free to incorporate them into regular practice if you like. They can be done before drawing the circle or after, to invite the powers of the Fey into your sacred space. After you use the call, you can then use the lit candle or taper to light the candle of that quarter if desired.

Hold up a lit taper or candle before you in the North of the circle, saying:

Hail to the North--
From the mountains of vision
Where the great Gods abide
To the depths of the caverns
Where the Mothers reside
Silent Ones
Old Ones
First of the Four
By Earth and by Being
Open the door

Proceed to the West and hold up the taper or candle, saying:

Hail to the West--
From the rush and the flow
That feeds the dream of the Muse
Where meets death and desire
Upon the bright shores of truth
Dark Ones
Cold Ones
Second of Four

By Water and by Daring
Open the door

Continue to the East and hold up the taper or candle, saying:

Hail to the East--
From the pattern of stars
To the song of first light
By the whirling of the winds
Where all stories take flight
Shining Ones
Watching Ones
Third of the Four
By Air and by Knowing
Open the door

Proceed to the South and hold up the taper or candle, saying:

Hail to the South--
From the call of the kindred
And the circle of the hearth
Wherein resides will
And the work of the art
Wise Ones
Cunning Ones
Last of the Four
By Fire and by Doing
Open the door

Take the lit candle or taper and turn to the altar and hold it up high so that all can see it. If desired, you can then use it to light your altar candles, or a particular candle prepared to represent the Fey powers. This candle can be red or green or black or white.

Faery Incense

The fairies are dancing
how nimbly they bound!
They flit o'er the grass tops,
they touch not the ground;
Their kirtles of green with diamonds bedight,
All glittering and sparkling beneath the moonlight.

--"The Fairy Dance," Caroline Eliza Scott

These incense recipes are for making smoke that will appeal to the Fey of the East, the Seelie Court. You can burn it during your rituals to help attract the Fey and also to attain the proper atmosphere for the rite. Unlike many incense recipes out there that call for a lot of ingredients, some of them hard to get, these are very basic incense recipes in order to make them easy to put together and use.

The recipes each have a foundation element, and then the rest of the ingredients are often found in your kitchen cupboard or supermarket. You can mix up a small portion (such as in the recipes below) or a larger portion. Store in an airtight glass jar, preferably one with amber or dark colored glass. As these are simple to make, you can mix them up right before ritual if desired so that they won't dry out as quickly.

Conversely, if you want to just buy incense, a good one is something that has both a smoky and a sweet scent to it. Palo Santo is a wood that, when burned, releases a very good scent that is appealing to the Fey. In general, sage is not for use in drawing the Fey to your rites, as it is a cleansing smoke.

Incense One—Spring

- Teaspoon of amber, finely crushed (or some small pieces)
- Half of a teaspoon ground cardamom

- Fourth of a teaspoon anise seed
- Half of a teaspoon ground mace*

Incense Two—Summer

- Teaspoon of dried fine sandalwood pieces
- Half of a teaspoon of dried rosemary leaves
- Teaspoon of dried basil
- Eighth of a teaspoon ground nutmeg

Incense Three—Autumn

- Teaspoon of dried patchouli leaves, finely chopped
- 3 whole cloves
- Eight of a teaspoon ground cinnamon
- Eighth of a teaspoon ground turmeric
- Eighth of a teaspoon ground allspice

Incense Four--Winter

- Teaspoon of frankincense, finely crushed (or a few small pieces)
- Fourth of a teaspoon ground ginger
- Fourth of a teaspoon ground cardamom
- Half of a teaspoon ground cinnamon

*If you can't find ground mace—a spice made from another part of the nutmeg, usually more readily available during the holidays for baking—then feel free to substitute ground nutmeg in its place.

∼ *Lament* ∼

Dust and dark what dreams they keep
Dancing in the silent deep
Round we turn and turn again
Try to wake them from their sleep.

Circles we make in wheat and corn
Show for what we are forlorn
Don't you remember, don't you care
For what's been lost cannot be borne.

Beyond the Veil we hear you sing
Strain to answer, enter in
The laughter and the tears begin
It is the way, the way we've been.

We feel despair, such hurt for thee
Longing for our love to see
In each other's eyes to find
Another reaching out to be.

Within us cries this empty place
Haunted by the ancient ways
To come again, to bind as one
This pain of parting never fades.

Round we've turned and turned again
Torn apart from what we've been
What it is to do, to know
They are us as we are them.

They are us as we are them.

Chapter 3

They Are Us and We Are Them

"One gift we have given is the gate to our home, if you dare seek it and it is drawn to you. You cannot find it if it will not be found. Just as you cannot find where it will lead you if you have not the courage and do not know what it is to be home.

We know you, but you have all but forgotten us. We expected such, for it is your curse to forget. She, who you name Pandora brought gifts as we bring them, yet her gift was not to forget but that of remembrance. If you do not remember you may not be a witch. This much is true.

Our blood causes remembrance, and it is our blood which marks the gate, the gate of the forest, that which grows from the earth of the Old Ones, those you name ancestor.

Where the blood of the gods falls, there grows up blossoms you name beauty. Our blood grows different, yet still resides within you, lying hidden in your stories, in that which poets tell, and artists paint. There are no coincidences—all that is, is."

-The Fey

The old stories show us that there has long been a link in the popular imagination between witches and Faery. This is portrayed both by the idea having witchblood—or, in other words, being *of the blood*—and the idea of having Feyblood, which is really six of one and half a dozen of the other. What it means is that when you are of the blood, you are also of Faery, that you are one of the Fey, even though you are in human form.

Witch and Fey have an intimate and familiar (familial) connection. In fact, when you are here in this world, you are essentially a Faery incarnated in a physical body. When this body dies, you are then released back to Faery. When you die here, you are "born" there and when you are born here, you "die" there. As we rejoice in a birth, so they mourn the loss of one of their own. As we mourn the death of a loved one, so they rejoice in a return of one of their own.

Thus, sadness and joy are irrevocably linked just as they are part and parcel of the two main sabbats that are the gateways between life and death, Earth and Faery—Beltane or May Eve and All Hallows Eve or Halloween. Some tend to see Beltane as being all about pleasure and joy and, yes, love and sex and flowers and feasting. Some tend also to see All Hallows about remembrance of those who have passed away from this world, about grief and loss and asking to see and know those loved ones through that veil this night if no other. But each is of the other when you stand on that boundary between witch and Fey. We may just as easily laugh as weep at All Hallows and weep as laugh at Beltane.

When we understand that connection, that we can be both here and there, witch and Fey. Then we can grasp that the true nature of time is not really linear, but encompassing both past and future in the moment of the eternal now. For we can and must learn to see past the illusion created by modern notions of time and past the illusion of separation not just between us and those who have died, but the illusion of the separation of all things. Yes, we are creatures of time as we spin back and forth between the worlds of life and death, transforming from quick to dead and back to quick, but our essence, our true self, is eternal. We whirl around this immortal point as we pass back and forth through the veil.

The Fey are sometimes called our elders, and one reason for this is because they, being spiritual entities, stand closer to the source of all things. Their power includes that of knowing, of sight, and this stems from greater vision granted by being of the spirit and having memory of what you have been and might be. Those of the body, we witches here in the material world are the younger children, yet our spirits remain of the elder. Thus, the younger children come together as one and create bodies for the elder children to reside within upon the Earth. We are ancestors and descendants of each other, of ourselves.

There also tends to be a high overlap of strengths and weaknesses and tendencies in folklore between the Fey and witches, both the benevolent and the malevolent. What protects you against the Fey usually is said to protect you against witches and what will please a witch will likely also please the Fey. There are commonalities of travel, of powers, of folklore.

Some say that witchblood is faeryblood, and so it is. For example, fire and iron or steel were said to be proof against evil works by both the Fey and by witches, specifically blades. However, that being said, there are also cultures that have stories of Fey who actually work with metals such as iron, so this is not universally true. There is also folklore that talks about putting a blade in the cradle to keep the child from being stolen by the Fey or that throwing a blade into a passing whirlwind, a sign that the Fey are flying by, will protect you from them.

However, perhaps it is not so much the particular metal of the blade that does the trick, for there are also old beliefs that blades "cut" relationships. So, it might well be that the folklore that cold iron and steel are proof against the Fey actually stems from the tradition of sharp blades cutting ties or bindings, not due to any inherent property of the metal itself. Iron is, after all, part of nature, just as the Fey and we are part of nature. Iron is also a grounding material, which means it can be used to stop spells—of particular use in protection—but iron is also used in some kinds of magick and spell work. Which means that intention plays an important role in the use of iron.

Both witch and Fey are essentially supernatural entities that must be honored and appeased at times in order to have their aid towards promoting the security and fertility of the community and the land. Small wonder that most Fey gods and goddesses who are linked to witches are also able to harm or cure, to bless or to curse. It's never good to anger the Fey or a witch. Yet, like the power of magick itself, the Elements and the spirits associated with them are neither good nor evil for we cannot judge any of the Fey by merely human standards. They have their own rules, just as the gods have their own rules. To condemn the Fey for what is right and natural to them is to fall into the same human-centric trap of morality that belongs to the worldview that believes that nature is evil and fallen.

The older stories of interaction with Faery shows it doesn't always end happily ever after. The Fey can be very dangerous, especially if you break your word to them or build things in their sacred places or on their sacred tracks or cut down one of their trees. The Fey could steal or sour your milk, cause misfortune or illness. Faery darts were said to cause strokes or to kill outright, the most dangerous of all of these darts coming from the Queen of Faery or the Fool of Faery because no one could heal you if one of those darts struck you down. Witches were also said to sour milk or poison wells, cause illness or death, steal away fertility, among a whole horde of other accusations that sometimes verged on the nonsensical. Like the Fey, witches could enter your home and eat and drink all your food. Sometimes, they did this with the Fey, sharing in their secret feasts.

Small wonder then that there are plenty of folktales and beliefs that speak to appeasing the Fey and witches, including giving them offerings. Out of such beliefs came trick-or-treating at Halloween. People would protect themselves by dressing up so that those Fey and witches and other supernatural creatures out and about on the night when the veil is thin would think they are one of them. At each home, then, people are offered the choice—to give offerings to these beings or to risk having tricks pulled on them. Of course, the tricks of today generally involve raw eggs and toilet paper and not invisible darts or spells that could bestow illness, misfortune, or death.

This dichotomy is also reflected in the riding of the Wild Hunt led by an Elf King, a pagan god, or a goddess of the Fey or of the witches. Those who rode in this hunt could include the dead, the Fey, the witches, along with any wandering soul that was swept up with them, even a living person who ran into them, often to their misfortune. Like the Fey and the witches, the Wild Hunt had the power to bestow fertility on the land or take it away. Its flight could mean good luck and prosperity or bad luck and disease.

Yet, like the Fey and the witches, the Wild Hunt is not danger for danger's sake. There is both purpose and necessity to its passage, in how it can come bearing destruction or creation. It's a representation of the sheer force of nature, of the volatile boundary where the living meets the dead, where this world interacts with the otherworld. The Wild Hunt, like the magicks of the Fey and witches, help balance the energies of the Earth and keep it flowing.

Still, it's not simple or easy. You don't get something for nothing. Not witches or the Fey alone can balance an imbalance that has grown too great to be corrected gently anymore. The "snap back" alone can cause vast amounts of destruction. Those witches who work weather magick can well understand this. You have to pay for sunshine and fair winds for that outdoor event you planned, and you have to pay for rain you drew to those parched fields and gardens. Whatever energy you coax or command creates a push or pull that causes a reaction, and this effects the larger world as it affects the pattern, both the seen and unseen aspects of it, of this world and Faery. This is true especially of great magicks, and we must ever seek to work these type of magicks with the greatest good in mind.

The old stories teach us we must never ask without giving, give without asking. It's important to learn how to receive with as much grace as you give, freely and openly. Don't promise something and then not carry through with it. Don't lie and dishonor both yourself and them. This is one of the big magickal no-no's. And don't imagine that the powers that be will never know. They always know.

The Fey are themselves drawn to those who are not just playful and imaginative, but truthful and generous and honest, both in heart and spirit and with their worldly goods. If witches want to work closely with the Fey, its best to foster within ourselves these traits that are beloved of the Fey. There are many stories about people being given abilities by the Fey—or about being "married" to supernatural beings, such as a Selkie—wherein they must not do or say something, for if they do then the "contract" and the relationship is void, often with dire consequences.

One rule of thumb in dealing with or bargaining with the Fey is to never promise something that you aren't absolutely sure you can give or do. It's better not to make the promise or deal at all than to break it, even if breaking it wasn't your intention. Keeping secret what the Fey wish kept secret is another must, the same as when witch traditions have oaths of secrecy. If you break an oath, the Fey will certainly know, and they will never forget it.

No matter what name you call them by or in what form you experience them, our interaction with the Fey remains strange, otherworldly, disturbing, frightening and dangerous. It's an experience that is outside the bounds of what is generally considered normal or natural and can have long-lasting effects, whether that interaction is primarily positive or negative. One of the keys to understanding this experience lies in not taking it literally. We cannot understand it purely from an intellectual, rational mindset, which can be a problem since that is the mindset we in the West are generally raised with. We don't have to toss it all out—science and technology and modern medicine have its uses—but we dare not deny Faery, for this is to turn away from a deep and abiding part of ourselves and our history.

Not only can our Fey experiences be "off the map," but it might just well turn the map right on its head. The ancient Greeks claimed that the witches of Thessaly could definitely act outside of what they considered the "cosmic order," by turning night into day and day into night, by altering the seasons, making rivers flow backward, and by walking on water in addition to flying. In this, you could just as easily be describing the abilities of the Fey.

Our interaction with the Fey lies in the "here be dragons" mindset, the one that understands that we don't know everything and that everything cannot be explained by science and logic. Instead, experiences with the Fey have to be looked at on multiple levels. They must be considered in a mystical, symbolic, metaphoric way as well as, on occasion, literally. What we see is certainly not all there is. With the Fey, there never is just one reason, just one answer, just one way of looking at things.

A greater reality exists both "out there," and within each of us. Our vision becomes constrained as we are born here and made to conform to the restricted view of reality that society demands. Those who refuse or are unable to do so well enough to fit in are often marginalized or even diagnosed with mental ailments. Which isn't to say that everyone who sees the world in different ways than the acceptable version that society has agreed upon is actually tuning into Faery and the world of spirit, but its difficult to discern at times the difference between a person who needs help and someone who is called by the gods or has the sight.

Still, we must seek that expansion of vision, something that isn't always easy. For Faery is not kind, not cute, not pretty or soft. The beauty of witch and of Faery is overwhelming and wondrous and terrifying. When we fully embrace the powers of the Craft, we learn how to see and how to feel as the Fey do. In experiencing Faery while still alive and in the body, we are enraptured by it, and there are, honestly, no words good enough to capture that sensation. It's incredibly addictive, especially for someone with a thirst to explore, to push the boundaries, to serve the forces of creation and evolution as emissaries of Dame Fate.

It's no coincidence that two of the traditional talents of the Fey and of witches have to do with spinning and weaving—a clear association with our connection with Fate—and from which we get the idea "spinning a spell" or "weaving a spell." Smithing is also associated with the Craft, mirrored by the forging of various magickal swords, armor, cups, plates, jewelry and other wondrous objects by elves or dwarves. Of old, smith-craft and witchcraft are among the most powerful supernatural forces in the community, needful yet feared.

Another essential ability is that of healing. Some witches and cunning ones were given powers of curing or were taught to cure by the Fey directly and were called "Faery Doctors." They served the people by using the gifts given to them by their interaction with the Fey or their sojourn in Faery to help heal those in need. Sometimes, this involved being able to heal with a touch, other times with ointments or herbs. It could even mean using dance to heal or trance to rescue the lost spirit of the sick or dis-spirited person.

One of the most famous of these Faery healers was Anne Jefferies in the 1600's. Akin to what happens in shamanic experiences, she fell seriously ill and claimed she had been whirled through the air to the land of Faery and back again. From this, she gained prophetic and healing abilities and was accompanied by the Fey for the rest of her life.

68

Other wise-ones and witches developed an even closer relationship to the Fey. They would be "initiated" by the Fey or by the Queen of the Fey and be given magickal and healing knowledge through dreams or by going into trance states, usually through ecstatic dance. This connection extended to being able to become possessed by the Fey themselves during rituals, similar to possession by the gods.

We and the Fey are meant to be together. The Fey know, and we act. Each of us is a node in the gleaming Web of Wyrd, the Web of Being. We are nexus points where change is possible, indeed, where it is probable. Just as there are such points where the ley lines meet on the Earth, forming crossroads of possibility, so each witch, each of the Fey, is a crossroads. We are each a bright star upon the Earth, and when we come together in a coven, we form a constellation...we tell an evolving story and create a powerful pattern, a pattern that can change what is collectively known as reality.

Our physical bodies are touch points for our light and spirit to actualize here and now. This is part of why we as Fey decide to be born to the flesh. The more we can allow that supernatural light to flow through us, to let our spirit inspire and inform our actions, our creations, our words, the brighter our star can be upon the Earth and the more we can heal and create and spin and divine.

In some ways, our bodies are shadows cast by our stars, patterns that can either hold true to the spirit that informs them or that are dragged askew by the demands, the fears, the shames, the desires, the societal expectations that this world is filled with. All too often, these drain away our knowledge and awareness of our Fey nature.

We need to remember we *chose* to be born, for it is always through conscious will and choice that we are reborn. Once we are here, it lies in us to, as Joseph Campbell would put it, "follow our bliss." Our bliss is our best chance at happiness, at feeling fulfilled and confident, to tap into our true self, our real purpose, and find a means of expressing that. We must connect to our kindred, both those who remain in the realm of Faery and who have joined us in incarnation upon the Earth, and take up our charge...whatever form that might take, whatever our clan demands, whatever the times require of us as agents of change.

We are collectively sowers and tenders and reapers of the seeds of transformation and during these times of transformation, especially the great,
even traumatic changes that come in the transition from one age to
another, we have to hold fast to our true selves. As the age changes, we
all need to change with it; the two are intertwined, as reality, and shared
belief about reality are bound tightly together. The Piscean parts of our
paradigm need to be sloughed off and the Aquarian to be embraced, all
without losing hold of our own inner foundation, the bones of who we
are. Thus, exactly how we express our inner light transforms from age to
age, just as it does from life to life.

We and the Fey are deeply involved, indeed, called to be part of these
great transformations. Some of us are brought to help end the old age
and some to aid in the birth of the new. In this, we can look to our
connection to our Fey-other to aid us. To become capable of looking at
yourself through their eyes means we can more easily see the true nature
of our light and where our foundation lies, our purpose. We will be able
to know ourselves as "other," and see past preconceptions and self-made
blind spots. Of course, this is a challenge, both to get to the point of
being able to let go of our ego-selves enough to step back and see what is
really there and in having enough courage to actually face what we might
see.

We all have darkness inside us—fears, shames, doubts, regrets, insecu-
rities, guilt, and sadness. When we peer within our own selves with the
aid of our Fey-other, all is revealed, all is laid bare. We see our issues, our
coping techniques, both good and bad, where we have failed and where
we have succeeded, missed opportunities, decisions that changed not just
our lives, but the lives of others. This inner vision can be frightening, to
say the least.

Still, we should remember that no matter our fears or discomfort in
this, our Fey-other knows us best and still loves us deeply. This is why
the relationship can be equated to having a Faery Marriage, having a
Faery "wife" or a Faery "husband." Not because it is necessarily sexual in
nature—though such things have occurred—but because of how intimate
it is, how intimate it needs to be. Our Fey-other can become one with us
in many ways, in mind, body, heart, and spirit, the "perfect" marriage,
where two become as one and greater than one.

Part of why the Seelie can and will help us in seeing what needs to be done is because the Seelie are our kindred, but also because—despite the boundaries between us—we form close, even intimate, relationships with them. The so-called Faery Marriage, wherein we call them "wives" or "husbands," even though the Fey really don't have a gender of their own but are actually both or neither gender. However, when one of the Seelie becomes attached to a particular witch in the Faery Marriage, they usually take on a gender in association with that relationship. They become yin to our yang, up to our down, dark to our light or light to our dark.

One accused witch of the 1600's acknowledged this by saying that male witches tended to have female spirits and female witches tended to have male spirits. This has nothing to do with the sexual orientation of the person involved, as we have known gay or bisexual witches whose Fey-other appeared of the opposite gender to them, though we have speculated what a transgender witch or one who has gone through a sex change would have as their Fey-other. It has to do with being a mirror image, the face that you see through the open gate to Faery, what will fulfill the gaps in yourself, what will make you a whole person, a better person, closer to your highest self.

Yet, the Faery Marriage is not just the union of an individual witch and Fey, but of our world and theirs. For just as we find reflection in the other, so the material realm and the realm of Faery contain echoes of each other. They need each other. We share in a sacred contract with our kin, the Fey. They push, and we pull, and we push, and they pull. When we go to Faery, we participate in their magick and rituals and patterns. some of which are meant to sustain this intertwined world. The same holds true when the Fey come here to aid in our rituals and spells.

The bridge we form with our Fey-others can bring the two worlds closer and closer. The more we work with it, the stronger it grows. Eventually, this overlap can create a pure point of connection. At that point, the gate stands open, and energies have free flow back and forth. This energy flow creates a pattern we can all recognize as the infinity symbol. It's also symbolic of our journey from birth in this world, to death, and the same in the realm of Faery. Where the two circles converge in the figure eight symbol of eternity, this is the point of transition. [1]

This same symbol can also be represented by the crossed arrows, crossed bones, crossed arms, and is the crossroads where witches and the Fey go to perform magick and to dance, a point where the past and the future meet as one. From there, the past and the future co-exist and we can not only know them but affect them. This is because the Fey see *what is* and we, as witches, can affect *what is*. The Fey see that moment, yet even as they see it, it is unchanging and changing at the same time...which seems like a paradox. But what is, what was, what will be are all connected.

We, as witches, are the wild card. We carry within us the power of choice, of change. This power is an intrinsic part of what makes a witch, a witch. Still, we need to see to be able to tip over that domino that will set all of the rest into motion. What we see, we can fix our will upon and alter. But without Fey vision, the second sight, we would be acting blindly, unable to focus all of the power of our will to the precise point that can best create change. It's our own inner Fey nature and our relationship with our Fey-other and our Fey-clan that help us gain the ability to see truly.

For just as there are clans and families of witches, so there are clans and families of Faery. These clans cross the boundary of the veil; when we are in Faery, we work to the purpose and under the auspices of our Fey-clan, and when we are born upon the Earth, we continue that work as witches. Our talents and skills are different on either side of the veil, but we share in the group consciousness of the clan. In this regard, each witch family, each Fey-clan, holds a piece of the puzzle. Just as some gods and goddesses are patient and some are stern, some are gentle, and some are demanding, so each Fey-clan differs in their approaches, and so we differ in our approaches, being a part of them.

The Fey-clans can also be a bit possessive of those who belong to them. A friend and I were once given a blessing by the Fey of another clan—all meant with the best of intentions—but our own Fey found it disturbing. I also was once tempted to write to someone who was having their own

---

1   See illustration page 212

Fey encounters and having a confusing time of it, but checked with my own Fey contacts first and was gently discouraged from the contact as how this person viewed his interactions with them was part of the purpose of that particular Fey-clan, not my own. Intervening in the workings of another clan would not be fulfilling my purpose

We can sometimes glimpse the greater picture that our clan is working towards, but we have a far better idea of it when we exist as one of the Fey, of course. Still, a close connection to our Fey-other can help us tap into that understanding, as well as choosing to consult our Fey-clan on a regular basis to make sure our path is in tune. Accordingly, if you or your group desires to work in close conjunction with the Fey, then involving your Fey-others in ritual is vitally important, which requires developing tools that work for you in order to contact and connect to them.

A coven of witches can create a group consciousness and share in a group purpose. This gift stems from our Faery clans, so the closer we each can come to our Fey-other—especially if we can be so close to each other that we are, in effect, standing within each other while in ritual or while performing magick—the greater our ability to also merge with each other as witches and call upon the whole of our own self, our familiar spirits, our totem spirits, our Fey-other, and our entire Faery clan.

Fey and witches all share in the ability to form a singular entity out of the many, what some might call a "hive mind." Though, more accurately, it might better be called a "hive spirit." When we, as witches, create a group mind, a coven spirit, what some call "the child of the art," we see and act as the Fey generally do, for this is their standard existence. They are the many who are one and the one who is many. But what comes naturally to them, we have to work at, for the material world's reality is strongly based on separation and individualization.

The Seelie are more weighted towards being the many who are one as opposed the Unseelie where the focus is more on the one who is many, if that makes sense. Whereas, you can form a relationship with a single Seelie Fey and interact with that one alone at times—even as they remain connected to all the others of the Seelie—the Unseelie Fey almost always are seen in groups and dealt with in a group. It would have to be a rare, special occasion for you to see and interact with a single one of them by themselves. In fact, they really don't have much of a concept of a *by them-selves*. This means that, when you form a relationship with the Unseelie, it is with a *them*, and not an individual. That would be truly rare.

To accept and embrace our path as a witch, we must accept and embrace our Fey nature, our connection to the realm of Faery, and the work of our Fey-clan. You don't get very far as a witch if you fear the Fey or try and keep them at arm's length. Over the years, I've run into a few pagans and witches who distrust and insist we should stay away from the Fey, who've actively tried to keep them at a distance, and it never made any sense to me. Hopefully, the Fey have been more amused than offended by such behavior. It is, after all, our choice between the *Gate of Terror* and the *Gate of Joy*. For myself, I'd rather open the door to Faery via joy and laughter and pleasure and ecstasy, rather than through fear and shock and pain and terror. But, either way, Faery will not be denied.

Still, it can be difficult for our physical bodies to handle that level of energy, so it not only takes practice to get used to it but also in learn-ing where our limits are. People who don't know how to deal with Fey power—how to shut it down, how to ground it out, how to channel it without lingering ill effects—can find themselves on edge, nervous, jittery, or even worse.

All magick has a signature. When we first learn to do magick, we begin to recognize the feel of magick. Different witch traditions have a slightly different feel but are still recognizable as witch magick. By working with the Fey, we can come to recognize the feel of their magick, as well. So, the magick of the Seelie differs from the magick of the Unseelie and from the magick of the witch. The magicks can, and should, work together, but they are not exactly the same.

Fey magick, like witch magick, has the potential to heal or to harm, to bind or to free, to create or destroy. Our role, with our Fey-others, is to know what the need is and focus the will to fulfill it. We use the sight to make the proper choices for the knowing within guides us. There is no doubt at that moment. You act on instinct or, rather, the witch equivalent of instinct—when we act out of truth we do with is necessary and take our rightful place in the four-fold crown of Fate.

Creation and Dedication of Your Faery Altar

And in their courses make that round
In meadows and in marshes found,
Of them so called the Fairy Ground,
Of which they have the keeping.

-"Nymphidia: The Court of Fairy," Michael Drayton

To be honest, the Fey don't really need an altar. They do have their sacred places, but they are part of the landscape, liminal spaces where our world intersects and interweaves with the realm of Faery.

We are the ones who most often feel the need to create sacred places to do ritual, mainly to get ourselves into the proper frame of mind to touch upon spiritual things and work our magicks. But that doesn't mean that we can't work with the Fey to create what will serve both our purposes.

Your Faery altar can be decorated with stones, feathers, shells, bones, pieces of wood, semi-precious stones, images with a spiral or star in it or even small statues of the Fey, anything that you are drawn to or that reminds you of the Fey you are working with or seeking out. For example, if working with the Seelie, you might want to set out feathers or bird bones and, for the Unseelie, shells or stones from a stream or river. Sometimes, you will find these objects out in the woods, or they might come to you as gifts from friends or family. Generally, it's best if the object is not something you have bought for that specific purpose but have found or received.

The best choice for a Faery altar is a large stone somewhere in a secluded wooded spot. If such a stone exists on your property, especially in an area where you can have some privacy, then you can set up your altar and leave it the way it is. But if you do leave some of the items there, obviously you risk them disappearing. If this is concerning, you can find a box or basket of some kind and keep the objects in there, taking them with you when you go to the altar, placing out what feels right and appropriate at the time.

In either case, drawing Fey signs on the stone with chalk is a good idea. You can use paint, but chalk means you will re-draw the signs and so renew them and more easily change them if need be.

To consecrate the Faery stone, pour cream or milk around the stone and then bury a token that represents yourself beneath or near the stone, touching the stone if possible. Bury a small mirror with the token.

If you decide to move the stone or move to another place and need to create a new Faery stone, then dig up the mirror and the token and wash both in moon water. Purify both with incense and then put some of your essence into the token for its next use.

For an indoor Faery altar, you can use a small table and altar cloth, preferably green or white for the Seelie, red or black for the Unseelie, or some combination. A cloth that is half white and half black can also be used, with the cloth draped over the altar so that the line between the two runs from the upper right-hand corner to the lower left-hand corner. This represents the veil between the world of the living and the realm of the dead, the realm of Faery.

You can create your Faery signs, on round pieces of stone or wood, pottery or glass, or you can paint them onto the altar cloth. Find a stone from the land with which you work or that you live on and pour cream or milk over it to consecrate it, before placing it in the middle of the altar. If you want, you can put the stone into a shallow bowl and pour a little milk or cream over it as offerings. The stone can be placed on a mirror with your token next to it, touching it if possible.

Use consecrated water when you need to wash the stone or bowl clean of any remnants of the cream or milk.

The Fey signs you can use include one for each of the Four Quarters, but you can also use any signs that the Fey provides to you or that are personally meaningful to you.[2]

---

2   See illustration page 56

Faery Divination Spreads

*"We have watched you. We have always watched you. What you
have long forgotten, what lies buried deep within, we have never forgotten. We **see** you, as you are, as you have been, all you could become.
Did you imagine you walk this path alone? Did you believe none
accompanied you, holding the will of the future, the blessed dictates,
the promise of She whom you name Mother of Fate?*

*When you forget, that part of us within you, **that** does not forget.
When you remember us, you remember yourself. As you are, as you
were, as you yet will be. This memory is old, old and old, back to the
beginning, back before what you now call modern humankind. This,
too, we have watched, as we watched those before you. What we love,
we do not forget."*

-The Fey

These spreads can be used with either Tarot cards or runes. If you have a
particular set of divination tools you maintain in conjunction with your
Fey work, they would be the best to use. You can also pick out a set of
cards or runes and consecrate them for your interaction with the Fey. A
simple blessing can be used such as taking the runes or cards and holding them in the incense smoke you use for your Fey rites.

Incense can be lit to provide the proper atmosphere while you are doing
the divination spreads, and you can also light a candle or set of candles.
If using a set of candles, picking a red one and a white one to represent
the blood of witches and the blood of the Fey, would be a good choice. If
using a single candle, a nice green-blue color (teal) that symbolizes the
connection between witch and Fey, can be used. A rainbow candle can
also be chosen as it represents the bridge across worlds.

You can also choose to place your Fey-token and your personal token
out when you do these spreads, placing them—such as in the case of the
Crossroads Spread—on the side that represents yourself (or witches) and
that represents your Fey-other (or Faery).

Crossroads Spread

For this spread, lay out a red cloth or piece of paper next to a white cloth or piece of paper, or you can use a red cord or piece of yarn and a white one. Your side of the spread will be on the red side, and your Fey-other will be on the white side. Where the two meet, this represents the veil.

The five cards for each side represent the four Elements and the fifth Element of Spirit. They also symbolize the five petals of the rose and the five points of the star.

Card One-Earth

The foundation, the basis, who you really are in this life, in this time and place.

Card Two-Fire

What you are meant to do, what you are meant to accomplish, how to express yourself through action.

Card Three-Water

Your feelings, your passion, the emotion that feeds your magick.

Card Four-Air

How you best see the world and yourself, true vision, your form of understanding, insight, and revelation.

Card Five-Spirit

Who you are deep down, what is eternal; your highest self.

There will be five cards for you and five for your Fey-other. Or this can be done as one set of five cards representing your coven or magick group and the other five the Fey who are your mirror, who work with your group.

The cards will be laid out in reflection of each other.

The final card, the 11th card, you should touch to the heart of each of the five stars/roses back and forth 7 times and then placed across the 2 spirit cards, across where the red and the white meet and form a line. This is the *Crossroads Card* that is the point of intersection, how you meet and know each other across the veil.

When the cards are all laid out, turn over each set of cards at a time. For example, turn over the Earth card (1 and 2) for yourself and your Fey-other and then look at them and their meaning, not just for the card alone but in conjunction with the matching card. Continue with this until you have reached the 11th card, the Crossroads Card.

You can also look at how the cards interact with each other across Elements, such as card 1 (your Earth, basic foundation card) reflecting your Fey-other card 4 (how they see and understand). In fact, this spread can be read in many different ways for, as we and our Fey-others are as one— or attempting to be so—thus we balance and teach and guide each other.

This spread is more to take a look at where you and your Fey-other are in relationship to each other over time and as you do the work to grow closer.

Star of Vision Spread

For this spread, you can lay out a piece of cloth that is black or dark blue. You can also lay out a piece of cloth that has stars on it or glitters like the night sky. Alternately, you can choose to draw out an eight-pointed star on a piece of paper or paint it on a piece of cloth and use that as a guide. The four main points will be longer and also represent the crossroads (the Four Quarters) we use in ritual and the shorter points will represent the Cross-Quarters.

A good incense for this spread is one that fosters insight and clarity.

If lighting a candle, gold or bright blue can be used.

Card One—How We See Faery

What is Faery to us, what are our Fey-others to us, how do we see what is normally unseen and part of the realm of spirits?

Card Two—How Faery Sees Us

What are we to the Fey? What are we as individuals to our Fey-others, and how do they understand the physical world?

Card Three—What We Can Do for Faery

What can we as an individual, or we as witches, best do for our Fey kindred and for the realm of Faery? What do they require that we can accomplish?

Card Four—What Faery Can Do for Us

What can the Fey as our individual Fey-others and the Fey as a group do for us and for our world? What do we need that they can provide?

Card Five—How We Can Be Closer to Faery

What do we need to do and to become and change about ourselves in order to become closer to Faery and to understanding the Fey and our relationship with them?

Card Six—How Faery Can Become Closer to Us

What the Fey need to do and to be, in order for our relationship to grow and strengthen, in order for the bond to best manifest.

Card Seven—How to Visualize Our Shared Goals

How do we see what we need to achieve? What is our purpose, and how does it manifest in the material world?

Card Eight—How Faery Visualizes Our Shared Goals

How do the Fey see what we need to achieve? How do they understand our purpose, and how does it manifest in the realm of Faery?

Card Nine—Our Commonalities

How are we and the Fey alike? What do we share, and how can we best understand each other in order to work well together?

Card Ten—Our Differences

How are we and the Fey are different? What do we have to try to get past in order to better understand and see each other? Where we might clash in an effort to achieve our goals?

Card Eleven—Our Strengths

What can we call upon in order to achieve our purpose; what we know and what we can do?

Card Twelve—Our Weaknesses

What is keeping us and the Fey from achieving what we need to achieve; what needs to be overcome?

Card Thirteen—The Key

This card represents the key to best working together with the Fey in order to achieve our shared goals, to bring about our shared purpose.

If desired, you can throw another three cards or runes on any answer that you have a question about in order to further illuminate the answer. This spread can be used and should be used more than once, as time goes by and things change and you and the Fey make decisions and take actions, so the picture of what is going on will change.

It might be a good idea to do this spread on a regular basis, such as around the times of the greater sabbats or, at the very least, at May Eve and All Hallows Eve.

True Path Spread

This spread is to best see not just what our path ahead is, the ways we are attempting to accomplish our goals, but also how that interacts with the path of our Fey-other and with the shared Family of Witch and Fey, our Fey-clan. Clearly, the best way for us to follow this path is for our goals to be as close to one as possible, and for the work we are doing to interact positively with the work of our Fey-other and the Family. Together, we can do what might not otherwise be done.

For this spread, it might be a good choice to lay out the cards or runes on a blue-green (teal) cloth. You can also use a blue cloth.

If using incense, a purifying one might be a good choice, such as sage.

When lighting a candle, a silver candle is a good choice or a purple or violet one.

Card One—My Work

Why I am here, my path, what I am here to do and to be?

Card Two—My Fey-other's Work

My Fey-other's path, what they are doing and need to be doing.

Card Three—The Work of the Family

The path of the greater Family of witch and Fey that I belong to, the work of my clan both living and dead.

Card Four—My Path So Far

What have I accomplished on this path so far, what has been done, what foundations have been laid.

Card Five—What Blocks My Path

What stands in the way of accomplishing my goals? What needs to be overcome and how do I need to change and act differently?

Card Six—My Fey-others Path So Far

What has my Fey-other accomplished on their path so far,? What have they done and what foundation have they laid?

Card Seven—What Blocks Their Path

What stands in the way of my Fey-other accomplishing their goals, what do they need to overcome? How do they need to change and act differently?

Card Eight—Our Family's Path So Far

What has our Family accomplished so far on this path? What has been accomplished, what foundations have been laid?

Card Nine—What Blocks the Path of the Family

What stands in the way of the Family accomplishing our goals? What do we need to overcome together and how does the clan need to change and act differently.

Card Ten—My Next Step on the Path

What should I be doing, what should I be focusing on? How can I re-think or re-visualize in order to take the next step?

Card Eleven—My Fey-other's Next Step on the Path

What should my Fey-other be doing? What is their focus and how can they transform in order to undertake the next step?

Card Twelve—The Family's Next Step on the Path

What should the Family be doing, what should the focus be? How can (or should) that focus change in order to best accomplish the goals of the path?

Card Thirteen—Transformation

What is coming that will be a crossroads of potential? How will the opportunity for change manifest itself? What should we be on the look out for in order to take the next step.?

You can also choose to lay out additional cards on the last card, the *Point of Transformation,* in order to fathom when this point might be coming. For example, ask will it be within the next month, the next year, the year after that and lay out a card for each time.

Faery Gate Spread

This spread is to help guide us to what will work for us to be open to Faery and to our role as one who is part of this world and part of the Otherworld. As everyone is different, so every gate is different. We and our Fey-others have to find what works best for us in being open and aware of Faery, of holding fast to this world even as we touch the Other-world, and what to expect as a result.

We can use the insights from this spread to show us the way forward and also to give us some ideas about how this will change our lives and how our friends, family, and coven brothers and sisters will see and experience that change. You can't open the door to Faery and not be transformed by it and, once that door is opened and you freely walk through it, you can't go back.

Opening the *Gate of Faery* is a very serious undertaking and some divination is always a good idea in order to provide clues about what to expect. Of course, it won't tell us everything. Not even the gods know everything. But it's always a good idea to be as forewarned as possible,

especially in making the choice to go through that door. We have to know enough on a deep, inner level in order to trust. That doesn't mean we won't be uncertain or afraid, but we can't be afraid in our hearts. There, we just have to know that this is the right thing to do.

Card One—How to Open to the Knowledge of Faery

This card to is provide some ideas about how best we can be receptive to Faery and what it can and will teach us. We all have blocks and fears and doubts which can make us fearful of opening up our hearts and spirits to the world around us, let alone the realm of Faery. This card might show us some of those fears and blocks or what path we should take to get past them. If it is unclear, you can come back to this card at the end of the spread and throw another card on it to provide insight into the first step.

Card Two—What Anchors You to This World

This card is as important, if not more so, than figuring out how to connect to and interact with Faery. It does no good to fly free of this world and be close to Faery and to your Fey-other if you have lost touch with your friends, family, and the land where you live. An anchor is very important. There are many stories of those who become lost in Faery, who lose themselves. Faery is very seductive, and it can be tempting to turn away from a world that can, at times, be hard and painful, so we need to know what we love here in order to hold fast to the world we chose to come to.

Card Three—The Gate of Joy, the Gate of Terror

This card will tell us the aspect that the gate will take. Extremes are what open us up to what is otherwise unseen, in part because it short circuits the rigidity of our rational mindset. We we feel is way more powerful than what we think when it comes right down to it, especially something that we feel that is echoed in our very body, blood, and bone. Its no coincidence that we talk in poetic metaphor about bone-chilling fear or that our very blood turned cold. Its a very real feeling. Just as powerful joy is also described as ecstatic...ecstasy stemming from a Greek word that means being out of yourself. We have some influence over what shape the gate takes, but it will also take on whatever form is necessary for it to work. Even if it starts in terror we can, through experience, learn to turn that terror to awe and joy.

Card Four—The Step to Pass Through the Gate

This card can help reveal the form our choice will take. Will it be a ritual act, a powerful meditation, a weekend event out in the woods that will allow us to not only glimpse Faery, but to become part of it? It could be anything, even something seemingly mundane on the outside that, afterwards, we feel different, we feel changed, we have within us an understanding that wasn't there before. The one thing necessary, though, is an act of will. We must willingly make our choice.

Card Five—How This Will Affect You

How will you change as a result of your choice. How will be be different from the person before now that you have communed with Faery. How will you change inside? How will you change outside? Will it effect just your spiritual life, or will it affect all of your life? This card will help guide you to see what might happen afterwards, the path you have undertaken. Of course, you are always changing, always transforming, so this will be but a first step. One of many.

Card Six—How the World Will See It

How others will see you after you take this step and make this choice may be good or it may be bad. People don't always understand and there are some who don't like to accept when someone they know changes. The larger community will also react to you becoming different and you will have to deal with that, as well. Some will be drawn to you and some will fear you. Some people will feel both ways at the same time, oddly enough. Being aware of how others will react to you will help you comprehend how much or how little to reveal of what you now know and its source.

Card Seven—The Key to Walking the Edge Between Worlds

It's not easy to balance between two worlds, between the realms of life and death, this world and the Otherworld. We each have to figure out how to walk that fine line without falling off of it, without being pulled too far to one side or the other. We need our anchor, but we also need not to become so bound to the mundane that we lose track of Faery. This key can take many forms, including that of a practice we need to maintain, such as regular meditation or ritual or concentration on a symbol or connecting to our Fey-other emotionally.

Card Eight—What You Bring Back

This card represents what you bring back to this world from Faery and also what passes through you from Faery to here. This is one of the roles of shamanic style practice, of the hedgewitch—to be the one with one foot here and one foot there and to allow the forces, insights, revelations, and whatever is needed to use you as a bridge. Faery and this world are intimately connected with each other and we can stand at the point of that connection. This card can also represent what you being to Faery and so can choose to throw a second card to provide insight into that question.

This spread can be done on a regular basis and should at least be done twice in the year, once at May Eve and once on All Hallow's Eve.

Faery Cakes

*"We make merry. We dance the dance of old, making and unmaking.
What is it to be merry? It is to dance in full knowledge of who you are,
to celebrate the patterns of moon and sun and stars and of the Earth.
We make merry. We feast, seated at the table laid out by those you call
Ancestor, Gods, mother and father. Your true home sits at that table,
your true family. Gather then, in each and every Circle, to dance and
to feast...to **know** you are not alone, you are beloved."*

-The Fey

One of the things that the Fey share with us is the love of a sweet, good
cake...or what we call a cookie today. There are old stories about food
offerings made to the Fey, such as barley or oat cakes, or even pancakes
"yellow as the sun." The point is that they should contain our blessings,
our best wishes, so that the same will be offered to us in turn.

You can make these cakes specifically as an offering to the Fey, or you
can use them in your Faery rituals to be shared. The most important part
of making them is to do it with a light heart and pour that happiness into
them as you mix up the dough and bake them. This is especially necessary when you are making Faery cakes for All Hallow's Eve, as part of
creating your feast for the Fey and for the ancestors.

There is a recipe here for each of the seasons—spring, summer, autumn,
winter—plus a few other recipes that include rose water and a recipe for
what is sometimes called a "wishing cookie."

Just a few notes:

You can try out these recipes for yourself and your rituals if you like, or
develop your own favored Faery cake for you and your Fey-other. Our
experiences are that the Fey aren't much for chocolate and prefer cookies
that contain little to no artificial flavors or preservatives.

Most of the following recipes are older recipes or based on older recipes.
I've also cut back on some of the sugar in a few of them. For example, the

Summer-Lemon Thyme Cookie has had the sugar specifically reduced in order to bring out the taste of the lemon. These recipes have not, however, been tested with sugar substitutes.

Importantly, for the *Winter-Fruit and Nut Jumbles* and the *Cherry Rose Delights*, please feel free to leave out any nuts that you or any of your coven members might be allergic to.

I have used both regular milk in these recipes and almond milk. It doesn't seem to make much difference in the final result. They have not, however, been tested with margarine instead of butter or with any kind of flour other than regular wheat flour unless the recipe indicates it is specifically gluten free. If you are wheat intolerant or need to be gluten-free, you will have to experiment with other kinds or combinations of gluten-free flour in order to make gluten-free cookies turn out.

Spring

Grandma's Old Time Sugar Cookie

- 2 cups sugar
- 1 cup butter, softened
- 4 eggs
- 4 tablespoons milk
- 2 teaspoons baking powder
- 1 teaspoon baking soda
- 1 teaspoon salt
- 4 cups flour
- 1 teaspoon lemon rind, finely grated
- 1 teaspoon nutmeg (best if fresh grated)

In a large bowl, mix together the softened butter, nutmeg, lemon rind, and salt. Add the sugar slowly to the wet ingredients and cream well. Add the eggs, one at a time, and finally the milk. In another bowl, sift together the flour, baking powder, and baking soda. Slowly, add the flour mixture to the creamed mixture.

Drop rounded teaspoons of the dough onto an ungreased baking sheet, let stand a minute, and then press down with the flat part of a glass that has been dipped into sugar. They will spread a little, so allow for about a half inch or so between cookies.

Bake in pre-heated 350 degree oven for approximately 10-12 minutes.

The cookie will be soft when it first comes out of the oven, so let it cool a minute before removing it to a rack to cool completely.

Makes approximately 4 dozen cookies.

The cookies are soft and good-sized. They are a Cummer family recipe and, when I eat them, they take me right back to my childhood. Very much a "grandma" cookie.

Summer

Lemon Thyme Cookie

- 1/2 cup butter, softened
- 1 ¼ cups sugar
- 2 eggs
- ¼ cup fresh lemon juice (approximately the juice of one lemon)
- Fine grated zest of one lemon
- ¼ teaspoon ground thyme
- ¼ teaspoon salt
- ½ teaspoon baking powder
- 1 ½ cups flour

Cream together the sugar and softened butter. Add eggs, then lemon juice and zest. Combine flour, baking powder, salt, and thyme. Add the dry ingredients to the wet ingredients, a half cup at a time, mixing well. Cover bowl and let chill in refrigerator for half an hour to an hour.

Preheat oven to 350 degrees. Drop by teaspoonfuls onto baking sheet.

Bake 13 to 15 minutes or until edges and bottom are firm. This cookie will not brown.

Let cool. Can be sprinkled with powdered sugar if desired. Makes approximately 2 ½ to 3 dozen cookies.

These cookies have a good strong lemon flavor and the thyme adds an herbal undertone. I tend to use a slightly less than 1/4 teaspoon of the ground thyme, but you can use more or less to taste once you've tried out these cookies for yourself.

Autumn

Sugar and Spice Snaps

- 1/3 cup white sugar
- 1/3 cup brown sugar
- 1/3 cup molasses
- 2 ¼ cups flour
- 1 teaspoon baking soda
- 1 ½ teaspoons ground cinnamon
- 1 ½ teaspoons ground ginger
- ½ teaspoon ground cloves
- ¼ teaspoon ground allspice
- ¼ teaspoon ground black pepper
- ¼ teaspoon salt
- 12 tablespoons softened butter
- 1 large egg yolk
- 1 teaspoon vanilla

Mix together the white sugar, brown sugar, cinnamon, ginger, cloves, allspice, and the black pepper. Add in the softened butter and molasses, stirring until creamed together. Add in the egg yolk and vanilla and mix well. Mix together the flour and baking soda and salt and incorporate a half cup at a time into the wet ingredients. The dough will be stiff.

Put some white sugar into a bowl. Take about a teaspoon-sized piece of dough and roll into balls, then roll in the sugar.

Bake in pre-heated 375 degree oven for approximately 10-12 minutes. The cookies will not spread too much, so you can put more than a dozen on each cookie sheet.

Remove to rack or paper towels to cool completely.

Makes about 4 dozen cookies.

These are small, very spicy cookies, and most people would never guess they have black pepper in them. Store the cookies in an air-tight container or they will get too hard.

Winter

Fruit and Nut Jumbles

- ½ cup softened butter
- 3 eggs
- 1 ½ cups brown sugar
- 1 tablespoon warm water
- 1 teaspoon vanilla
- 1 teaspoon baking soda
- 3 cups flour
- 2 cups chopped dates
- ½ cup chopped nuts, pecans or walnuts

Mix together the brown sugar and softened butter until well creamed, then add the eggs. Put the baking soda into the warm water and stir to dissolve. Add to the creamed sugar mixture, then add the vanilla. Add the flour, a half cup at a time. Finally, stir in the chopped dates and the chopped nuts.

Drop by spoonfuls onto the baking sheet.

Bake in pre-heated 350 degree oven for approximately 10 minutes. Remove to let cool completely on rack or paper towels.

This is a variation on the old-fashioned "jumble," a cookie that goes back to at least the 1700's. You can choose to add some chopped citron or chopped candied fruit to this recipe in order to make it more like the much loved (or dreaded) fruitcake and cut back a bit on the chopped dates.

Honey Spice Wishing Star

The following recipe is for making a cookie you can hang on your Faery tree or for specific rituals where you are doing magick to bring something to you or both. They can also be used at the New Year or at your birthday, because you break off one point of the star at a time as you concentrate on making your wishes come true.

- 1½ cup sugar
- ½ cup honey
- ½ cup water
- 1/3 cup softened butter
- 1 egg
- 2 cups flour
- 1 teaspoon ginger
- ½ teaspoon salt
- ½ teaspoon baking soda
- ½ teaspoon nutmeg (best if fresh grated)
- ½ teaspoon cinnamon

In a large bowl, cream together the sugar and softened butter, then add the egg, honey, and water. Sift together the flour, ginger, salt, baking soda, nutmeg, and cinnamon. Add the dry ingredients slowly to the creamed mixture and blend well. Cover the dough and put into the refrigerator for at least an hour.

Roll out dough onto floured surface and cut into star shapes. Place onto an un-greased baking sheet.

Bake in pre-heated 400-degree oven for approximately 8 minutes.

If using for your Faery tree, poke a hole in the cookie that you can later thread a ribbon or piece of thin cord through in order to hang it later. If the hole closes up some during the baking process, just use a straw to re-open it gently before the cookie hardens as it cools.

Pryaniki-Russian Gingerbread

I have included a recipe for Russian Gingerbread, also known as Pryaniki, because it is one of the oldest sweets and is traditionally used to celebrate and mark great occasions such as marriages, births and deaths, as well as the holidays.

This cake can be used for any of the sabbats, but especially for Beltane and Sovane rituals.

- 1¾ to 2 cups flour
- ¼ teaspoon baking soda
- ¼ teaspoon ground cinnamon
- ¼ teaspoon ground ginger
- ¼ teaspoon ground cardamom
- ¼ teaspoon ground mace
- 2 tablespoons softened butter
- 2 tablespoons crushed blanched almonds
- ½ cup honey
- 1 egg
- ½ cup of a thick jam (one with a sharp flavor such as cranberry or wild plum or gooseberry is best)

Glaze:

- ½ cup powdered sugar
- 2 tablespoons fresh squeezed lemon juice

Crush the blanched almonds. Blend together the softened butter and honey in a bowl, then add in the egg. Take the cinnamon, ginger, cardamom, mace, baking soda and crushed almonds and mix in well. Slowly add flour until it forms a soft dough. Wrap up the dough with waxed paper and put into the refrigerator for at least an hour or overnight.

Preheat the oven to 350 degrees.

Roll out the dough on floured surface to 1/8-inch-thick and cut out rounds of dough with a 2 ½ inch cookie or biscuit cutter. Spread the jam on one of the rounds, leaving an edge of dough all around. Place a second round on top of the first and seal the two edges together by hand. The edges can be decorated with the flat of a fork or a crimper if desired.

Place cookies on greased baking sheet and put into oven at the 350 degrees for the first 10 minutes and then reduce the oven temperature to 325 degrees for approximately another 8-10 minutes. Put cookies on a rack to cool.

For the glaze, mix together the powdered sugar and lemon juice. Brush over cooled cookies.

Instead of a lemon glaze, you can also try an almond flavored or vanilla flavored glaze. For this glaze, take the ½ cup of powdered sugar and mix with 2 tablespoons of milk and a drop of almond or vanilla extract or to taste.

You can buy blanched almonds at the store, but if you want to blanch them yourself then boil the whole almonds in water for about 1 minute and then plunge them into ice cold water. This loosens the skin so that you can easily remove it.

Rose Water Cookie Recipes

The following recipes use rose water in them, which is not to the taste of everyone, but the Fey enjoy them. As they've expressed it—it's like having a scent that you can eat. When in doubt, for yourself to consume, go light on the rose water until you know if you like it or not. If you try them and really find you don't like the flavor of rose water and intend to eat them yourself, then you can always choose to leave out the rose water and substitute another flavor.

Food grade rose syrups and rose water can bought on-line or from Indian or Middle Eastern grocery stores. You can also go ahead and take a shot at making rose water or rose syrup yourself. If you are making anything with fresh roses, pick out the ones with the strongest fragrance, but make sure that they have not been sprayed. When in doubt, leave it out.

If you are offering them to the Fey and aren't going to eat any yourself, then use the full amount of rose flavoring for a nice strong-scented cake.

Rose Water Cookies

- 1 cup unsalted butter, softened
- 1 cup sugar
- 2 ½ cups flour
- 1 teaspoon baking powder
- 1 large egg
- 1 tablespoon heavy whipping cream
- ¼ teaspoons food grade (edible) rose water
- 1/8 teaspoon salt

Mix the butter with the sugar in a bowl. In another bowl, mix the flour with the baking powder and salt. Combine the wet and dry ingredients, then add the heavy whipping cream, egg, and the rose water. Cover and let chill in the refrigerator for at least one hour.

Roll dough out on floured surface to ¼ inch thick. Cut out cookies with whatever cookie cutter shape you desire.

Bake in preheated oven at 375 degrees about 10 minutes, or until the cookies are firm and lightly browned at the edges.

Let cool. Best kept in an air tight container.

These are rather crispy cookies and thin, so be careful not to let the edges get too done. You might want to try this recipe with just the ¼ teaspoon of rose water if you want to eat them yourself, or you can up the amount to ½ teaspoon or more for the Fey.

Lemon Rose Water Cakes

- 1 cup of unsalted butter, softened
- ½ cup powdered sugar
- 2 ½ cups flour
- ¼ teaspoon salt
- ½ teaspoon ground nutmeg
- 2 tablespoons milk or heavy whipping cream
- ½ teaspoon freshly grated lemon zest
- ½ teaspoon vanilla extract
- ¼ teaspoon food grade (edible) rose water
- Sugar crystals (optional)

Mix together the softened butter and sugar in a mixing bowl. Add in the vanilla, the milk or heavy whipping cream, and the rose water. In another bowl, mix together the flour, lemon zest, salt and nutmeg. Combine the wet and dry ingredients, adding additional milk or heavy whipping cream if need be if the dough is touch too dry.

Roll out on a flour surface ¼ inch thick. Cut out with whatever shape cookie cutter you desire. Put on cookie sheet and sprinkle with some sugar crystals if you wish.

Bake in preheated oven 350 degrees about 15 minutes or until the edges are firm and slightly golden brown.

Let cool and keep in airtight container.

This recipe has a blend of more flavors with the rose water. It also contains less sugar. This cookie might make a good choice for a ritual where both you and the Fey will be consuming the cookies.

Cherry Rose Delights

- ¾ cup softened butter
- ¾ cup sugar
- 2 tablespoons milk
- 2 eggs
- ¼ teaspoon food grade (edible) rose water
- ½ teaspoon vanilla
- 1 teaspoon baking powder
- ½ teaspoon baking soda
- ½ teaspoon salt
- 2 ¼ cups flour
- 1 cup finely chopped dates
- 1 cup chopped pecans
- 1/3 cup chopped maraschino cherries (well drained)

Mix together the butter and sugar, then add the milk, eggs, vanilla and rose water. In another bowl, mix together the flour, baking soda, baking powder, and salt. Incorporate the wet ingredients into the dry ingredients. Fold in the pecans, dates, and cherries. The dough will be very sticky. Cover the bowl and put into the refrigerator until well chilled, six to eight hours or even overnight.

Preheat the oven to 375 degrees. Take pieces of the dough and roll into 1 inch size balls and put on the cookie sheet. Flatten down the dough slightly with the bottom of a glass dipped into sugar. You can also use a blend of regular sugar mixed with colored sanding sugar. If desired, you can press a half of a pecan into the top of it.

Bake approximately 8-10 minutes or until slightly browned. Let cool 1 to 2 minutes on the cookie sheet before removing to wire rack to cool completely.

Makes approximately 3 ½ dozen soft cookies.

If you are leaving out the rose water, you can up the vanilla extract to 1 teaspoon instead. But this cookie has a nice blend of flavors and most people would never guess it contains rose water unless you tell them.

This one is my favorite rose water cookie to date and it has gotten good reviews from others, as well.

The following recipes are for gluten free rose water cookies for those who have issues with wheat or gluten.

Gluten Free Rose Water Shortbread

- 1 ½ cups white rice flour
- 1 stick of butter, softened
- 1 large egg
- ¾ cup powered sugar
- ¼ teaspoon food grade (edible) rose water
- ½ teaspoon cardamom
- 1 teaspoon poppy seeds (optional)

Mix together the cardamom and the rice flour in a large mixing bowl. In another bowl, mix together the softened butter and the sugar. To the liquid ingredients, add the egg and rose water. Combine the wet and dry ingredients and cover the bowl. Let chill in the refrigerator for at least six hours.

Preheat the oven to 300 degrees. Flour your hands with rice flour and take pieces of the dough and roll into 1 inch balls. Place on cookie sheet and use either a fork to flatten the dough or the bottom of a glass dipped into sugar. Sprinkle the cookies with poppy seeds if desired. Bake for 20-25 minutes or until the cookies are firm, but not browned. Remove from oven and let cool. Keep stored in airtight container.

These cookies, like many gluten free ones, can be a bit dry and crumble more easily. If making a regular version with wheat flour, use a cup of white flour and a half cup of rice flour. It really does help to chill the dough well before making the cookies. You can also use one of the cookie presses with a pattern on them to flatten the cookie rather than the bottom of a glass.

Gluten Free Rose Water Sugar Cookie

- 2 cups white rice flour
- 1/3 cup sweet rice flour
- 1/3 cup tapioca flour
- 1/3 cup cornstarch
- ½ teaspoon salt
- ½ teaspoon xanthan gum
- 1 teaspoon baking soda
- 1 ½ cups sugar
- 1 cup butter, softened
- 2 eggs
- 1 teaspoon vanilla
- ½ teaspoon almond extract
- ½ teaspoon food grade (edible) rose water

Mix together the rice and tapioca flours, the cornstarch, salt, xanthan gum, and baking soda. Cream together the softened butter and sugar, then add in the vanilla and almond extracts and the rose water. Add in the eggs once at a time and mix well. Slowly add in the dry ingredients to the wet until a dough is formed.

Chill the dough for half an hour to an hour then roll the dough by hand into teaspoon size balls and dip in some sugar or sanding sugar. A colored sanding sugar such as pink, green, or silver would be nice. Place on a baking sheet and flatten a little with the bottom of a glass that can also be dipped in sugar.

Bake the cookies 12-15 minutes in a pre-heated 350 degree oven until they are lightly golden in color. Do not over bake.

The cookies will be a little soft when they come out, so let them sit a minute on the baking sheet before removing to let cool completely.

If you decide to leave out the rose water, increase the vanilla to 1 ½ teaspoons instead.

~ *The Secret Kin* ~

Time and tide take heed of no one
Least of all
Those would throw rocks at it.
One must face the undertow
To find the secret moon
Which calls them forth
And sets them back again.

When yesterday comes
Its is already today
Tomorrow does not wait for the dawn
For night is eternal.

Our fingers are long
You know their touch
Our hearts are open
They know much
Of what is dreamt of as history
But not yet taken place
A city rises but is already
Crumbled down to dust
The bones, the shell, the passing knell
Of death
Is but an illusion as much as life.
You all be ghosts
Who dream of life
You never die
But return to life.

Thunder calls

The sky glows blue
Dark space vanish
The tides renew.

One cloud an edge
Over bottomless flight
What fear to plunge
To steal the night.

Time and tide what life endures
A precious promise whispered sweet
One jewel to keep and two to bear
A necklace of tears, a cup of air.

Dewdrops press upon the flesh of roses
A thorn pieces bright
Madness entangled
It takes more than a kiss to break the spell
Of light enchanted
In dreams of life
Beyond the masque of death
To dance with one's self
And see one's true heart, one's
True love revealed.

What do you wish to know of Faery?
Of the clan of air and the family of darkness?
From dusk to dawn, their powers call
On the sickle moon
When all hangs in balance.

Chapter 4

Through the Veil

"We have been silent for many years, speaking to few, misunderstood by most, standing aside to see...is it time? What will they do? Where will they go?

We have been silent, but not gone away. We would not go away. Where would we go? We are of this place as much as you are. What you love, we love. What we love, you love. At least so long as you listen to your heart.

It is through the heart that we are. It is through the heart that we may touch and be with you. Close your heart, and we are gone, as though we had not been. Invisible. All around, but not seen. To see us, see through your heart. To hear us, listen to your heart. We are silent no more."

-The Fey

The night came alive, the full moon casting shadows among the trees as the wind swayed the branches. There was no one there that we could see, but we were not alone. The shadows walked, they watched just out of the circle of our firelight. We had walked the maze at twilight, and they had witnessed our journey inward and out. We had held our rite as night began to fall and they had guarded our circle, even as the haunting sound of the whip-poor-will echoed through the forest. Later, while we slept, we had been called and gone out to the river, waking in the morning to find our feet covered with sand and grass, with vague memories remaining of what we had done in our dreams, of waters red as blood and laughter and dancing.

We had been Faery-led at Lammas, and we talked of it around our fire the next night, nervous about it, excited and afraid, and as we talked, Faery drew close around us. This was our sacred place...the enchanted world of old, half here and half there, reclaimed, a covenant that bridges across worlds, across time, across the veil.

But what then is the veil? We tend to talk about it as that which separates this world from other worlds, the realm of Faery or the realm of the dead from the land of the living. But the veil can also be described as that which keeps us from seeing the Otherworld, that which makes it unseen. To pull back that veil is to learn how to see the unseen, that which lies all around us, though we normally lack the means to recognize or acknowledge it.

The Fey indicate that the veil is *"what keeps us from seeing what we ought not see."* The word ought means "obligated." So, the veil keeps us from seeing what we are not obligated to see, what it is not necessary for us to see. So, you can say that the veil keeps us from seeing what is not required for us to see. For those of us who are called to be witches and cunning ones, for whom it's needed to see what others do not normally see, it is proper and necessary then for us to see through the veil. We *will* see what we are *required* to see.

This does not, however, mean that we must take what we see and experience absolutely, literally. That's one of the mistakes that some make when they have visions or experiences that are outside of the ordinary. This goes not just for witches, but for mystics of all religions. Such visions must be looked at in multiple ways, symbolically, poetically, mythologically, and artistically. What we experience in the Otherworld and what we see in the Otherworld, whether via meditation, ritual, dreams or by journeying there in flesh or in spirit, rarely means just one thing.

We are required to translate what we see into this world, to help it take shape here. We are the ones who need to see the greater reality that our own is a part of, but not the all of. Faery sight can help gain us that clarity of vision, and it's not so much the world we live in that changes, but that we come to see the greater rather than the lesser. Our eyes are opened to the spirit realm that lies beyond the material world, and out of which the material world arises.

It's like the light spectrum, where we can only see within a certain range, yet there are other forms of light that exist that our usual visual senses cannot pick up. Accordingly, we must expand beyond the evidence of the five senses to "see" more of the spectrum. But, because how we sense the realm of Faery is not tied to the five senses, it can take myriad forms. It can come by means of visions, but it could be voices, sounds, smells, colors—some that we have no name for—or a feeling or sensation.

This can make our experiences and understandings of Faery difficult to describe and hard to remember, for as the expansion of our senses fades to what is considered normal, what we have "seen" can also fade away and become lost. Accordingly, the veil is as much within us as without us. For we could attend a ritual, journey to a sacred site, and yet not have the unseen revealed.

For most people, the veil only parts rarely, perhaps a few times in a lifetime, if even that, and in many circumstances, they end up denying what they have seen or not using it for good purpose because they have no context within which to place it. So, for those of us who more routinely see through the veil, who are obligated to do so, we need to not only believe in what we have seen but place it within the context of who we are and what we are engaged in and make good use of what we have seen. It takes practice to retain as much of this experience as possible, and this is all the more vital since we need to "see" in order to "go" to Faery. We get to the Otherworld, to Faery, by jumping the hedge, taking the dread bridge, the sword bridge, or, in other words, crossing the veil.

To some, this bridge can be seen as the Milky Way arching across the night sky, a bridge along which ancient witch and Faery goddesses such as Dame Holda, Nicneven, Herodias, and Diana traveled. With them various night-riders in the form of birds such as geese, screech owls, and nightjars. The idea that witches traveled on brooms came later; originally, witches transformed themselves to "fly" or flew on the backs of animals, especially the wolf, and thus journeyed to the sabbat along the paths of power known as the corpse roads, the ways of the dead, or the old straight tracks. It was a wild rushing journey to the Witches' Mountain, the Vale of Roses, the walnut tree of Benevento, all names and images for the same gathering "place."

Obviously, it's no coincidence that the Faery Rade and the Wild Hunt travel on these same lines of power, for all across Europe and in England, the Fey, witches, and the dead are traditionally tied together. They and we journey to the same sacred place to be together.

For instance, there are many cases where accused witches of the past talked about their interaction with Faery and this ended up being part of the proof needed to convict them of being witches. They related how they went to dance and feast with the Fey in the Otherworld, to have sexual relations with them, to be granted powers of healing or prophecy. One woman of the late 1500's was accused of going with the *Good Neighbors* and the Queen of Elfhame and admitted that she had friends in the Queen's Court who were her kindred. The Scots self-professed witch, Isobel Gowdie, also talked about how she was out "flying" and dove into a barrow and ended up meeting the king and queen of the Elves. Though it was night in her world, once she had entered the realm of the Elves, she found that it was day there, emblematic of the mirrored nature of the two worlds.

The close association of witch and Fey can also be seen in the traditional title for the high priestess—the Queen of Elfhame. For the true witches' circle lies in Faery, taking place neither here nor there and so those who got there must be witches and are "Fey" in nature—a little wild, a little strange, even a bit mad. This Fey nature is because faery blood and witch blood are essentially the same.

Other outward signs indicating those of Fey blood is that they tend to have red hair or were born with six fingers on their hands. Of course, there is also the traditional indication of having the Sight or Faery Sight by being born with a caul. Being born into a witch family also increases your chances of being a witch and interacting with the Fey. Those who arrested accused witches also knew this and eagerly looked for signs of others in an accused person's family that might be suspect.

Of course, you can also be taken through the veil by the Fey, the infamous *faery-abduction* scenario. It was a common belief that the Fey would steal people and keep them with them in Faery. So much so that, in Scotland, if you had gone away for a long time, people might say you were in Elfhame. Of course, one of the most famous of these stories is that of the author of *"The Secret Commonwealth of Elves, Fauns, and Fairies,"* Reverend Thomas Kirk, who apparently was taken away to Faery. Other famous tales include that of Tam Lin, Thomas the Rhymer, and the Erl-King, who made a bargain with a small man on a goat and got caught up in the Otherworld for his troubles. He eventually became one of the leaders of the Wild Hunt, while Thomas the Rhymer became a bard after he returned through the veil.

In folklore, the Fey are said to be particularly apt to take away those who are beautiful or interesting or odd or have golden-blond hair, which predilection has probably given rise to the modern Christian stories of Satanists liking to steal blond children for their "sacrifices." Of course, some Christians even equate the Fey directly to demons, which is part of explaining any experiences of what is other, of the unknown as coming from "the Devil." They see the experience through the paradigm of there being only good and evil, God and Satan, and so the faery-abduction must be evil and Satanic unless they somehow manage to paint the Fey with the face of angels instead.

Another modern form of the experience is the alien-abduction. Most find this disturbing, if not downright terrifying, though some return with a renewed spiritual interest or focus on environmentalism and protecting the Earth. While in the hands of these "aliens" in their "UFO's," people are sometimes given visions or are apparently experimented upon or studied. Much of these seems a recent development based on today's emphasis on science and technology—both the way that the Fey appear and how their Hollow Hills are now flying saucers.

The abduction tales retain the aspect of Fey interaction though; that tells us of how someone goes there for what seems like a short period of time only, upon returning, to find out that years have passed in the mundane world. A familiar span of time is finding out that 100 years have passed in the meantime and all of your friends and family, all you have known is long gone. There are also stories of having spent months or even years in Faery, only to return and find no time has passed at all in the normal world. The veil, then, not only represents a boundary between worlds but also a shift in time, or understanding of time.

Because Faery is thus outside the boundaries of place and time, then to come back from it you not only need to know *where* you are returning to but *when*. You can return from it to any time and any place. For certainly, journeying to Faery is dangerous but so is coming back again, since there is always the chance you can get lost. It helps if you have a connection with the local land spirits and if your blood is tied to that land—whether by ancestors having lived and died there for generations or by deliberate blood rituals to bind yourself to that place. You can then follow that thread back through the veil from Faery or any other world you might journey.

There are, of course, certain special nexus points where such transitions are more common and easier to undertake. Sacred springs and forests and hilltops are some of the traditional places, but when you return from Faery through them, you need to know the feel of the place to which you belong, the land you are a part of. You need to follow the pull of your own home that can draw you back again through the veil.

When it comes to the times when these nexus points are most active, we can find clues in the stories of attempts made to recover those who had been taken by the Fey. The best times were thus the *Quarter Days*, what is known today as Beltane Eve, Lammas Eve, All Hallows Eve and the Eve of Imbolc. These were the times when the Fey were said to ride out, which clearly also implies that the veil is thinner at those times. Of course, All Hallows Eve remains the premier time the veil is said to be thin, but the other three evenings are also transition points when Faery can be accessed more easily.

At All Hallow's Eve, we tend to use the open gate to bid our loved ones, our ancestors, to return to us. The one who facilitates this is no less than Old Hornie, the horned god of death, the Lord of Faery. While, at Beltane Eve, we use that gate to travel to Faery and celebrate under the auspices of the Lady of Faery, the Rose Queen. Lammas Eve and Imbolc Eve are more like potential times when the gate is accessible, for the veil is not

quite as thin at those times as at All Hallows and Beltane. They will open
if there is need for them to open.

The Fey can also open the veil if they choose at other times, but it takes
work on their part, so it's better if you use a natural Quarter Day if you
can. For instance, we have asked the Fey a handful of times to open the
veil at a Cross-Quarter day for a particular ritual, and they have obliged,
but it takes a whole day for them to open the gate and another whole
day to close it again. During those three days, strange things happen.
People have had odd dreams and experiences, visions and insights, and
you can sense the wild energy unleashed. It's hardly surprising that any
rituals done while the gate is open are more Fey in nature, edgy and even
unnerving.

The *Faery Sabbat* and the *Witches' Sabbat* are two halves of a whole.
When we go to the sabbat in the Otherworld, we meet there with our Fey
kindred, taking part in feasting, dancing, battles, and magicks done in
that "place." We desire to be with them, and this desire helps span the
gap between and, once we have gone there, the sense of homecoming, of
belonging, helps guide us back again. Once we have traveled through the
gate of Faery to our true home of the heart and spirit, we can more easily
find our way back there ever afterward.

When we go to our sabbats here in the physical realm, it's an echo of that
other sabbat. We can make it a true sabbat, a greater sabbat, by connecting to our kindred both quick and dead, seen and unseen.

When we draw a circle, we create our ancient landscape, our compass.
We summon the powers to watch and guard and lend their energies to
our ritual, using the images, the symbolism, that we share with them. We
create a space that takes place in and outside of time, a place that is not
a place, between worlds and part of all worlds. Any circle can become a
gate to Faery and a node of possibility if that circle is awakened if we are
awakened.

For the true witches' crossroads is where our world and the world of
Faery cross, creating a moment filled with the potential for change. The
Faery Circle is the *First Circle*, the *First Pattern* of which all other circles
are an echo. It's the original pattern from which all others take their form

and purpose, from which all witch circles derive. So, each time a witches' circle is raised, it taps into that power, creating patterns within patterns within patterns from the macrocosm to the microcosm and beyond.

According to the goddess of Faery:

> *"all blood is the crossroads. This world and Faery both*
> *inside us, in our blood. To know that and become that..."*

To know that and become that means understanding something so well that we almost become what we understand. It can even mean that we actually do become what we understand, which, in this case, means that we become the crossroads. It means that we interweave with the Fey and the strands cross to make nodes in the Web of Wyrd, each node a beginning point where light meets dark, past meets future, time meets eternity; the mystical crossroads that's within each of us and without us.

The energy that pours through the *First Circle* comes from what some call the Abyss or the Void, the realm of chaos and infinite possibility, infinite impossibility. Faery sets the first order upon that outpouring of chaos; then we bring that pattern through into the physical world. This is done upon the dictates of Lady Fate, the true Queen of the Crossroads, the dread weaver of the Web of Wyrd.

When we journey to Faery, to the *First Circle*, we work with the pattern there. When we return to our world, we bring that pattern back with us. We seek to bring the dreams we dream there to realization. What we know as ideals, beliefs, and dreams are felt far more powerfully in Faery. When we come back through the veil to our physical bodies, we try to bring back a focus for those ideas, beliefs, and dreams so that they can manifest themselves in the material.

For these ideas and dreams can take root in our world, in people, in cultures and nations, and become real and immediate and alive. They can spread from person to person, place to place, culture to culture, and give rise to actions and creations of all kinds. They can take on a life of their own, transforming through time, sometimes fading away only to be resurrected once more. Or they can simply die off because the times no longer support them and people are no longer open to them. Sometimes, it can take only a short while for this idea to grow and sometimes it can take centuries to manifest fully.

When many witches, many dreamers, many artists bring through similar ideas, similar patterns, there is a much greater chance that they will take root and grow quickly and strongly. We can see this in action when common ideas come to being through many people in many places, people who have had no contact with each other. Clearly, its something whose time has come for it to be born and it expresses itself through those who are open to it. When these things happen it's a good idea to pay attention to them for such expressions hide a greater truth, something that each artist or dreamer or witch is manifesting a small portion of in their own way and to the best of their ability. Each has a piece of the puzzle, a clue to what lies beyond the individual manifestation.

Of course, everyone has it within them to become a gateway for something to be born from Faery. So, one might ask, what are witches for if everyone can potentially be a portal? The big difference lies in one thing—consciousness. Conscious will and intent and purpose. Most people, if they bring through ideas, dreams, patterns, do it without conscious intent. They may also have little, if any, concept of what effect this will have on them, on the world, on the future. They do not know how to *see*, to perceive the myriad aspects and effects of what they are doing.

There have always been those born with the potential to see and know more than what the five senses allow, but those who are born with the potential to be witches are *called* to gain that power to see. Anyone can learn to do spells and doing spells does not make someone a witch. There is much more to it than that. The potential within, the ancient ancestral knowledge, and divine flame must be awakened. A witch is someone who has died to their old life and becomes re-born, whether through a ritual initiation or one by the gods or the Fey. Witches are called to journey beyond the *River of Blood*, past where most are forced to stop and turn back lest they never return.

Witches go beyond and return because we must. We must go, and we must return. More than that, we are also drawn to pursue the great mysteries. We hear the great rushing voice of the beyond and have the courage to dare to seek out and bring back what is needed the most from what is otherwise unknown. In this, the Fey are our partners, our companions, our guardians, and our guides. We can't get there without them.

The more in tune we are with our Fey-others, the more we can serve our shared purpose. A witch working in conjunction with an entire Faery clan and with other witches who are part of that Faery clan, in the past, the present, or the future, and so take part in great magicks, especially the magick of transformation, transformation that has its beginnings through the veil and beyond.

For the winds of change have their starting place in Faery—they flow from where witches and the Fey meet and dance the patterns. Old patterns end and new patterns begin, while others are re-fashioned or built upon the bones of the old. There are small patterns and large patterns, but all the patterns interact with each other. What a pattern represents is a way of being, of how things are, and how the world is seen, its paradigm. The true world is much more, of course than what we can see of it, but as the paradigm shifts, different aspects come to light.

Witches need to lead the way. As change begins in Faery, being able to see and connect across the veil means we can know more about what is coming, about the interactions and echoes that otherwise might remain invisible. Working with our Faery contacts and our Fey vision grants us the ability to take the clues, the omens, and signs all around us, and know when we have reached a vital juncture, an important turning point. At those points, it is our right and our duty to act. We use that knowledge granted by our Fey-sight to work magick and make sure that magick is grounded in the material.

We are here to do what the Fey cannot; else we would not need to leave the lovely realm of Faery to be born here.

Ritual to Dream with Your Fey-other

In the hinder end of harvest, at All-hallowe'en,
When our good neighbours dois ride, if I read right,
Some buckled on a beenwand, and some on a been,
Ay trottand in troops from the twilight;
Some saidled on a she-ape all graitlied in green,
Some hobland on a hempstalk hovand to the sight;
The king of Phairie and his court, with the elf-queen,
With many elfish incubus, was ridand that night.

-"Flyting Against Polwart,"Alexander Montgomery

Witches through the centuries have been known to "fly," to travel out of their bodies. Many of us do this while dreaming. The dreams that result from actual travel are stronger, stranger, and do not feel like regular dreams. It's always good to pay attention to such dreams and, quite often, they can lead to the creation of magick or rituals or artistic expression. They also can lead us to deeper understandings and answers to questions that we need for ourselves or others.

It would be good to keep a notebook or journal near your bed in case you wake during the night and need to jot something down or to write it down once you get up in the morning. The more powerful images and impressions will remain, but some of what you dream of will fade and so should be recorded as soon as possible. It may not be easy to capture everything, and some of it might not make sense, but looking at it for clues will often lead to insight and even further questions. Sometimes, things that are not clear at first will reveal themselves over time, or you will be able to piece together a picture eventually from many dreams and through a combination of dreams and divination.

The best time to undertake this ritual is during the three nights of the full moon—on the night before the moon is at its full, the night of the full moon, and the night after. Other traditional times would be the nights of the sabbats, especially on the eve of the Spring Equinox and at

Beltane Eve. You can also use this ritual if you have a particular question for which you need insight.

This ritual is for right before you go to sleep so that you can travel in your dreams with your Fey-other with them as your guide or guardian. It makes use of your charged token and the token of your Fey-other, though you can do it without the tokens if need be.

The tokens can be placed into a small bag together and tucked under your pillow for the evening. If that won't work well for you or if your tokens are fragile, then place them or hang them on the headboard or near the head of the bed or on a nightstand near the head of the bed.

With the tokens in your hand, touch the left side of the bed, saying:

> *In sleep to dream*

Touch the right side of the bed, saying:

> *In sleep to fly*

Touch the foot of the bed, saying:

> *Between the earth*

Touch the head of the bed, saying:

> *Between the sky*

Hold the tokens to your forehead and then over your heart, concentrating on your wish to travel with your Fey-other.

Place the tokens under your pillow or above or near the head of your bed.

As you relax to sleep, keep holding the desire to travel or your particular question in your mind.

In the morning, touch the tokens again to your heart and your forehead and express your thankfulness and affection for any experiences and knowledge gained. Do this, even if you don't remember much when you wake up, for often we do travel in our dreams, but sadly do not recall much or all of what we saw. That takes time and practice and openness.

If you do get a particularly strong vision or insight from these dreams or in answer to your question, follow your instincts if you feel drawn to make an offering to the Fey in return for their aid. Gifts should inspire gifts because this honors the balance.

You will know when a dream is a "true dreaming" by waking with some knowledge, an innate understanding that retains its power and immediacy. It might take the form of a connection you haven't seen before, of a ritual or spell that you need to do, a chant or song you need to sing, a place you need to go to, a symbol you need to start using, or an awakened memory of Faery.

Each night, we do not simply rest, but explore the Otherworld and expand the spiritual boundaries of understanding. We learn how to catch hold of those hidden memories to become more aware and powerful as a witch as we learn how to exist in two worlds at the same time.

Meditation to Journey to Faery

"He whom you know as the Dark Man, the Black Man, we call the whispering one. You go to hear His voice, yet never reach it. He leads you on, calling you after Him, for that He is destined to do."

-The Fey

There are many ways of journeying to Faery.

To go there in the flesh is rare and dangerous, but it does happen. People have stumbled into Faery by driving down a road that you can't find when you look for it later, or by stepping through a gap in a wooded bluff that disappears once you emerge again. Or you step between two trees in the darkness or between two lit torches, the boundary marked by a broom or blade laid over the gateway and find the night has transformed and that you are able to see what was unseen. When this happens, you find yourself outside what is considered "normal" reality and, once you return, often find yourself doubting what happened, what you saw, what you felt, if you don't already have a context to place it in.

In this case, we are talking about traveling there via trance, where you work to enter an altered state of consciousness in order to send out your spirit from your body. This is not necessarily easily done and can take practice, but it's a worthwhile endeavor, even if you can only manage it for a moment or two.

You can incorporate this into your regular ritual practice, such as by using a guided meditation at each full moon circle and, should the opportunity arise, doing a ritual in some woodland spot where you can set up the proper gateway. You can choose to use it during your circles either as-is or with your own personal or coven symbology.

In a group setting, each person can take a turn in reading it, so that everyone gets a chance to experience it. This can be done in a ritual context, or simply in a darkened room. At first, it might be better to set the mood, so to speak, by the use of candles, incense, whatever you might need to get into the proper frame of mind. Later on, these things can be dispensed with once you know how to get into the proper trance state without them.

If working alone, the meditation can be recorded to be played back later.

Get comfortable and do some deep breathing, letting the worries and stress of the day drain away. Some grounding and centering work would be useful here, whatever you or your group generally uses.

Once everyone is settled down, the chosen person can read this meditation, or you can start the recording:

It's night, and you stand in a forest of great, old trees. Their branches frame the sky overhead where you can see the stars creating swirls and patterns. The air is cool and fresh. You can hear the song of crickets all around you. In the distance, an owl hoots softly.

A mist begins to rise from the ground between the trees. It moves in swirls and patterns. A faint light begins to come from the ground beneath your feet. As you watch, it winds its way out before you, forming a silvery pale path.

You start down the path, following it as it twists and turns between the roots of the great trees, between huge moss-covered stones. The light of the path unwinds before you, fading off behind you back into darkness.

The path takes you to a stream, lined with tall grass and reeds. You can hear frogs in the reeds, singing in tune with the water as it makes it way over the rocks. Tiny yellow lights move over the water, fireflies flashing on and off, weaving their own dance.

Several flat stones bridge the stream, and you step out onto the first one. Cold air comes up off the water, and the fireflies drift around you as you cross, stepping from one stone to the next until you reach the other side.

Before you, an old stone staircase leads downwards into the earth, the steps are worn away by the passage of time. To either side stands a large pillar, one of black stone and one of white. As you look up, you see that there are figures on top of the pillars.

A hooded, cloaked figure stands on top of the black pillar, hands outstretched to hold a skull. Pale light comes from the eyes of the skull and the fireflies hover over it, forming a living crown. You can't see the face within the hood, but you feel his eyes upon you.

He knows you as you know Him.

You name him: The Horned One, The Lord of Twilight, The Lord of Death, the King of Faery

A naked figure with long wild hair stands on top of the white pillar, hands holding a broom woven of wood and vines and flowers. You look into Her eyes as She gazes at you. You see darkness and the light of a thousand stars. She knows you as you know Her.

You name her: The Rose Maiden, The White Lady, The Pale Lady, the Queen of Faery

You acknowledge the Lord and Lady of Faery, then step between the black and white pillars and onto the stone staircase. As you descend deeper and deeper, you feel coolness and the smell of damp earth around you. The walls to either side of you begin to glow faintly.

Down and down. Deeper and deeper. One step after another. Down and down into depths of the earth.

As you approach the bottom of the stairs, the walls pull back, and you find yourself in a large cave. The walls of the cave glisten, and there are strange symbols etched and painted on the stone, horned beasts and circles and bees and lions and eyes.

In the center of the cave, there is a dark pool of water. As you approach the pool, a mist rises from it. Shapes move in the mist, forming and reforming, twisting and transforming, always changing, never still.

You begin to hear a distant sound from somewhere beyond the mist, a murmuring, a whispering, a soft buzzing.

A bright white light appears in the center of the mist, getting brighter and brighter as it approaches. Brilliant colors spark out of the mist, glimmering on the walls of the cave. You know this light. It is blinding, beautiful, strange, welcoming, familiar.

A glimmering bridge appears across the pool, leading towards that light. To step onto that bridge is to seek the world that lies beyond, to pass through the gate of Faery.

You step out onto the bridge. As you walk towards the mist, towards the light, the pool of water beneath you turns darker and redder, becoming a pool of blood. The blood of the generations, the blood that bears the divine power of the heavens. You feel its power growing as you cross the bridge, as you approach the gate. You have walked this way before. You have always known this path.

The gate is before you, the spiraling light opening to welcome you. Step willingly into the Realm of Faery...

(silence for a time)

It's time to return. You turn and face another gate, this one made of darkness—not fearful, but warm and familiar. It is the darkness of the cave, of the Mother, of the earth where you belong.

You walk towards the darkness, feeling the warmth rising around you, surrounding you.

In the distance, a light appears, not the brilliant white light of

Faery, but orange and red and flickering. As you walk towards it, the darkness pulls back, and you find yourself in a large cave.

In the center of this cave is a great fire, the flames casting shadows across the ancient stone walls, illuminating carvings, and paintings of the moon, of the sun, stars, human figures, and hands.

At the far side of the cave is a tunnel framed by rough rock niches. You walk past the fire, feeling its heat against your skin, and approach the tunnel.

You see one niche contains the skull of an ancient cave bear; the bone yellowed with age, the skull wreathed by flowers and fruit.

In the other niche sits the skull of a great ram, its horns painted red and black, the skull wreathed by leaves and acorns.

You pause to acknowledge the Lord and Lady of the Land, then step into the tunnel beyond.

As you walk, you begin to sense the weight of your body, feeling your breathing, the flow of blood in your veins, the steady beat of your heart. You begin to feel more and more awake and aware.

The passage is growing lighter and lighter as it rises upwards, ever upwards.

In the distance, you can see the cave opening, sunlight streaming inwards. As you approach the entrance, your breathing quickens, and you become more and more awake, more and more aware.

You reach the mouth of the cave and find yourself looking out at a forest of great, old trees. The air is fresh and sweet, and you can hear birds singing, feel the warmth of the sun on your face. The sky is blue overhead, framed by soft white clouds, and a breeze moves through the leaves of the trees, a green dance, shadow, and light.

You know this place. You are home. You are here. You are awake.

At this point, you all should move around or clap your hands if you need to wake yourself up fully. It would be good to eat something if you still don't feel grounded.

If you are working in a group, the experiences can be shared with each other, especially since they sometimes reflect each other and this can lend insight. It is always a good idea to write them down either in your own journal or a coven book or both.

Road to Elfhame Charm

Faeries, come take me out of this dull world,
For I would ride with you upon the wind,
Run on the top of the disheveled tide,
And dance upon the mountains like a flame.

-"The Land of Hearts Desire," William Butler Yeats

The strongest charm to facilitate your journey to Faery is your personal bond to your Fey-other. That being said, as we are creatures of the material world, we tend to use physical "tools" to aid us in accessing the metaphysical both within and without. Not only because it works, but we enjoy using them. We like what we have created, what we have put together to celebrate rituals and to do magick. They are—or should be—expressions of aspects of ourselves and what we want to accomplish. So, a charm meant to help us get to Faery should have a personal touch to it, something meaningful to us.

The form of the charm can be that of a bracelet, an anklet, a necklace, a bag of herbs and other items, even a mask and a veil or a headdress or crown. The important thing is to invest the object with intent and the ability to be a "trigger" to get you into the proper mode to travel. This charm can be used during ritual when you want to journey to Faery. You can also use it during meditation or if you are going for a walk in a natural area where you want to catch a glimpse of Faery or the Fey.

A good charm should include a holed stone, also called a hagstone. A naturally holed one is the best and should be treasured and never given away, for they are also considered to be lucky, and if you give them away, you are giving your luck away. Traditionally, hagstones are also good protection stones, especially against spirits who might come to harm you in the night. A holed stone is considered by some to be a gift of the goddess Diana, Queen of Faery and, by looking through the stone, it is said you can see the Fey.

Barring finding a natural holed stone, craft stores often have little stone circles of stone for use in jewelry making.

Another good choice for putting on your charm for protection is a bright blue bead or the image or emblem of a blue eye. These are traditionally used as protective symbols against the *evil eye*. You should also put a token of your totem on the charm as your totem is one way you travel to Faery. Generally, you can find small charms in the shape of most things, including animals of all kinds. You can also use a charm in the shape of a broom or staff.

Other beads can be put on the charm as desired. Amber beads or rose beads are good choices. You can also use beads you have gotten off a piece of family jewelry. Another sort of object to add to your charm would be a strange or unusual item, preferably one you have found or were given as a gift.

The items can be simply placed into a bag or strung on a strong piece of thread. If using a bag, the bag can be tied with a cord so that you can wear it around your neck or, if a small bag, around your ankle. When it comes to the bag, one made of cotton or linen is best rather than silk. You can also choose to attach the objects to a length of chain. If the charm is made with thread or a chain, you can also wear it around your neck or ankle, depending on the size and length. The best color for the thread is red.

To charge the charm, set a cup or goblet of cream or another liquid offering on your Faery altar, along with a plate that contains three Faery cakes. This can be done on your altar in your home or outside or by your Faery tree. You can also choose to light one red and one white candle.

Cleanse the charm with consecrated spring or moon water and pass it through incense smoke. If you have items on the charm that cannot go into water, then just use the smoke.

Hold the charm within your cupped hands or place it on the altar and lay your hands flat to either side of it.

Concentrate on your Fey-other or use whatever means you have worked out between you for contact.

Ask your Fey-other, either out loud or silently, to connect the charm to Faery, to render the blessing that shall make it a true Faery gift.

When you feel the energy of Faery fill up the charm, saying:

> *So mote it be*
> *By blessings three*

Give the liquid offering to the Fey, either on the ground or, if indoors, into a libation bowl. Pour it in three portions. Give the three cakes to the Fey, again laying them on the ground or the outdoor altar or putting them into the libation bowl. The offering should be libated later in your normal place.

Keep the charm hidden away when not in use, preferably somewhere on your Faery altar. If anyone else touches the charm for some reason, cleanse it again before use. If it still doesn't feel right, then you might want to take it apart and put it back together again, then re-cleanse it.

If one of the objects falls off, don't put it back on, but look for something else to replace it. We have had this happen multiple times. For example, a token just disappears or keeps breaking, seemingly without cause. In one case, a coven member had a small animal token and, even though it was stored securely in a padded box, when she would pull it out for ritual she would find one of the legs was broken off and was nowhere to be found. After the third leg broke off, she finally switched tokens.

∽ *Woodland Sprites* ∽

Cross-legged he sits
The toadstool boy
Crooked hat and small as a toy
His skin is poison
His mouse fur clothing ragged
His eyes wicked and black
If you licked him you would die.
All the while
The moss-green girl dances
Before him
In a veil of last autumn leaves
And thorns
Delicate and quick as a bee
Her hair a wisp of spider silk
Her face marked
By the blood and spark
Of a stolen firefly
Her mask divine.

Who are they really?
The toadstool boy and the moss green girl
Curiosities of some long past age
Imaginary childish things
That somehow never passed away
They don't care
That they should not exist
That you should not spy them there.
Dancing and leaping and twirling
With the coy
Little lights of Faery
Those that have long led astray
The unfortunate

And fortunate alike.

If you dared believe
If you'd dare creep through the night
Close enough to bite
You would know they smelled of mold
Of old and rotting things
Of stagnant water
And wet leaves
Of the fallen paint from sleeping
Moon Moth's wings
The shredded tails of squirrels
And other crawling things.

For these sprites are made patchwork keen
Thin and pale like sloughed off skin
Brown and green as acorn shells
Mushroom dust
And scarlet berries
The kind that even birds won't eat.
Their eyes purple-black
Dark and sweet
Unkind and wild
Who can tell what they really think?

The red feast and the white
Might well lead you to their land
But by the end of the night
Who knows
If you'll come back again
The ancient woodland gate
They guard
Is not for those who dally
Who think that sprites are cute
And that no Fey are deadly
The toadstool boy would laugh
His laugh
And the moss green girl just giggle

If you would name them something tame
A tiny winged butterfly thing
Sweet as honey dew
And golden sparkling on the wind.

Oh, the toadstool boy would laugh
As he danced upon your body
And the moss green girl giggle
To see your spirit wander
Between the worlds 'til lost and gone
Twilight pale, thin and wan
Never but never
To find your home once more.

Chapter 5

The Light and Dark Courts

"Look less upon us as a light court and a dark, for each is as one
to the other. Light and dark are not opposites as you would have it,
but complementary. One cannot exist without the other, so they are
each of the whole. Call us such if you will, but know it is but a means
to understanding. We are different each to the other, but it is not so
simple as light and dark.

Some say the place you name Faery lies between and so it is so. A
dawn world, a twilight realm; they are shades of that which never dies,
and we are shadows of that which passes away only to rise again. We
are as you are and they, those you name of the dark, are keepers of the
ancient secrets that lie in the dark and shrewd builders of tomorrow.
They build on the bones, and it is the bones that they know well."

-The Fey

Light and dark. Bright and black. Dawn and twilight. Pale and grey.
The light Elves and the dark Elves. The shining gentry and the rushing
hordes. Essentially, the Fey that we tend most often to encounter fall into
one of these two camps. Which isn't to say that these are all the Fey there
are, only that these two types are the ones we interact with the most. The
light so beautiful their beauty can seem terrifying. The dark, so terrifying
that they have their own wild beauty.

In Norse belief, the Elves or *Alfs* were split into two types who lived in two different realms, the "Light Elves" or *Liosalfar* and the "Dark Elves" or *Dockalfar*. In Scandinavia, they also separate the Elves into light and dark, the light Elves living in the air and the dark Elves in the underworld. In ancient Persia, the Fey were seen as *Deevs* that were considered ugly and shaggy and horned or as *Peris*, who were beautiful, bright and fair, and lived off the scent of perfume.

Of course, being tricksy shapeshifters, the Fey can appear in any guise they desire. But to give some attempt at description, the light Elves or the Seelie Fey tend to appear as very tall and thin, with long limbs and long fingers that can move in ways that are decidedly not human. Their faces generally are very pointed and their eyes incredibly large and also very pointed. The Seelie are also pale and white and bright and, sometimes, it may even seem that a light is shining out from them, as though they are lit from within.

People through history have glimpsed them and their shining court, seeing them as impossibly beautiful, dressed in brilliant white clothing or the traditional Faery green. The overall impression of the Seelie is that they are ethereal beings, almost seeming to float at times. Occasionally, people will see them with pointed ears and slightly more human-shaped eyes, but the general impression of the Seelie is that they are long and sharp, pointed and spindly, thin and angled, seemingly fragile-looking.

The Unseelie Fey, on the other hand, are generally seen as shorter and smaller, though their eyes are equally large and dark. The key here is that the Unseelie Fey tend to have round eyes rather than pointed and their mouths also appear rounded. They like to appear in groups and will move almost as if they are one. Their skin appears to be darker than that of the Seelie, though still strangely smooth. They can appear almost grey in color, though some see them as more greyish-green, almost like moss. They can also take a seeming not unlike that traditionally imagined as imp-like.

The Unseelie tend to scurry or hurry around or even rush right at you. They have a certain scent to them, that of mingled sweet decay and dark, fertile earth, which is hardly surprising since they are associated with the Underworld. Some might even say that they smell a bit like death and they wouldn't be far wrong. They can also take on the seeming of hounds at times, participating in the Wild Hunt. Still, the Unseelie can look like short humans if they desire, down to wearing clothes and caps. From them, we get the goblin look sometimes favored by movies and artwork, the small gnarled creatures with striped or red hats.

Folklore tells us that the Unseelie Fey enjoy working with metals and can fashion fabulous things. Old stories tell us how they make shoes, forge weapons, goblets, and jewelry, among other marvelous bits of treasure that they guard deep underground. It makes sense, then, that they have come down to us not only as Brownies but as Dwarves. The word Dwarf is descended from the words *duergar* and *zwerg,* and, in Swedish, the name *dverg* is also the name for a spider. As the Unseelie are spinners of the world, working for the Queen of Weavers, Destiny herself, it makes sense that they are linked to spiders and building.

The Unseelie make an appearance in the poem, "The Fairies," by William Allington:

> *Up the airy mountain,*
> *Down the rushy glen,*
> *We daren't go a-hunting*
> *For fear of little men;*
> *Wee folk, good-folk*
> *Trooping all together;*
> *Green jackets, red cap,*
> *And white owl's feather!*

Both the light and the dark Fey can harm or curse people, but we cannot really judge them as being "good" or "evil." They are not like us. We cannot hold them to our standards or expectations.

They are powers with a consciousness that is, in some ways, similar to our own and, in others, very, very different. They are more akin to a natural force that is set into motion, so we cannot say they are wicked any more than a thunderstorm, or a flood is wicked, for no act of nature is moral or immoral—it just is, and so are the Fey. For nature can be destructive, but also creative. The wind and hail and down-pouring rain of a thunderstorm can cause damage, but they also release the pent-up energy of the Earth, the same as with earthquakes. Forest fires can destroy homes and property and result in loss of life, but they also make way for fresh growth and are part of the natural cycle necessary for the health of the forest and grasslands. Similarly, the Fey, both light and dark, are a necessary force that acts in and upon and through our world.

Of course, the Seelie and the Unseelie also have connections to each other, but the Light Court and the Dark Court definitely do not always see eye-to-eye. This can be a tempestuous relationship, to put it mildly. In fact, there is usually a powerful push-pull going on between them. They certainly do not think and react the same. They don't always agree. To be honest, it might be said that they rarely agree. On those occasions that they do—look out! When the Light and the Dark Courts agree and act together on the same goal, the same purpose, this results in powerful magick that cannot be denied.

Our interaction with them must also differ, though there are certain commonalities that we must obey, for the Fey share in the same code of honor. As they put it,

> *"your rules are not our rules, yet this does not mean that we are without rules. All live by rules, even those you call the Gods. You have your own magicks, and we have ours, and the gods have theirs. Look to your own rules and look to your own magicks and you will best know whose honor we all serve."*

In the old fairytales, we see the ramifications of breaking one of those rules with the Fey, light or dark. For example, there is a terrible price to pay if a bargain with the Fey is broken or if someone dishonors their word or good name among the Fey. Accordingly, we need to be careful what bargains we make with the Fey, what promises we give. We need to be forthright and honest, both with them and with ourselves, for they know what is in our hearts even if we might not. Of old, we base our relationship with the Fey upon such agreements and trust. We give to them, and they give to us. They give to us, and we give to them, exchanging energy, power, knowledge, gifts, and affection.

If such trust is ever forfeit, then our prosperity, our homes, our families, our friends, even our lives can be forfeit. There is plenty of folklore about the bad luck and ill fortune that happen to someone who betrays the Fey or who proves unworthy during a spiritual quest or who messes around with what the Fey consider sacred, such as their trees, wells, springs and standing stones, their hollow hills and mounds. The betrayer's fields and orchards will no longer be fertile, their family can become barren and be prone to illnesses, and they can even be struck down by strokes or seizures or simply vanish.

Another rule we find in the old stories is that of never telling the Fey "thank you" for any gift given for saying "thank you" breaks the current of mutual giving and receiving. Instead, we must give for the sake of giving, not for the sake of getting. That doesn't mean that we can't ask the Fey for things, but we can't look it in the same light as a monetary exchange. I give you ten dollars, and you give me this pizza. In that case, the exchange is done, and there is nothing more. Instead, with the Fey, this an ongoing process, one that is tied to things being done in the proper time and proper place.

A further old rule is that, in making deals with the Fey, the deals we make should be proper ones, born out of necessity and not just mere desire. For example, is it appropriate to feed the Unseelie a whole lot of cakes and cream and then demand they help you win a big lottery? It might not be in the best interests of the world, or even of yourself, in the long run, to win a big lottery. Are you even sure what it is you really want? A lot of money or happiness? Will winning a bunch of money bring you want you need to grow spiritually? Will it bring you security? Will it give you the means to fulfill your purpose in the world, or actually make it harder to accomplish?

The Fey will honor the deals we make, but they might not always warn us of the consequences of those deals. They are not obligated to warn us. Out of affection, some of them might give us the head's up on occasion, but they might also let us go on our merry way, knowing we will learn a lesson from our mistakes. Those warnings often come in the form of riddles that we need to figure out, but if the warning ever comes in plain language, then we seriously need to pay attention. If the Fey tell us that something we are asking isn't what we should be asking for, then we would be fools to just blithely continue on without a care.

We need to be responsible for our choices. Dealing with the Fey is the same as doing magick; we need to be sure of what we want and if this is aligned with the necessities of Fate. Which means we need to think wisely when we ask the Fey, light or dark, to get or do something for us. Be sure of what you really require and your intent. Be sure it is something you are willing to pay for, to take responsibility for. For, as we are not the final arbitrators of justice, so we can't get everything we want, even if we think we are right. We have to more than think we are right; we need to *know* it, to be aware of it the same way the Fey are aware of things. We need to *know*, deep down, this is the proper course, the proper path. Not the only path, but the proper one.

Anyone who refuses to take responsibility for their magick should never make a deal with the Fey. They are just setting themselves up for a hard fall. The Fey might be our brothers and sisters, but they will not let us get away with being irresponsible with knowledge, powers, and gifts gained from them. It's not that they are here to punish us and they certainly respect that we have the ability to choose our own path, but once we enter into a bargain with them we need to uphold that bargain or face potentially dire consequences.

When we work with the Fey of the Light and Dark Courts, we must neither plead nor imperiously command them. We work within the boundaries of the bargains our ancestors have set with them, until and unless we are in such a time and place to re-draw those boundaries. Some of those boundaries go back to the beginning and constitute a vital part of the foundation of our interconnectedness with the Fey. Some of them change as times change, as cultures change, rewriting our relationship with the Seelie and Unseelie.

Just as our paths are built upon the bones of the ancestors, and we seek to tap into that, so we must also understand our ancient bargains with the Fey, light or dark. When the time comes to reset those boundaries, to make new bargains, we need to take a good hard look at them before committing ourselves to the deals we are about to strike.

As for the Unseelie, they especially, will not ask first if this is what you really want. They won't tell you that you might be better off not asking for that or that you should ask for something else instead. They won't warn you that the path you are about to choose is not going to turn out the way you think it will, or that it might lead to pain and suffering and loss and hardship. They also won't tell you that it is the right choice, the right bargain, and will bring about what you need. That's not their job. They don't ask why. They don't say "no."

She who is Mistress of the Unseelie is the Lady of Darkness and Dreams, the Lady of the Realm of the Dead. She tells us that to deal with the Unseelie Court

> *"life seeks death as death seeks life. To taste, to touch,*
> *to know—offer the best of what you are, of who you are.*
> *Offer life, the taste, the touch, the knowing of it. Strike the*
> *bargain, but know what it is that you desire. For if you do*
> *not rightly know the needs of your heart, your wish may*
> *well go astray.*
> *They—they do not take advantage. They do not wait in*
> *the shadows to make you rue your wish. The error is yours*
> *if what comes to pass is not what you imagined it to be.*
> *They spin, they weave, they build. But it is your desire that*
> *sets them to motion. Beware what you set in motion.*
> *My children do not hear your words, but the words writ-*
> *ten in your mind, in your soul, those they hear. Be true to*
> *both, and they will be true to you. Be false, be unknowing,*
> *think to fool them and you will be the fool for it. They are*
> *not called the gnawers of bones for nothing. They do not*
> *wear the mantle of terror for nothing.*
> *Eternal death or eternal daring...what they will be to you*
> *depends upon your understanding of what is true. Not*
> *mortal truth, but the truth of the gods. Seek the truth of*
> *the gods, and my hounds shall freely come to your hand,*
> *and my shadows be yours to command."*

For the Unseelie, the bargain is all. It's the basis of our relationship with them, the basis of our understanding of them, such as it is. For, unlike the Seelie, the Unseelie have never been and will never be born to this world. They have never been alive in the material world. This means that our understanding of them is more problematic; for while the Seelie can and have experienced life as material beings, the Unseelie have no such experience. We simply can't connect to them in the same way, for they remain "alien" to us, permanent denizens of the Otherworld.

This does not make them inherently bad, even though Christianity has sometimes painted them as such. This historical reliance on the bargain has led to the stories of deals being struck by ceremonial magicians with their "imps." Taken even further, it has given rise to the idea of the dread "Satanic pact," wherein you make a deal with the devil, and he gives you various spirits to help you in your dire magicks, spirits that you need to feed and care for. From this, we get the idea of witches having an extra nipple in order to feed their little demons, one of the signs that the witch-finders looked for to make an accusation stick.

But the Unseelie are not evil or demonic. Sure, they are tricksy, even downright dangerous at times, but if we deal honestly with them, they will deal honestly with us. Part of that involves making offerings to them. Traditionally, these offerings were not the horrible kind the Christians would accuse witches of making, but would consist of milk or cream or butter or honey or various kinds of bread, oaten cakes or pancakes. Though it's true, they are sometimes offered blood, which is perhaps what gave rise to calling them evil along with any Pagan gods who were once offered blood. Any acceptable and honest offering can help keep you in the good graces of the Unseelie, which is right where you want to be.

Clearly, there are similarities between the Unseelie as creatures of the realm of death, and of the dead themselves, who also need to be honored and appeased lest they become the angry dead …the hungry dead. It's from the idea of not honoring your ancestors, of not remembering the dead, that gave rise to the folklore of the vampire. Not the charming, even sparkling, vampires of today's movies, but the original vampires who gnawed on their burial shroud and made family members sick, who left their graves to suck the life out of their victims. The Unseelie, as enti-ties of death, have much in common with the human dead and we owe them respect and risk much if we don't give that respect.

Unlike the Unseelie, the Seelie are more like us in many ways and understand our needs far better. They also appreciate offerings of milk and cream and cakes, but also accept other forms of offerings, such as songs, poetry, ritual and the simple sharing of energy. What we give, they will give in turn, though the form of the gifts will not be exactly the same. As we are kindred, the Seelie will step in if what we've gotten up to might unknowingly or knowingly cause harm to the family and the clan. It's not something they do lightly, but they will do it.

We as witches have the divine power of choice, but we sometimes make bad choices and, because we are witches, these mistakes can have profound and far-reaching consequences. Witches, like anyone else, can be seduced by desires and become blinded by fears and lies. One can just as easily make a mess of things when doing magick or taking action at a vital point, rather than making things better or steering them onto the proper path. We might even think we are doing right, when we are doing wrong, especially when we are following truth rather than sooth, following man's law instead of divine law.

Despite this, we definitely shouldn't rely on the Seelie saving us from our mistakes. We need always to take responsibility for our actions, even if we didn't foresee what might happen, even if what happened wasn't what we wanted to happen or expected to happen. The ancestors expect this from us. The Fey expect this from us. The gods expect this from us. And we need to expect this from ourselves. Which is why we should be as sure as we can be when we work magicks, especially the greater magicks, and use the knowledge the Seelie can give us in making our choices.

The relationship we have with the Seelie are like the ones we have with our family, with our covenmates, with those we love and who love us. Their strengths become our strengths, just as their weaknesses can become our weaknesses. Together, we can work to become greater and bring out the best in all, to learn the lessons we need to learn in order to take hold of our hidden treasures and gain our gifts and powers. Together, we can become a force that can undertake greater magicks than we ever could alone.

On the other hand, the relationship we have with the Unseelie are more akin to being business partners. Our connections are through the bargains we have made. This also creates a bond, but it is not that of "wife" or "husband," not the intimacy of our other selves. But as all gifts create a connection, so we do create links with the Unseelie through our offerings and with what we ask in return. The more we bargain with them and honor those bargains, the more changes we make and things we build and ideas we spin into reality, the stronger our connection to them becomes. We can then use that as a foundation for ever greater bargains, even greater magicks.

Of old, the Fey are said to respect bravery, hard work, honesty, humility, compassion, dedication, and generosity. Certainly, those who lack those qualities never fare very well. Even as they congratulate themselves for their cleverness, for winning one over, they end up holding a handful of crumbling leaves instead of the Faery gold they imagined they had gained. They have undertaken the mystical journey and abjured the companions and guides that they need to win out, showing themselves to be unworthy of the covenant. They fail the challenge, fail the quest. They fail themselves.

Just as we, as witches, work magick that spans the light and the dark, so we need to know and work with the Light and the Dark Courts of Faery in equal measure. We need to involve both aspects into our path, thus bestowing great power and thus requiring great responsibility for that power and its repercussions. We have to uphold our end of the deal, to keep the balance, to forge and re-forge lasting relationships that will benefit us all in the end.

The gifts and powers and knowledge of Faery is a wonderful, precious gift, but it never comes without a price. If we are willing to pay that price, we can gain much. If we are unwilling, we have much to lose.

Beltane Faery Ritual

"What we love, we love. What we know, we know. We know you. We love you. We never forget. It is not of our nature to forget. When you know us, you shall not forget. In mind, in body, in bone, in spirit,

we will be as one, and we shall remember. As one, we shall remember. The red rose pricks white and the white rose, red. We dance. You dance. As one, we remember. As we dance upon the field of roses, the field of blood, within and without the bounds of all...we remember."

-The Fey

The eve of May Day is known by many names, including Beltane Eve and Walpurgisnacht, and is traditionally the time that witches fly out to celebrate their rites. Of old, they traveled to the sacred mountain, the sacred hills, the sacred valley, and there danced and feasted with other witches, the gods, and the Fey.

At this time, we journey to the realm of Faery for the veil is also thin at Beltane. We pierce it to go there just as we invited them to be with us here at Sovane, All Hallow's Eve. As witches, as cunning folk, we can go deeper into Faery than anyone yet living. In fact, this journey is part of what makes a witch, for to be able to travel to the other side and return again is an art.

For this ritual you will need:

- Altar table or stone
- Center candle holder and candle
- Taper or candle to light the Four Quarters
- Candles for the Four Quarters
- Black piece of cloth
- White piece of cloth
- Piece of green cloth cut into a round
- Different colored ribbons cut about 12 inches in length
- Small slips of paper with a hole punched through each end
- Goblet or bowl of red wine
- A plate of Faery cakes
- Additional food and drink to be shared
- Floral or leaf wreaths that can be tied so that they fit many head sizes
- Bell

The slips of paper should have messages written on them beforehand and then be folded up and the end of the ribbon slipped through the holes and tied off.

The wreaths can be made several days beforehand or earlier in the day. There should be one for each person attending. When you make them, be aware that the one you make may or may not be the one you will end up wearing.

Place altar in center of ritual space.

Lay the black cloth on the left-hand side of the altar (the West side) and a white cloth over the right-hand side (the East side). Put a round green piece of cloth in the center of the altar and have a candle holder in the middle of the green cloth.

If you have a tall candle holder, you can tie the ribbons around it, or they can be laid out in a starburst pattern around the central candle.

You can, if desired, decorate the altar with flowers, buds, and small mirrors or crystals. You can even scatter sequins around on the altar. Representations of the traditional red and white spotted Faery mushrooms are also a good addition.

Light the West and East candles, saying:

From West to East

Light the South and North candles, saying:

From South to North

Carry the lit taper around the circle, saying:

Weave and spin and spiral forth
Between light and dark
Between dusk and dawn
Red river

White stone
Rose and thorn

Light the candle in the middle of the altar and blow out the taper.

Place goblet of red wine and plate of Faery cakes on the altar, along with more food and drink as desired for feasting (not all of it needs to be on the altar, but you can place a representative amount).

Ring bell three times.

Priest or priestess or chosen person says:

> *Stars above and stars below*
> *Between the worlds, we must go*
> *The secret gate*
> *The open door*
> *Our kin await*
> *The Lady pale, green, adored*

Cense all with incense and mark each person's forehead with a mix of soot and wine in the form of a + or crossroads. Or you can mark each person's face with the mix of soot and wine, both cheeks and the forehead.

Put on or hold your traveling bags or stones.

The priest or chosen person goes to stand to the North-East of the circle.

The priestess or chosen person takes the wand and faces them with wand raised, saying:

> *He who walks between*
> *Life and Death*
> *Dark and Silent One*
> *Traveler of the tides*
> *That ebb and flow within*
> *The great Web of Wyrd*

Master of smoke and mirrors
Broom and pole and blade
We wait upon the threshold
We would know the way

Allow the God who *opens the way* to speak as He chooses or He may just choose to join the circle.

Dance around the altar deosil, slowly at first and then building in speed. A song or a chant may be used, or laughter is even better. Feel free also to spin and whirl as desired and as space will allow. The point is to get to a giddy, dizzy state, one of breathless joy and lightness.

Stand around the altar and let each person pick up one of the wreaths and crown another with it until all are wearing them.

As each person is crowned by another, have that person say to them:

With joy
With love
We wake to the world
Within the circle
Cast by the dance
Of our brothers and sisters
Blessed be

Other person responds:

Blessed be

Pass around the goblet or cup of red wine and have all drink.

Pass around the plate of Faery cakes and have all eat.

You can all sit down then and share in the feast.

When done, each person takes a ribbon from the altar and looks at the message it contains. These should be kept to yourself as gifts from Faery.

All to dance widdershins then, slowly and deliberately, concentrating on returning home.

At the end, you should sink down and touch the earth, grounding yourself back in the material realm.

Blow out the candles—North to South to West to East.

You can place the message from Faery on your Faery altar later or put it under your pillow if you want to dream about it or get further insight in how to bring it to fruition. It's best to keep the message to yourself if at all possible, at least until it has been fulfilled. You will know when its time to reveal it.

For instance, we were all given such messages in a coven I was in years ago, and some of the coven members shared their messages within a few months or a year after they were obtained. Other messages are still being held secret, for some of these messages may take years to unfold, even a lifetime. Don't feel compelled into sharing what is yours and yours alone, for the results of your actions will ripple outwards, even if the seed of the idea remains kept within your heart.

Outdoors Beltane Faery Ritual

For this ritual you will need:

- Altar table or stone
- Center candle holder and candle (with hurricane shade if needed)
- Taper or candle to light the Four Quarters
- Torches or lanterns for the Four Quarters
- Black piece of cloth
- White piece of cloth
- Piece of green cloth cut into a round
- Different colored ribbons cut about 12 inches in length
- Small slips of paper with a hole punched through each end

- Goblet or bowl of red wine
- A plate of Faery cakes
- Additional food and drink to be shared
- Floral or leaf wreaths that can be tied so that they fit many head sizes
- Bell

Put the wreaths and cup and place, as well as the food and drink for feasting, in another location than where you will be creating the circle. A second altar can be set up there, preferably on an old stump or large stone.

Light the West and East torches or lanterns, saying:

> *From West to East*

Light the South and North torches or lanterns, saying:

> *From South to North*

Carry the lit taper around the circle space, saying:

> *Weave and spin and spiral forth*
> *Between light and dark*
> *Between dusk and dawn*
> *Red river*
> *White stone*
> *Rose and thorn*

Light the candle in the middle of the altar and blow out the taper.

Ring bell three times.

Priest or priestess or chosen person says:

> *Stars above and stars below*
> *Between the worlds, we must go*
> *The secret gate*

The open door
Our kin await
The Lady pale, green, adored

Cense all with incense and mark each person's forehead with a mix
of soot and wine in the form of a + or crossroads. Or you can mark
each person's face with the mix of soot and wine, both cheeks and the
forehead.

Put on or hold your traveling bags or stones.

The priest or chosen person goes to stand to the North-East of the circle.
A broom or blade is placed on the ground there to mark the gateway.

The priestess or chosen person takes the wand and faces them with wand
raised, saying:

He who walks between
Life and Death
Dark and Silent One
Traveler of the tides
That ebb and flow within
The great Web of Wyrd
Master of smoke and mirrors
Broom and pole and blade
We wait upon the threshold
We would know the way

Allow the God who *opens the way* to speak as He chooses or He may just
choose to join the circle.

Dance around the altar deosil, slowly at first and then building in speed.
A song or a chant may be used or shared laughter.

If the *God of the Gate* is there, let Him lead the dance and, when the time
is right, He will take all over the broom or blade bridge to Faery.

Once outside the circle, travel to the feasting place set up in advance. If possible, following a twisting trail there.

Stand around the second altar and let each person pick up one of the wreaths and crown another with it until all are wearing them.

As each person is crowned by another, have that person say to them:

> *With joy*
> *With love*
> *We wake to the world*
> *Within the circle*
> *Cast by the dance*
> *Of our brothers and sisters*
> *Blessed be*

Other person responds:

> *Blessed be*

Pass around the goblet or cup of red wine and have all drink.

Pass around the plate of Faery cakes and have all eat.

You can all sit down then and share in the feast.

When done, each person takes a ribbon from the altar and may look at the message it contains, your gift from Faery.

The priestess or a chosen person then should lead all back to the first circle space.

All to dance widdershins then, slowly and deliberately, concentrating on returning home. At the end, you should sink down and touch the earth, grounding yourself back in the material realm.

Blow out the candles—North to South to West to East.

For an outdoor ritual, instead of the ribbons with messages, you can use stones that are placed around the feasting place or even have people look to find objects placed along the way to the feasting place. A message can be written on the stone, or the stones themselves can be chosen for what they represent. For instance, clear crystals, amethyst, azurite, amber, aquamarine, prasiolote (green amethyst), lapis lazuli, and other white or green or blue stones are good choices for connecting to the Otherworld. While stones that are good for grounding include dark or red stones such as obsidian, red agate, black tourmaline, smoky quartz, garnet, onyx, and jet.

If you intend to journey a fair way to your feasting place, you might decide not to place any stones along the way, but instead, let each person find what they will along the way.

Sovane Faery Ritual

Come, heart, where hill is heaped upon hill,
For there the mystical brotherhood
Of hollow wood and hilly wood
And the changing moon work out their will.
And God stands winding his lonely horn;
And Time and the World are ever in flight...

-"Into the Twilight," William Butler Yeats

Even more so than May Eve, All Hallow's Eve is associated with the supernatural, it being a time when witches and spirits of all kinds fly free, requiring people to protect themselves with charms or by making offerings. Whereas May Eve and May Day celebrations have faded from what they once were, even around the turn of the century, Halloween has only grown in popularity. Perhaps, this is due to its deep connection to remembering and honoring the dead or maybe, as some have put it because people like dressing up and kids love candy. Certainly, Halloween has become extremely secular in nature, despite some Christians protesting that it is, at its heart, a "Satanic" holiday.

Yet, this fascination with Halloween with its links to the dead, to the wearing of masks, to the strange and the unusual, even the frightening, shows it has an enduring quality, that it fulfills a need in our lives and our society. For if Beltane is about celebrating life, then Halloween is about embracing death. While, both are about love, a love which bridges the divide of the veil.

At Halloween, this love is shown by calling together the *Great Family*. We reach out to our ancestors, our loved ones, our kindred, who have passed beyond and we seek to honor them, to remember them. We offer them gifts, thus renewing and continuing our bond with them. A bond that will draw us to them when we pass away, and a bond that will bring us back to our families when we are born again.

For an indoor ritual, you will need:

- Altar table
- Center candle holder and candle
- Taper or candle to light the Four Quarters
- Candles at the Four Quarters
- Drums, bells, rattles
- Set of horns or stang
- Black piece of cloth
- White piece of cloth
- Piece of red cloth cut into a round
- Lightweight veils you can see through
- Goblet or bowl of red wine
- Goblet or bowl filled with heavy whipping cream
- A larger bowl for libations
- Plate of Faery cakes, one for each person in the rite to use as an offering
- Messages for your loved ones on small strips of paper or leaves
- Large bowl or cauldron
- Scrying bowl or mirror

Place altar in center of ritual space.

Lay the black cloth over the left-hand side of the altar (the West side) and a white cloth over the right-hand side (the East side). Put a round red piece of cloth in the center of the altar and have a candle holder in the middle of the red cloth.

Place the large bowl or cauldron to the West

You can, if desired, decorate the altar with apples, small pumpkins, acorns, and autumn leaves. Representations of the traditional red and white spotted Faery mushrooms are also a good addition.

Light the East and West candles, saying:

> *From East to West*

Light the North and South candles, saying:

> *From North to South*

Carry the lit taper around the circle, saying:

> *Weave and spin and spiral down*
> *Between light and dark*
> *Between dusk and dawn*
> *Red river*
> *White stone*
> *Rose and thorn*

Light the candle in the middle of the altar and blow out the taper.

You can do scrying at this point with a mirror or bowl of water. Have each person come around and gaze into it, saying or having all say:

> *Mothers and fathers of the beginning*
> *By darkness and light*
> *By breath and flame*
> *By virtue of the blood*
> *Show me*
> *Show me*

From whence I came

Take around the plate of Faery cakes and have each person take one and concentrate goodwill and good feelings, charging them with energy

Place the empty plate before the central candle and have each person come around and place their charged cake on the plate. Each can speak to their Fey-other or ancestors or any loved ones as so moved.

Place the goblet or cup of red wine to one side and goblet or cup of cream to the other side of the plate of cakes.

Set the libation bowl to the north of the central candle.

A chosen person stands to face the West, holding the horns or stang aloft, while the rest cover their heads with the veils, pick up their drums, bells, and rattles, and also face the West.

The person to the West says:

> *Lord of Elfhame*
> *Open the gate*

All repeat:

> *Lord of Elfhame*
> *Open the gate*

All repeat louder, sounding the drums, shaking the rattles, and ringing the bells:

> *Lord of Elfhame*
> *Open the gate*

All dance around the altar, singing, using the drums, bells, and rattles, basically making as joyful a sound as possible for you are welcoming your family.

When the energy peaks, all sink down and lay their hands on the altar or grip the edge of the altar and all say, or one chosen person says:

> *We welcome our family*
> *We welcome our loved ones*
> *The feast is laid*
> *The cup is filled*
> *The gate stands open*
> *Come in*
> *Come in*
> *Blessed be*
> *The chosen company*

All repeat:

> *Blessed be*
> *The chosen company*

All take off the veils. Each comes around and places their message into the bowl or cauldron to the West, speaking of their loved ones if they will.

The horns are placed on the altar near the libation bowl, or the stang is laid down to the West.

A chosen person holds up the goblet or cup of red wine, saying:

> *Red blood*

A chosen person holds up the goblet or cup of cream, saying:

> *White blood*

Each pours a small amount into the central bowl, saying:

> *Be as one*

All come around and repeat, pouring a small portion of red wine and a small portion of cream into the bowl and repeating:

> *Red blood*
> *White blood*
> *Be as one*

All sit-down, reaching out to commune with your Fey-other. Let each person speak as moved or as messages come from their Fey that are meant to be shared. Any personal messages should be kept private.

When done, all rise and a chosen person picks up the libation bowl with its mingled wine and cream and holds aloft.

All say:

> *We are one blood*
> *We are one family*
> *We are one across worlds*
> *Never forget*
> *We are one*

One at a time put the Faery cakes into the wine and cream and set the bowl down on the plate.

Blow out the candles—South to North to West to East.

Take the cakes and red wine and cream to your normal offering spot to Faery, such as the Faery tree or the altar you have set up. If not able to do that right away, leave the bowl on the altar until you can libate it.

Take the messages to a running stream or river and put them into the water or burn them on a fire at a later time.

For the feast that follows, and for the next three days, you should have a libation bowl or plate and cup into which you place a small portion of each meal you have and also make that an offering to the Fey and your greater family.

Feasting should not be done in the circle for this ritual, for its a time of offerings. None of the food or drink being given to the dead, to the ancients, to the Fey, should be touched. As the goddess of the Seelie once chided us during ritual, "*do not eat the food of the dead.*"

Outdoor Sovane Faery Ritual

For an outdoor Sovane Faery ritual, a place where you can have a fire is best. Better still, if there is a large flat stone that can also be used for an altar. If using a stone, forgo using cloth on the altar. You can choose to use the veils for this ritual, or you can paint yourself and go skyclad (if possible). Masks are also a good addition.

- Altar table (if no stone available)
- Center candle holder and candle (with a hurricane shade if need be)
- Taper or candle to light the Four Quarters
- Torches or lanterns at the Four Quarters
- Drums, bells, rattles
- Set of horns or stang
- Black piece of cloth
- White piece of cloth
- Piece of red cloth cut into a round
- Lightweight veils you can see through
- Goblet or bowl of red wine
- Goblet or bowl filled with heavy whipping cream
- Cauldron with water
- Plate of Faery cakes, one for each person in the rite to use as an offering
- Cards or written messages for your loved ones who have passed—on paper or on leaves

Place altar to the North of the ritual space if you have a fire in the center.

Lay the black cloth over the left-hand side of the altar (the West side) and a white cloth over the right-hand side (the East side). Put a round red piece of cloth in the center of the altar and have a candle holder in the middle of the red cloth. Use leaves and apples, small pumpkins and acorns to decorate the altar.

Place the cauldron of water before the altar, decorated with leaves or vines or apples if desired.

Light the East and West torches or lanterns, saying:

>*From East to West*

Light the North and South torches or lanterns, saying:

>*From North to South*

Carry the lit taper around the circle space, saying:

>*Weave and spin and spiral down*
>*Between light and dark*
>*Between dusk and dawn*
>*Red river*
>*White stone*
>*Rose and thorn*

Light the candle in the middle of the altar and hand the taper to each person as they come around to kneel down and gaze into the cauldron, the person or all saying:

>*Mothers and fathers of the beginning*
>*By darkness and light*
>*By breath and flame*
>*By virtue of the blood*
>*Show me*
>*Show me*
>*From whence I came*

Take around the plate of Faery cakes and have each person take one and concentrate goodwill and good feelings into them.

Place the empty plate before the central candle and have each person come around and place their charged cake on the plate. Each can speak to their Fey-other or ancestors or loves ones as so moved.

Place the goblet or cup of red wine to one side and goblet or cup of cream to the other side of the plate of cakes.

A chosen person stands to face the West, holding the horns or stang aloft, while the rest cover their heads with the veils, pick up their drums, bells, and rattles, and also face the West.

The person to the West says:

> *Lord of Elfhame*
> *Open the gate*

All repeat:

> *Lord of Elfhame*
> *Open the gate*

All repeat louder, sounding the drums, shaking the rattles, and ringing the bells:

> *Lord of Elfhame*
> *Open the gate*

All dance around the fire or altar, singing, using the drums, bells, and rattles, basically making a joyful, welcoming sound.

When the energy peaks, all sink down and place their hands flat on the ground, facing the flames.

If the ritual does not have a fire, all lay their hands on the altar or grip the edge of the altar, and all say, or one chosen person says:

> *We welcome our family*
> *We welcome our loved ones*

The feast is laid
The cup is filled
The gate stands open
Come in
Come in
Blessed be
The chosen company

All repeat:

Blessed be
The chosen company

All take off the veils and stand and reach out to commune with your Fey-other. Let each person speak as moved or as messages come from their Fey that are meant to be shared. Any personal messages should be kept.

When done, all say:

We are one blood
We are one family
We are one across worlds
Never forget
We are one

The horns are placed on the altar near the libation bowl, or the stang is laid down to the West.

At this time, any written cards or messages can be thrown into the flames.

A chosen person holds up the goblet or cup of red wine, saying:

Red blood

A chosen person holds up the goblet or cup of cream, saying:

White blood

Each pours a small amount into the central bowl, saying:

Be as one

All come around and repeat, pouring a small portion of red wine and a small portion of cream into the bowl and repeating:

Red blood
White blood
Be as one

Take the central bowl and pour it out to the West of the circle. Place the plate of cakes to the West of the circle with it.

Blow out the lanterns or torches South to North to West to East.

Follow the same three-day offering cycle as indicated for the indoor Sovane ritual. Be sure to feast outside of the ritual, not within it.

Beltane and Sovane Bread

A little mushroome table spred,
After short prayers, they set on bread;
A Moon-parcht grain of purest wheat,
With some small glit'ring gritt, to eate...

-Robert Herrick

Part of your feasts for Beltane and Sovane can be an historic bread called the *bannock*.

Bannock is a Gaelic bread that was made with yeast and usually fried in hot oil or grease, much like fry bread. Even though it was a common bread that people used to eat, it was also made for specific occasions, sacred holidays that included the greater sabbats of Beltane, Lammas, Sovane, and Imbolc. Bannocks can be made in a round or triangular shape and, traditionally, no metal was used while mixing up the dough. They also can be made with nine knobs of dough on the top of the loaf. Those knobs then can be ripped off of the baked bread and either thrown over your shoulder or placed into a libation bowl as you state for whom you are making the offering.

For Sovane, you can bake the *Dumb Bannock* or *Hollowtide Bannock*, making two loaves, one to offer to the Fey and the ancestors and a matching one for your feasting after the ritual. This serves to echo the connection between you and the Fey and your beloved ancestors. It was called the *Dumb Bannock* for its relation to the *Dumb Supper*, the meal you laid out for your loved ones from the other side. This bannock could also be broken up into pieces and put upon the graves of your family members who have passed away. The *Hollowtide Bannock* was usually plain, not containing any fruit or nuts, but if you did add fruit, the traditional ingredient was currants.

For Beltane, the bannock can be the main focus of the feast in the Otherworld, perhaps served on a platter along with fruits and flowers. It can be made into a round and knobs of dough placed around the outside, thus reflecting the rays of the sun. This bannock also can be broken up into pieces, and one of the pieces dusted with soot. All of the pieces are then put into a bag or basket, and each person takes turns pulling out a piece of the bread. The person who gets the bannock with soot on it has chosen what is called the "Beltane Carlin" and can be the chosen "sacrifice" for the ritual.

These bannock recipes use baking powder rather than yeast and are baked in an oven. Accordingly, they are easier to make, take less time, and don't involve messing around with hot grease or oil. You can also reduce the sugar by leaving it out of the dough entirely and by not dusting the loaves with the sanding sugar.

Beltane Bannock

- 3 cups flour
- 2 tablespoons sugar

- 2 tablespoons baking powder
- 1 teaspoon salt
- 2 ½ cups golden raisins
- 1 ½ cups water
- ¼ cup butter, melted
- Sanding sugar (optional)

Preheat oven to 350 degrees. In a large bowl, mix together the flour, sugar, baking powder, and salt. Add the melted butter, then add some of the water, mixing until the dough turns into a soft ball. You might not need all of the water. If you end up adding too much water and the dough becomes too sticky, add some more flour if necessary.

Work the golden raisins into the dough.

Put dough on floured surface and lightly knead about a dozen times.

Place the rest of the ball of dough on a greased baking sheet—one with a raised edge, such as pizza pan can also be used. Flatten out the dough into a circle with the center about 1 inch high.

If desired, sprinkle some sanding sugar on the top of the dough.

Bake about 30 minutes or until the bottom of bread is golden brown.

Gluten Free Beltane Bannock

- 2 ½ cups brown rice flour
- ½ cup tapioca flour (starch) or arrowroot starch
- 2 tablespoons sugar
- 2 tablespoons baking powder
- 1 teaspoon salt
- 1 ½ teaspoons xanthan gum
- 2 ½ cups golden raisins
- 1 ½ cups water
- 6 tablespoons butter, melted
- Sanding sugar (optional)

Preheat oven to 350 degrees. In a large bowl, mix the flour, sugar, baking powder, xanthan gum, and salt. Add the melted butter, then add some of the water, mixing until the dough turns into a soft ball. You might not need all of the water. If you end up adding too much water and the dough becomes too sticky, add some more flour if necessary.

Work the golden raisins into the dough.

Put dough on floured surface and lightly knead about a dozen times.

Place ball of dough on a greased baking sheet—one with a raised edge, such as pizza pan can also be used. Flatten out the dough into a circle with the center about 1 inch high.

Sprinkle top of dough with sanding sugar if desired.

Bake about 30 minutes or until the bottom of bread is golden brown.

Bannocks are not an overly sweet bread, and they taste great with honey-nut cream cheese spread on them, but also are good with butter and honey.

You can also cut back on the golden raisins by ½ a cup and add chopped walnuts to the dough. Walnuts traditionally were believed to contain precious gifts, and this is perfect for a bread eaten in the Otherworld as part of the gifting of the Fey, just as we gifted to them at Sovane.

Sovane Bannock

- 3 cups flour
- 2 tablespoons sugar
- 2 tablespoons baking powder
- 1 teaspoon salt
- 2 ½ cups currants
- 1 ½ cups water
- ¼ cup butter, melted
- Sanding sugar (optional)

Preheat oven to 350 degrees. In a large bowl, mix the flour, sugar, baking powder, and salt. Add the melted butter, then add some of the water, mixing until the dough turns into a soft ball. You might not need all of the water. If you end up adding too much water and the dough becomes too sticky, add some more flour if necessary.

Work the currents into the dough.

Put dough on floured surface and lightly knead about a dozen times.

Place ball of dough on a greased baking sheet—one with a raised edge, such as pizza pan can also be used. Flatten out the dough into a circle with the center about 1 inch high. Sprinkle with sanding sugar if desired.

Bake about 30 minutes or until the bottom of bread is golden brown.

Gluten Free Sovane Bannock

- 2 ½ cups brown rice flour
- ½ cup tapioca flour (starch) or arrowroot starch
- 2 tablespoons sugar
- 2 tablespoons baking powder
- 1 teaspoon salt
- 1 ½ teaspoons xanthan gum
- 2 ½ cups currants
- 1 ½ cups water
- 6 tablespoons butter, melted

Preheat oven to 350 degrees. In a large bowl, mix the flour, sugar, baking powder, xanthan gum, and salt. Add the melted butter, then add some of the water, mixing until the dough turns into a soft ball. You might not need all of the water. If you end up adding too much water and the dough becomes too sticky, add some more flour if necessary.

Work the currants into the dough.

Put dough on floured surface and lightly knead about a dozen times.

Place ball of dough on a greased baking sheet—one with a raised edge, such as pizza pan can also be used. Flatten out the dough into a circle with the center about 1 inch high. Sprinkle with sanding sugar if desired.

Bake about 30 minutes or until the bottom of bread is golden brown.

Currants are traditional for the *Soul Cakes* given out at All Hallows. Sometimes, these were made with currants, and sometimes they included seeds and were called *Seed Cakes*.

You can also choose to cut back the currants by a ½ cup and add chopped hazelnuts to the bread. Hazelnuts mean fertility and good luck, but also protection against spirits that might ill-wish you. As there are all sorts of spirits wandering around at Sovane, protection represented by the hazelnut, as well its blessings of good fortune, make an excellent addition to your feast and this bread.

Faery Drinks and Consecration of Salted Wine

Blood and dust and honey'd wine
Blossoming my heart's desire
Blood to call the star within
Dust that wakes and stirs and spins
Honey'd wine so wild, so sweet
Once again to know, to meet

The oldest form of offering for the Fey is something in which the spark of life exists, such as blood or semen, but that may not always be possible or desirable. Hence, giving milk or cream are a traditional sacrifice, especially cream. If you do not have heavy whipping cream, then regular cream or half and half will serve in a pinch. I have to admit that I have used all-natural coffee creamer on occasion, the sort made with real milk, cream, and sugar.

Salted red wine or simply red wine can also be used, being representative of blood. Other forms of alcohol besides red wine are also acceptable, for its no coincidence that many alcoholic drinks are called "spirits," for they are said to have life in them. Accordingly, a mix of whiskey and cream can also be a good choice, or you can just use a good whiskey, rum, beer or ale. If you already make wine or beer or ale yourself or can get it from someone you know who does, that's even better.

For more options, the following recipes can be made and used for a drink in ritual or as an offering. Conversely, you can also choose to mix some of the following in a bowl with milk or cream, perhaps adding some honey.

Blackberry Cordial

- 3 quarts fresh or frozen blackberries or 4 pints of blackberry concentrate
- 4 cups water
- 3 cups sugar
- 1 tablespoon whole cloves
- 1 tablespoon whole allspice
- 2 cinnamon sticks, broken
- Brandy (optional)

Crush blackberries if using fresh or frozen. Put into a large pot on the stove and add water. Bring to a boil and boil on medium heat for 10 minutes.

Strain the liquid, reserving the juice. Add water if needed to make 2 quarts total.

Put back into the large pot and bring up to simmer. Slowly stir in the sugar and add the spices in a cheesecloth bag. Simmer for 30 minutes, stirring on occasion.

Bring back to boil, then remove from heat and discard the bag of spices.

Once cool, add brandy if desired, to taste. Store in a sterilized bottle or jar in the refrigerator for up to a week.

The blackberry is one of the plants hallowed by the Fey and, in fact, some folklore says you should not eat blackberries because they belong to the Fey, while other stories tell us you can eat the berries, but only until the end of September, after which they no longer belong to us.

This recipe for traditional blackberry cordial can also be made as is or with the inclusion of brandy if desired. If you prefer to be able to drink the cordial without alcoholic content, you can leave the cordial as is and then add the "spark," the "spirit" in the form of brandy just before making the offering. Of course, the cordial will keep longer if it includes alcohol.

Alternate Blackberry Cordial

- 2 quarts blackberry juice
- 1 lb sugar
- 4 grated nutmegs
- ¼ oz ground cloves
- ¼ oz ground allspice
- ¼ oz ground cinnamon
- Pint of brandy

Bring all to a simmer in a covered saucepan.

Let mixture cool.

Strain and add the brandy.

Put into sterilized bottle or jar and keep in the refrigerator for up to a week.

Rather than using blackberries, you can also use other fruit and fruit juice from the sloe family, such as peaches, apricots, or plums. If buying juice that is sweetened, you will want to cut back on the amount of sugar added to the mixture. If you are making juice from fresh fruit, you will likely want to keep the same amount of sugar, but it really is to taste.

Almond and Honey Milk

- 1 ½ oz blanched almonds
- ½ lb sugar
- Grated lemon peel of 2 small lemons
- ½ quart whiskey
- ½ tablespoon honey
- 2 pints milk, whole milk if possible

Grind up the almonds in food processor or chop finely.

Mix the almonds in well with the sugar.

Boil the milk and let cool.

Mix the almond-sugar mixture in with the cooled milk, strain, and put into a sterilized container. Best used the same day.

Almonds are in the same family as the sloe, so this recipe includes almonds and also two other Faery favorites—milk and honey.

Milk Punch

- 2 quarts water
- 1-quart milk, whole milk if possible
- ½ pint lemon juice
- 1-quart brandy
- Sugar to taste

Warm the milk and water and mix together. Add the sugar and stir to dissolve. Add the lemon juice and brandy and stir.

Strain the mixture. Pour into a sterilized bottle or container and keep in the refrigerator. Best used the same day.

Honey or Rose Cream

- Pint heavy whipping cream
- ½ cup honey or ½ tsp of food grade rose water

Mix together and beat until soft peaks form. Use immediately or keep in the refrigerator for a few hours before using.

You can also mix both the honey and a ½ tsp of the food grade rose water into the cream to create a rose honey cream. As an offering, this looks very nice if placed in a bowl or cup and decorated with fresh red rose petals.

Rose Milk

- ½ to 1 teaspoon rose syrup
- 1 cup of cold milk or cream
- Sugar to taste

Mix the ingredients, adding the rose syrup and sugar to your taste or to the taste of your Fey-other or your Faery clan's preferences.

Keep in the refrigerator and serve cold the same day. Do not add ice or it will water down the milk.

If you intend this rose milk for a Fey offering, it would be best to make it with cream rather than milk.

Consecration of Salted Wine

"If you would seek us, seek the darkness. Come not afraid but be as one with it. Listen...listen...without courage, you are lost. We will not deny the fearful ones for our Lord you know as Death is Compassion. Come in darkness with open hands, emptied heart, and the darkness

will fill you, and you will know the light through the darkness. Come
dancing, come singing, come silent of tread and voice, but come...we
are necessary to you. We are needful things, precious dreams, brave
hopes, the bread of the land, the fruit of the harvest, seeds of the future.
Sow us...sow us...sow us...it is needful."

-The Unseelie message as given through the Seelie

You can, of course, use red wine or salted red wine without any kind of
consecration, but when possible, this ritual blessing or one you create
yourself can be used when salting the wine to make it appropriate for
offerings.

Be careful not to mix in too much salt, but just enough to give it a slightly
salty taste. When done correctly, the salted wine oddly ends up tasting
akin to blood...so this is a ritual drink that you will want to use sparingly
if you aim to partake of it yourself, and only if you feel you can receive it
with true understanding and respect. Otherwise, just use it for a ritual
offering, in particular for the Unseelie.

This doesn't have to take place in circle, but you can choose to perform
this consecration during one of your normal rituals.

Take the red wine and pour it into a bowl. Put sea salt into another bowl
and set the two bowls side by side.

Hold one hand over the bowl of red wine and one over the bowl of sea
salt, palms downward, saying:

> *Salt and wine*
> *Wine and blood*
> *Make of mine the life*
> *Bless the blood*
> *Bless the fire*
> *Stolen from the breath*

Lean down and breath three times into the sea salt, then take the salt and stir some into the red wine, concentrating on the fire within you going down into the salt.

Use your fingers or small spoon and put an odd number of pinches of salt into the wine, such as three or seven or nine or eleven or thirteen. The more pinches, the less salt per pinch you should use. The idea is to lightly salt the wine, not to make it completely undrinkable.

If not using immediately, store the salted red wine in a bottle or jar and keep it in the refrigerator for just a few days.

**Be very careful not to drink too much of the salted wine if you have a medical issue with salt and, even if you do not, only take a little. The taste is very strong, and many people find it overwhelming. We use it extremely sparingly, for special occasions, and only take tiny sips.

∼ *Lord of Shadowfall* ∼

Rabbit rabbit
Whirling dervish
Black eyes form a ring
And summon up the night
To watch as the dark comes rushing in
On soft, cool wings
As specters prance across the sand
Hounds and jackals
A black cat speckled by ancient waters
The rush of deep rivers
Unknown to man
Where every drop knows a mystery
And shares it only with
His brother
Dreams and spells blend and sink
Below the earth the decay
Of languid spider webs and dust
Each grave keeps its red cap

Its fragrant green coat
Of mushrooms and clinging moss
Oh but there just there
One sits upon a rock and strokes
The rabbit in his lap
Mottled grey and brown and white
As the fickle moon
Their smile the same
White white white and black
Sharp as flint
And what came before the dawn
Of man
Leaping flirting gamboling
Round and over and in and out
Scurrying in at the last
Never just one to appear
Lest the whole troop come rushing after
Carrying the unwary off to drown
In a pool
Where the black geese call out
To their lord and master
As he sits in a cloak of air
Upon a ragged-maned horse
Of thorn and shadow
His crown of horn
And alabaster
The owl feathers in his hair
Stained blood upon black
As the horn he raises up
To make the silent sounding
As through all the worlds, they run
He calls
They come
Hungry furious forlorn
The little ones.

The song below was written by a friend of mine, Beth Hansen, who also is involved with the Fey. We have circled together many times over the years, including one May Eve ritual where we journeyed to the Otherworld and drank May Wine and shared the laughter of Faery. She is deeply inspired by the Gods, the Fey, and the Muse, and when I first heard her sing this song, it just felt so perfect it had to be included here in this book."

The Fires of Samhain Eve

The moon will rise behind the bare branches.
The crows take rest high in the trees.
Watching below the witches will gather
Lighting the fires of Samhain Eve.

The songs begin, calling the Others near;
singing the tales of long ago
when Elfkind were kin, our sisters and brothers
singing together on Samhain Eve.

Come! Come! Dance with us,
put your hand in mine.
Come! Come! Sing with us,
our magick is en-twined.

Around they go dancing the magick in
by the fires of Samhain Eve.
High in the hills, the crows watch knowingly
under the moon on Samhain Eve.

The ghosts guard the doors of only the fearful
so witches can dance under the trees.
Weaving their magick with the Good People
around the fires of Samhain Eve.

Come! Come! Dance with us,

put your hand in mine.
Come! Come! Sing with us,
our magick is en-twined.

The moon will rise behind the bare branches.
The crows take rest high in the trees.
Watching below the witches will gather
Lighting the fires of Samhain Eve.

Beth Hansen is a singer/songwriter and mixed media artist dedicated to making paintings and necklaces of the Goddess in every facet of nature. She can be contacted through her website: www.harmonygoddess.com.

Chapter 6

With a Whirl of Leaves

"One gift we have given is the gate to our home, if you dare seek it and it is drawn to you. You cannot find it if it will not be found. Just as you cannot find where it will lead you if you have not the courage and do not know what it is to be home.

We know you, but you have all but forgotten us. We expected such, for it is your curse to forget. She who you name Pandora brought gifts as we bring them, yet Her gift was not to forget but that of remembrance. If you do not remember, you may not be a Witch. This much is true. Our blood causes remembrance, and it is our blood which marks the gate, the gate of the forest, that which grows from the earth of the Old Ones, those you name Ancestor.

Where the blood of the Gods falls, there grows up blossoms you name beauty. Our blood grows different, yet still resides within you, lying hidden in your stories, in that which poets tell and artists paint.

There are no coincidences. All that is—is."

-The Fey

Faery rituals *flow*. There is no need to talk, to plan; it all comes naturally, in tune with the ritual and the purpose of the ritual. If we seek to interact with the Fey, to participate with them in a ritual context, we must be in tune with them in the same way they are in tune with each other. When that happens, what it feels like is a mingled sense of urgency, of rightness, of bone-deep excitement, of being wrapped up in a moment of powerful transformation. We just know when to act and what to do, as if called by some internal force that we cannot deny. Conscious thought doesn't enter into it. You go on instinct, an instinct guided by destiny.

All of this is very much related to the idea of the *Call;* when you are drawn out of your body to attend the witches' sabbat. You have to go, and you want to go, and you could no more not go than you could deny who and what you are. The Call lies in our blood and in our bones, just as Faery exists in our blood and in our bones. When we experience the Call, the rituals we do, the magick and actions we take are happening both within and without of Faery, both within and without of this world. Of course, we always have a choice, to go or not to go, though there is a cost for either choice. By denying it, you deny part of yourself, part of what you were born here to do. By accepting, you seek to embrace Fate.

When the Call comes, you are pulled out of your normal, mundane life and consciousness, and it's like you have finally awakened, can finally *see.* You feel perfectly at peace, calm even, even as your body is filled with energy. You sense the Unseen world around you, and when you put your focus on something, you can understand it deeply. It doesn't feel strange or unnatural, but perfectly right and, so long as you follow that feeling, what you do will flow as Faery rituals flow.

It will all make sense as long as you remain in that Fey frame of mind, as long as you remain in tune with the magick you are doing and with the forces around you. It's almost as if your conscious mind has shut itself down, except that it's not as simple as that. Only the questioning, the doubting, the ego-centric part of your conscious mind drops away, leaving an utter surety of what to do and a sublime sense of well-being and having a vital role in a larger purpose.

This happened to me several times, beginning in the coven I trained with. We heard that Call, and we responded. We came together in shared magick with each other and with the gods and the Fey. The pull was irresistible, beautiful and wonderful. While we remained in that state of mind, we had no fear at all. Our bodies, our minds, our spirits just *knew* and were bound together as one. We knew what we needed to do, where we needed to go, what we needed to accomplish. This sense of pure knowing and action is part of what it means to be a witch.

The best thing to do when this feeling, when the Call comes, is to accept and to revel in it; to act out of the sense of calm joy, the still heart at the center of the whirling fire, the whirling wind. It's this pure, quiet sense of surety and centering of self that allows us, as witches, to work with great powers and not be destroyed, not be burnt up by our own gifts. Without this...well, we all know those who have paid a dire price, physically, mentally, spiritually, for summoning beings and forces that they could not handle.

This focus and flow should be courted not just to interact with the Fey, but to further any magickal group or coven work. We can come to be like a "hive-mind," form a group-soul, as much as we can, and this should be one of our goals. If not with a coven we are working with, then at least in accord with our spirit familiars, our past-future lives, and the other spirits that we have relationships with. For we are many and one and one and many, the same as Faery is.

The creation of a group spirit with those in your coven or group or with your spirit familiars and contacts is no small thing. When working in a group, it can get even more complex, for then it involves not just the other members of the group, but all of *their* spirit familiars and contacts. Once you add in everyone's Fey-other, it becomes even more difficult to achieve, but more powerful because of that. Together, we can handle and work with powers that we could not undertake alone or with just a handful of others. We become mighty, capable of just about anything.

Of course, when we work with the Fey, we have to remain aware that the magickal rules of Faery are different than ours in some ways. There are things that they will tell you they can't or shouldn't do, just as there are things that we can't or shouldn't do. Of course, there are also certain rules to magick that apply as much to the Fey as to witches. There, we can certainly find commonality. For the flesh we give the magick might be variable, but the bones beneath are similar. But there comes a time when the Fey venture into landscapes we are unsure of and might never be able to understand completely. At that point, we simply have to trust in them and the depth of our shared history.

The magick of the Fey of each of the Elements have their own focus, their own currents of power, their own techniques and stories to tell. When

we understand the Fey of each Element, we can better understand their
magick, for the two are bound together in much the same way that we
can see into the heart and mind of an artist through their art.

Our magick is Fire-based, involving strength of will, focus, concentration, and intent. It is primarily powered by the energy in our bodies, that
can be strengthened by our emotions and focused via our wills. Our
magick is active, fiery, and based upon the gift of the heavens—the power
of choice. It also has an element of longing within it, of seeking to grasp
what is beyond us, of ever striving for more. This has its own strengths
and weaknesses, for we can also find it hard to be content, to be happy
with what we have.

The magick of the Witch is, thus, the magick of the eternal quest, the
flame of desire and discontent that burns within each of us inspiring
us to explore the unknown. So we are drawn to keep looking beyond
farthest horizon, to push past our limits, to strive for what might seem
unattainable.

Out of all of the Fey, our magick best meshes with those of the Seelie. In
fact, some of our magicks are specially forged to interact and intertwine
with the magick of our Fey kindred. Where our magick ends, theirs
begins and vice versa. For example, as we raise power, it spirals upwards,
coming to a single point, a single focus. At the same time, the Seelie create a power that spirals downwards—very much appearing like a whirlwind, which they are commonly associated with—and the two powers
wrap around each other, the single point where they meet becoming part
of both worlds.

The power raised then pours between the above and the below at the
same time. Where the two meet just about anything is possible, for the
point that is created is neither here nor there, neither in time nor out of
it, neither the past nor the future, neither made or un-made. This point
exists and doesn't exist at the same moment, and unreality can pour
through it and be made real, just as reality can be poured through it and
be made unreal.

If this sounds wild and crazy, it should. It's hard to explain how witch
magick interacts with that of the Fey, especially to today's rational and

scientific mind. The closest you can come to it sometimes can be found in the theories of quantum physics, where the mystics and prophets of the "religion" of science reside. When you look at these theories through the eyes of the Fey they can seem obvious, even simple. What the conscious mind of today is only beginning to grasp the questions of, the mystical mind of the Fey and of witches have long known, intuitively and naturally.

Witches make decisions, and the Fey see the shadows that stretch out from those decisions, all of the consequences, the reactions that arise from each action. The Seelie say...*this is how it is. Absolutely.* But then there is that sly half-smile, that sideways twist of the head, and they add... *unless it is not.* What this means is that witch magick is, in many ways, a wild card. We can achieve what might be considered impossible, and the Fey are aware of that. Those of us with the power of choice have the ability to change *what is*, to make something else *what is*, instead.

For example, some say that all things are fated, that our decisions are not really that of *free will*, but stem from who we are, what we know, what we have experienced. All we have seen and all we have done and hope and fear for predisposes our decisions and, of course, that is true to a great extent. Our past experiences will lend themselves towards affecting our decisions in the future. Quite often, this influence will be on an unconscious level, so we're not even aware of it. Unless we become conscious of those influences and make our decisions based off that deep inward awareness, based off a greater sense of truth and need, we will remain so influenced.

As witches, we have the *will*, but to make it *free*, we need to break away from the biases and blindnesses born of this lifetime and act out of the inner knowing that is Fey for the Fey see past all of that, just as they can see many potential paths. For many times, there is no one particular way, one particular right path, and the Seelie perceive and work with the ebb and flow of those many ways, those countless paths. However, what is considered "good" in the eyes of the Seelie Fey can often be defined to a certain extent as what is *meant to be.*

Rarely do the Fey see but one way and know that one way as the only way. Accordingly, they do not tend to fixate on one particular road over another. They know only too well how quickly it can change, how the currents can shift and flow, often based upon but one decision, one single action or inaction. To the Fey, many of these paths are generally not seen as being any different than any other, but there is sometimes one particular path or another that may have more benefits, that may lead to what will turn out better. These are the paths that they would, obviously, prefer that we pick. They accept what is *meant to be*, but might nudge us if they can into a different version of what is *meant to be* if they see what is set into motion is not for the best.

Certainly, some choices can lead to bad things happening. The Fey do have *preferences* when it comes to that. They would much rather we learn our lessons and evolve with a minimum amount of destruction of each other and of the planet we share. But, when it comes down to it, they know that the choices are ours...and so are the consequences of those choices. If we will not learn the easy way, then it must be the hard way. If pain and suffering are called for so that people will learn what they need to learn, to make the choice to change and evolve, then they understand that. They would be sad for our pain but carry on all the same.

Certainly, that has happened in the past, is happening now, and will happen in the future. For people find it hard to change, to accept transformation, to learn to see through the lens of a different paradigm. Those who do accept change become, then, the vanguard for change and that is also a difficult charge to take up, for sometimes it causes anger and hatred and those people who are meant to be guides become, instead, targets. History is filled with examples of those who espoused a new way of the world, new spirituality, and often paid with their lives for it.

Even those who work in the shadows, as witches often do, find difficulties in guiding necessary transformations, for there are also forces that work against change, that fight the future.

Magick comes in many forms, and one such example is the "spiritual warfare" of some modern-day Evangelical Christians who seek the fabled *End of Days*, rather than face the change from the Piscean to the Aquarian Age. They would rather die than change and they would rather the world end than change and the practices and prayers they use are little different from the occult forces that they rail against as being "Satanic."

This religious movement finds echoes in other fundamentalist and extremist movements that seek control over people and countries, often with similar end goals as the Christian extremists.

There is also the magical force that has created a "god" of money, greed, and dominion that endeavors to keep the world just as it is so that the rich get richer and the poor get poorer or at least remain poor and in their place. This force is fed by an engendered fear, by a belief in a lack of prosperity, by convincing people that they do not have any hope of change or even any right of change. It denies this change because it must ever grow, ever consume, even at the cost of destroying the environment that supports us all. This is the spirit that denies the god of free will, the god of the divine flame that burns in the blood of witchkind.

Some people are quite happy to try to tell you that life has no purpose. Or they will try to convince you that they and only they can tell you what that purpose is, usually to their own benefit. The Fey will never tell you that.

Some people are quite happy to tell you what you need to be happy and feel fulfilled, also usually to their own benefit. The Fey will never do this to you.

The Fey know only too well what we need to feel happy and fulfilled, to sense we are part of a higher purpose—and that is to be our true selves. In fact, the Fey need us to be our true selves, for then we are capable of doing our jobs. There are plenty of paths, religious, political, financial, that seek to make us feel powerless and purposeless, all so that they can use the resulting confusion and anger and fear to further their own ends.

As witches, we must strive never to do this, hard as that can sometimes be. We need to light the way for others, and that is best accomplished by leading by example. The Fey can show us the way, but we show the way for others through what we do. Our actions and accomplishments affect this world, even as they are inspired by the Otherworld.

All people have the right of choice and witches doubly so. Witches who have formed strong bonds with the Otherworld, with their Fey-others, can learn to work with them to raise magickal energy that can cause change, that can affect just the right place and set the right actions into motion. For if you know just where to apply the correct amount of pressure, you can effect change with far less effort and with a far greater result. It's like pushing over that first domino that will set all the rest into motion.

The shining nodes of light in the Web of Wyrd that are these turning points can be highly visible to the Fey and to Witches who have tapped into the Second Sight. But to know how to put pressure on them so that change will go one way or another requires Fey-sight, Fey-knowing, as there is never just one way things can go, never just one possibility. There are shades of potential.

These points of possibility can be times, places, circumstances, events, and even people. Some are combinations of the above. If you have the Fey-sight, you can foretell and feel these points when they occur, where they occur, and how they occur. There is a power to them, a sensation, electricity, that once felt you will know it when you sense it again. You will be able to sense what sort of keys are necessary to turn them, to set change into motion, be it actions, rituals, art or magick. Changes then will ripple across the web, across worlds.

What the Fey offer us is a means to reclaim not just the knowledge of our past, of our ancestors, but an understanding of how we can bring what is necessary into the world. We can do this via engaging in trance states as part of our ritual practice, seeking to gain such visions, dreams, mystic experiences that can show us future possibilities, future paths. Some of these Fey gifts provide inspiration for magick and rites we should do, specific ritual actions, songs or chants, symbols or objects to be used. We also sometimes get glimpses of other witches, other covens, who are being equally inspired to action, thus gaining a deeper understanding of the bigger picture we are involved with.

One such vision led us to perform a Midsummer ritual where we called down the powers of inspiration and sent them out through the currents of the Earth. We were shown what colors to use, what to decorate our staff with, who we should call upon, and where we should get the four stones meant to mark out the four Quarters. We worked together as a coven to flesh out the ritual but were still amazed at the final form it took, at what the result was.

That's because what we did was but a part of a greater whole, of what was being set into motion at that time. Clearly, that Midsummer ritual took place at one of those points of possibility. Some of the people involved were frightened by what happened that night and, as another witch sister of mine put it, they got scared because it was *real magick*. It was wild magick, powerful, demanding, creative and destructive at the same time, Witch, Fey, Elemental.

Fey-witch magick can all too easily pull us off balance. It's for this reason that we need a good strong foundation. We must adapt to changing times and cultural transformation, for without change we risk losing touch with the world and cannot lead the way forward, but it is equally vital to retain a sense of deep communion with the past, with ancestral wisdom. If these roots are lost or abandoned, we can too easily drift with the winds of change.

As witches, we need to keep one foot not just in Faery and one foot here, but on foot in the past and in the future. We need to be able to ride the storms of change, not be swept away by them. The best way to do that is by willingly and consciously taking an active role in those changes. We must also understand and be sympathetic to the fear of change. For, certainly, it's not hard to become concerned or scared of change, for change represents the unknown.

Yet, for witches and cunning ones, the unknown is also a powerful attraction. That doesn't mean that, in our personal lives, we might not like security—a home, a means of paying the bills, food on the table—but in our spiritual lives, we revel in the mysterious. We dance up the storms of change, whirling with them as do our Fey kindred.

As the Goddess of the witches says,

> *"storms are a sign of the Fey, rushing air and whirling*
> *water. You cannot stop it. You cannot control it. You may*
> *well dare summon it, but do not imagine it is yours to*

command. Those you name Fey or Faery, the Gentle and
Kindly Ones, are not to be trifled with, nor ignored, nor
discounted as mere phantasms.

Storms are a sign of change and what sort of change do the Fey intend? Air and water flow in accord with the tidal waters, transforming, traveling along the secret currents of the Earth, the veins of the Mother. You, too, are part of the Mother. The storms are signs of the rising of the new day. Flow, flow with the true currents..."

With Fey-sight, we can access a deeper understanding of the evolution of the human race and the great unfolding of Fate. We can better sense the whole of the web through its permutations and continual transformations, for there is a natural flow to the currents of time, of energy, of life, of magick.

To work against the flow of Fate is very difficult and takes a lot of will and force and can be dangerous. To work with the flow of Fate is easier for it is working in tune with how things are meant to be, which is why the Sight and the Call are extremely important to being a witch. We need to be able to look behind the curtain, as it were, not only seeing the dominoes but comprehending how those dominoes fit together and what will be the result if you choose to tip this one or that one over.

Fey Introduction Ritual

Love is a power.
Love is a creative power.
Love is why the universe came into being.
Together, beauty and strength create love.
Beauty and strength are the two pillars, one white and one
black,
and the path of the Witches lies between them.
To be able to call upon and use the power of love,
you must contain both pillars within you.

To walk the path of the Fey is to walk the path
that lies between these two pillars,
between light and dark,
between night and day,
between this and that.
Some call it betwixt and between and so it is.
Learn to be betwixt and between and you shall be Fey.

This ritual can be done within a circle or without one. However, the ritual is *only* to be done at All Hallows, either the evening before, the evening of, or the evening after.

It is meant for you to pledge yourself to your Fey-other, to honor and strengthen your commitment to them.

Go the East and stand facing that direction. Concentrate on letting down all your guards and opening your heart.

Take a few breaths and express a welcoming feeling as strongly as you can. You are here to meet and remember a friend, a lover, a protector, and a guide, your other self, one who loves you. To be wedded to your Fey-wife, your Fey-husband.

If desired, you can say:

> *By the call of the dawn*
> *By the whirling song of the heart*
> *Between fire and air*
> *Between night and day*
> *Of old and forever*
> *I claim the unbroken bond*
> *I call upon you*
> *Brother (Sister)*
> *Blood of my blood*
> *Breath of my breath*
> *Bone of my bone*
> *Come to me*
> *Let us remember*

Let us love and be as one
Let us love and be as one

This is best repeated at each All Hallow's Eve, even if you already have formed a good connection with your Fey-other.

During the rest of the year, you can get up at dawn and face the East and say:

By the call of the dawn
By the whirling song of the heart
Remember remember remember
To love and be as one
Or you can choose to use these words:
By love come to me
By light I am here
We who have been parted
Shall part nevermore
Together we shall walk
As together
We have always been
For what makes us as one is all
The rest illusion
The tides grant us this time
Eternal as we live the dream
And eternal reside
In each other's arms
Our hearts the bridge
Our hopes the path
That lies before us

The most important part is not the actual words, but the sense of welcome and the ability to open your heart to your Fey-other. For some, this comes quickly, and it grows stronger over time. For others, they have had to work at it.

In addition, the communion with your Fey-other can also be more powerful at times and fade away at other times. It's not as if they have gone away, for this they will not do, but they are busy at times, and we are busy at times and our ability to contact them can ebb and flow as a result. When there is a need, they will always come.

Invocation of Your Fey-other for Ritual

"All in nature have spirits, just as you have a spirit. There be no trick to this, no magick as you know it. It just is. The magick, what you name magick, lies in connection. One spirit to another. One to the many and many to the one. We know this, and we are as the magick. You know it, and you are as the magick. Without this, there is no magick, only illusion. Only the lie of loss."

-The Fey

As part of using this ritual to call your Fey-other for ritual practice for the first time, you should make a braid. This braid will represent the communion between each witch and their Fey-other. Once made, it can then be used as a ritual trigger. Yours is the red cord or yarn, the blood of the witch, white is the color of Fey blood, and the blue-green yarn or cord represents the binding, the magick, the power of Love.

If you are putting charms, bells or holed stones or crystals into the braid, these can be charged with energy beforehand. One good choice is a charm that represents your totem. Another is a small pendant that is a mirror or shaped like a star.

For the ritual you will need:

- Red candle
- White candle
- Altar cloth, green is best
- Large bowl
- Two smaller bowls
- Cream

- Red wine
- Wand or ritual blade
- Incense of choice
- Red yarn or cord
- White yarn or cord
- Blue-green yarn or cord
- Any charms you wish to attach to the yarn or cord

Set up an altar with one red candle and one white candle. You might want to use an altar cloth that is green.

Fill one of the smaller bowls with red wine and one with cream. The rest of the altar can be left bare or be decorated with flowers or leaves or stones.

Take the red, white, and the teal or blue-green yarn or cord and cut them to even lengths. They need to be long enough to braid into a necklace or a bracelet or anklet.

Draw a basic circle with either wand or blade.

It would be especially good to cense the circle well with a rich-smelling sweet incense or leave a stick of incense burning on the altar for the rest of the ritual. You can use the incense made from recipes included in this book or burn a small piece of frankincense or amber.

Light the red candle, saying:

> *By the blood of this world*

Light the white candle, saying:

> *And by the blood of the other*

Take the three portions of yarn or cord and begin braiding them together, concentrating on it binding together you and your Fey-other.

Tie any charms into the braid as you make it.

When done, run the braid through the incense smoke and then hold it out before the candle flames, saying:

> *By fire and air*
> *By breath and body*
> *What is love if not this*
> *That which bridges all worlds*
> *And reaches beyond understanding*
> *As the two become one*

Pour some of the wine and then some of the cream together into the larger bowl, saying:

> *By the blood of this world*
> *By the blood of the other*
> *Two become as one*

Put on the braid and concentrate on your breathing, on raising energy. A song or chant can be used at this point or even simple humming or toning. The point is to rouse the joy within.

See or sense the Fey in the room, your Fey-other as he/she moves closer and closer to you.

Allow yourself to sway, to dance, to whirl, as much as space will allow. When the Fey energy goes into you, and through you, it will be bright and sharp, ecstatic and even frightening. It will make you feel as though you are drunk with intense sensation.

Dance until you become dizzy and then allow yourself to sink down and touch the earth.

If any visions come, let them flow through you. Don't try to understand them at the time or even to hold onto them. If you are meant to remember, you will remember.

You may feel the physical touch of the Fey during the dance or when you are lying there. It can feel like an actual material sensation or like energy is moving through you. You might see their eyes staring into yours, even if your physical eyes are closed.

Afterward, be sure to ground out any excess energy.

Take the mingled wine and cream and libate it.

Afterward, you can use this braid when you want to contact your Fey-other during ritual or to have them participate in ritual or join with you.

The Fey might give you a few words or a charm to say when you do this, or you can say:

> *By the blood of this world*
> *By the blood of the other*
> **Two become as one**

You can also use a more formal invocation if desired, such as:

> *Between the Gates*
> *Of light and dark*
> *Between the Gates*
> *Of night and day*
> *Seen, Unseen*
> *I call you by the blood of this world*
> *I call you by the blood of the other*
> *(Brother) (Sister) of the Art*
> *I summon thee*
> *To be as one with me*

Open up your arms and your heart to your Fey-other. Welcome them to the ritual and welcome them to your body. Your Fey-other can then participate with you in divination, magick, and ritual.

When you are done with the ritual, acknowledge the contribution of your Fey-other, and take some deep breaths, grounding yourself. If need be, have some food to eat to help ground out the energy. A tiny pinch of salt can also help you back to yourself.

Below is a similar ritual for invoking a Fey-other into someone else.

Have the other person put on their braid, close their eyes, and cross their hands over their breast. Let take a few deep breaths to relax and get into the proper state. When they are ready, they can open their hands up, palms held outwards.

Point your wand at the person and say:

> *By life and love*
> *By death and dream*
> *By what is bound*
> *And what is free*
> *I summon thee*
> *Seen, Unseen*
> *Oh Brother (Sister) to She (He) within the Art*
> *Open wide the way*
> *Between the Gates*
> *Of light and dark*
> *Between the Gates*
> *Of night and day*
> *Oh Brother (Sister) to She (He)*
> *Enter in we pray*
> *The body of your most beloved*
> *(name) here*

If you are working in a group where you might want to invoke your Fey-others at the same time, you can all put on the braids you have made, concentrate first on your breathing and relaxing, then say together:

> *By life and love*
> *By death and dream*
> *By what is bound*
> *And what is free*
> *We summon thee*

Seen, Unseen
Oh Brother, Sisters of the Art
Open wide the way
Between the Gates
Of light and dark
Between the Gates
Of night and day
Oh Brother, Sisters
Enter in we pray
Body, spirit most beloved

Once all have conjoined with their Fey-other, you can then dance and raise energy for various magickal workings or tap into the inner knowing of the Fey.

Afterward, all should do take some deep breaths and ground the energy as the Fey leave. A shared feast is a good idea.

You can also use the braid you have created in a basic ritual to renew the relationship through the sharing of Fey cakes and milk or cream or other drinks that can be done as part of your normal rituals or once a month, for example at the full moon.

Have cakes ready, enough for all and three for the Fey, and a bowl or goblet of something to drink.

Put on the braid you have made.

All stand and say:

Between the Gates
Of light and dark
Between the Gates
Of night and day
Oh Brother, Sisters
We call you

Place the feast on the table or altar or stone and say:

We meet
We cross
All hail
All hallows
Witch and Faery
One is the circle
One is our name
Kindred all

Take up the cakes and set either one or three aside for an offering for the Fey.

Pass around the rest of the cakes and have everyone take one and eat it.

Take the drink and make a libation to the Fey. Share around the rest with each other.

If there is any left at the end, pour this out as an offering.

Dancing is a good idea at this time, or you can proceed to what is next in your normal ritual.

Consecrating Moon Water

The shining threads,
the swirl of the stars,
the deep darkness,
the fire in the heart of the Earth,
the fall of a single leaf,
the cool breath of the caves,
the sharp lightning cast from creation.
The poets know the Mystery.

For the creation of consecrated water for rituals or blessings, the best source is from a local spring. Springs are not only places where water wells up from beneath the ground, but where there is an outpouring of energy, prosperity, creativity, and magick. They are where the currents deep in the land come to the surface and have long been seen as sacred and powerful sites.

If you cannot obtain local spring water, then water from a clean local lake or river will do. Rainwater is also a good choice, especially rainwater that came from a passing thunderstorm. If you do not have access to a local clean water source and cannot collect rainwater, then buy some spring water, if possible from a spring that is close to your area.

Fill a clear jar with the water and wait until the night of the full moon. Go outside and stand under the light of the moon, holding up the jar to let the moonlight shine through the glass, through the water.

Say:

> *By moon and stars*
> *And motherlight*
> *Bless this water*
> *Bestow the sight*
> *To see and know*
> *The worlds between*
> *Bless this water*
> *To ride the dream*

This water can be used for consecrating people or objects during ritual.

It can also be used before you go to sleep at night when you want to "ride" or "fly" in your dreams to the Otherworld. For that purpose, take some of the water and touch it to your heart and your forehead and you can also put a small amount into a bowl or clear container at the head of your bed.

If you are using this water to "fly," then it is a good idea also to have a small bag of earth nearby that comes from your local sacred land or place in order to find your way back. The bag can be put into a larger cloth bag and placed beneath your pillow or hung above or near your bed. It can also be put under the bed, preferably below the foot of your bed. Rather than local earth, you can also use a stone or token that you have charged with the feeling and essence of "home" to be an aid to getting back again.

∼ *Water Wicht* ∼

She cleans her teeth with a ragged fish.
The hair gets caught
And pieces of plaid;
Highlanders taste the best of all,
Feral and free and sharp
Like wild honey and thistle flower.
But they who yet remember her kin
prove wary as well
So a feast is a rare thing
To be savored
And remembered on the leaner days;
once all knew her ways.

She tore a claw on a buckle once
A thing of gold and carved
Serpentine cats and ravens
Blood picked out on the arch of their backs;
The spitting frenzy
And the subtle gleam of these
Who pluck and wear their fortune
Upon the field of doom.
She's seen their hard-won coin as well
And held their gifts of gold and bright stones
Seen the beauty of the sun-fired ones
As they were strangled, cut and bled
For the dark earth to swallow,
The offering of kings and queens
Sealing the bond between
Life and death.

Unlike those now who refuse to see
Who imagine a cross held tremblingly

In their grasp
Will protect and defend from doom,
While cats and wolves fear her honestly
And ravens taunt her from the safety of the trees,
Waiting and wishing
For her to grant them their due--
The carrion of the ford,
The toll of the river's grave,
A bit,
A bone,
A speckle of red,
All those of the New Faith
Who thought her kin
Long cursed and long dead,
Refuse but are unable to refuse
The Lady of the Bogs
Of the mud and blood and flood
Of water's wish and water's end.

Chapter 7

Within the Garden of Mysteries

Each fairy breath of summer
as it blows with loveliness
inspires the blushing rose

-Anonymous

The Queen of Roses is one of the names for the Queen of Faery. She and Her consort, the King of Shadows who is the Lord of Death, dance together as light and day, night and dark spin around them, as the stars above make and unmake patterns. In their realm, rises the great branches of an ancient tree, guarding the waters that rush from beneath it, the waters of memory. All around the tree, the brambles of the wild rose twist and twine, leaves, buds, and delicate pink blossoms with hearts of gold. This is an old image of the *Land of Faery*, where witches celebrate the otherworldly sabbat, a place known by many names—Blockula, Venusburg, Benevento, the Valley of Josephat, Mount Athos, the Plain of Aphrodite, and Akelarre, among many others.

Traditionally, roses are considered to belong to the Fey, who are protective of them. Its said that one should always ask permission of the King or Queen of Faery before picking a rose. But then roses have a long connection to the ancient magicks of life and love and death. Roses are

bound up with the domain of witches and with the realm of Faery, and
the intimate bridge between the two, where they and we are as one.

The old rose has five petals, and these petals symbolize the five-pointed
star, the Elements of Earth, Air, Fire, Water and that point within the
center of the circle where the four Elements unite, what some call Spirit
or love or mystery. Roses symbolize the highest ideal of spirituality as
well as the depths of physical passion. They are the romance of the soul
and the body, not setting one above the other as some religious paradigms do, but embracing them both equally.

In ancient Rome, roses grew on their grave sites, and the Swiss called
their cemeteries, rose gardens. Some say that the rose is the flower that
grew on the famed tree in the mythical Garden of Eden, the Tree of
Eternal Life that Adam and Eve were denied. Not eternal life as in living
forever, but coming to the knowledge of what is *eternal*, just as the fruit
of the Tree of Knowledge granted the understanding of time.

The rose is related to the heart chakra and also represents secret keeping,
hence the term *sub rosa*, or beneath the rose, due to the custom of keeping silent about what is said when a rose has been hung above a meeting
place. The rose is also the purity of perfection. Not perfection as is often
described today—meaning being without fault—but the perfection of self
that means you strive to become what Fate has chosen you to be, to best
play the role required of you.

To grasp the folkloric and occult aspects of the rose, we can look to a
familiar fairytale, that of "Sleeping Beauty" or "La Belle Du Bois Dormant." There are many versions of this story, all of which are, to a greater
or lesser extent, based on the one written (or put together) by Charles
Perrault whose story in English means "Beauty Sleeping in the Wood."
This title gives us a deeper understanding of the magickal significance
of the tale. The beauty lies dormant, sleeping, unaware in the woods, the
woods in this case taking the form of a great wall of thorns and brambles. Clues to what kind of brambles lies in the Brothers Grimm version
of the story which was called "Brier Rose."

Due to a misfortune with the Fey who came to bless her birth, the princess in the story is cursed to prick her finger on a spindle on her birthday and fall into a deep sleep akin to death. While she sleeps, a brier grows up around her castle, both to protect her in her sleep and to keep others out.

It was the princess's destiny to die—or fall asleep for 100 years—by the hand of Dame Fate. To be awakened from this death (or sleep) required the kiss of a prince, whose charge it is to break through the guardian thorns and awaken the sleeper within. After which, depending on the teller, they end up together eventually after many more trials. They also have twin children, Le Jour and L'Aurore (Day and Dawn) or, in some other versions, the children are named after the Sun and the Moon. All of which tells us that this story is filled with older symbolism that has lingered.

One way of looking at it is that the sleeping princess is the mystery sleeping within the blood, protected by the thorns of sacrifice. She represents the dread and beautiful inner mysteries that need to be awakened. In this, we are all both the sleeping princess and the daring prince. We seek the mystery beyond the rose, beyond this single lifetime and beyond death—the mystery of who we are and what we are and all we can be. We seek Faery, the land of roses, that which lies beyond the veil, the realm of ancient mystery. We seek the Rose Maiden, the Lady of the Sabbat, the Queen of Faery.

It also isn't coincidental that the briers that grew up around the sleeping castle and princess are representative of the hedge. Hedges mark out boundaries, including that between life and death, this world and the Otherworld. Those witches who jump this hedge or walk it or ride it can be said to be embracing the meaning of rose and blood and bramble, the experience of being of two worlds at the same time.

The rose guards this mystery and is also the secret to unlocking it. To master the rose then is to master ourselves. The kiss that the prince bestows once he breaches the hedge is the moment of true rebirth. For though we exist in the world of the living many of us remain "asleep" to our magick, to the potential in our blood, to our true being and purpose, to our ability to walk in both worlds. Beauty sleeps and is roused by the kiss of strength. The blood sleeps and is awakened by the touch of Faery.

We then become the blossoming of passion and love and death and our scent rises to attract spiritual guides and helpers, including the gods. For the scent of our blood is intoxicating to the Fey, the same as our flesh is beautiful to them. We are the rose and a shining star, and as we realize our own inner knowing, we blossom, and our light grows brighter. We dare the thorns, we dare the veil, reclaiming our sleeping powers, our sleeping selves. The story of Sleeping Beauty thus speaks to our need to "awaken" our inner knowledge, our inner powers, to have the courage to face dangers and undergo challenges.

The white rose stands for Faery, for this is the color of their blood, while the red rose represents the witch, the blood, and in the old stories is a blossom associated with fire. Together, they make up the pink rose, the wild rose, with its golden heart; the rose that is found in the wilds of the Otherworld. The golden heart of this rose that is the inner knowledge that marks us as one of the blood, gnosis, true resurrection. These other-worldly roses blossom from the blood of the witch and the Fey, red and white co-mingled.

A rose garden is a good place to contact the Fey or a clearing in the woods where wild roses grow. Roses are also a good choice to decorate a Fey altar and to use in ritual practice, especially one white and one red rose that are bound together. Even if you do not draw a circle or call the Elements, you can simply place those two roses on a stone or the altar as the simplest means of marking the crossroads of their world and our world and the relationship that binds the two together. It's also proper to use roses to mark births, deaths, and initiations, to make a crown for a priestess who will speak for the Faery Queen, and to place a single red rose or a red rose for every member of the coven with any offering made on All Hallow's Eve.

Besides places where wild roses grow, the Fey are also associated with the wild and unknown, sacred and dread places of this world—the deep forests and the hills and the mountains and deserts, the rivers and lakes and marshes and moors. Folktales tell us of Faery hills, Fairy trees, and Faery stones. They also warn us that it is dangerous to linger or sleep on those hills, beneath those trees, or within the bounds of such stones.

For the sacred places where the standing stones dwell, where the barrows and cromlechs mark out the boundaries between the living and the dead, are linked to the ancestors and the Fey. Old stories and accounts describe how the Fey dance around the stones or even reside within them, as they also reside within certain trees or groves. Some beliefs indicated that the stones were made by the Fey. Other tales indicate the stones themselves can move and dance or that they were once people who have been transformed to stone, often by the magick of witches. Some of the more famous stones linked to the Fey include the Stone of Scone, the Scottish stone of kings, and the Irish Stone of Destiny, as well as the stone made into the seat at King Arthur's Round Table, the *Siege Perilous*.

Of course, it was risky to move or destroy such stones, the same as it could bring down the wrath of Faery if you dug up their sacred trees or removed branches or fruit without their permission. Even today, there are stories of roads that are altered to avoid having to destroy traditional Faery trees or groves, especially in the countries where the Faery Faith of the past remains strong. In one older story, a standing stone was moved to a garden setting, only to have a terrific storm brew up that resulted in a landslide that destroyed the garden, after which the people could hear the Fey laughing about what had happened. In other tales, we were warned that if you moved or destroyed a Faery tree or shrub that you would be visited with ill health and bad luck if not worse. The Fey might well strike with one of their deadly darts, paralyzing or killing the one who crossed them.

Another sacred Faery spot is where holy trees stand near a well or spring. People would come there to tie ribbons and strips of cloth on the trees or throw a coin into the well and ask for a boon. Clearly, this is where we get the idea of the wishing well. They had to know which well to go to, though, for there are both blessing and cursing wells, wells said to have healing properties and wells where you can do work to harm your enemies. This reflects the abilities of Fey and witches to do harm or to heal, to give or to take away, depending upon the intent behind the energy or offering or spell.

One tree is directly said to be a gift of Faery, the apple tree. Apples and pigs are said to have their origins in Faery, which makes the Yule tradition of the roast pig with the apple in its mouth emblematic of the blessings of the Otherworld. Apples are also tied to All Hallow's Eve, the

ending of the old year and the beginning of the new. The island of Avalon
where the divine king, Arthur, was taken after he died is said to be an
island of apples, the land of the immortal ones from which he is to return
someday. Apples, then, are a good choice for ritual, though when picking
apples in the fall, one should always leave one last apple on the tree as
an offering to the future and the Fey. One should also be careful about
falling asleep beneath an Apple tree for it makes you vulnerable to being
kidnapped by the Fey.

Another sacred Faery tree is the elder or elderberry. These shrub-like
trees were sometimes specifically planted in order to attract the Fey and
folklore tells us to wear elder sprigs on May Eve. Elder-Flower goddess,
Frau Holle or Mother Hulde is one of the goddesses of the Fey. Her
followers are the wild, dancing Fey called the Hulden. She is also one of
the gods who leads the Wild Hunt and a wreath made from an elder is
supposed to let you be able to see the Fey on their wild rides or rades or
the witches riding out on their elderberry poles. The elder is a gate to the
realm of Faery, just as Mother Hulde has power over the gates through
which we pass from death to life and from life to death. It's said that
where elder trees stand, the Fey, the witches and the spirits of the dead
can travel and you should never keep a baby in a cradle made of elder for
then the Fey could pinch the poor child.

Other stories tell us that witches could transform themselves into elders,
so a single elder tree could either be a gate to Faery or it might actually
be a witch in disguise. The wood of the elder tree is also powerful protection against negative magick and people of the past sometimes buried
hair or fingernails or afterbirth beneath elder trees to guard against those
personal items being used against them. The red berries of the elder can
be made into jam and wine or baked into pies and has numerous medical
uses, hence its nickname as the "county medicine chest."

Besides the elder, another set of trees sacred to Faery are the *Oak and
Ash, and Thorn,* especially when all three are found growing together.
Accordingly, this is one of the best places to hold your rituals and a good
place to pick to consecrate your Faery tree if possible. If you take a small
branch or sprig from the oak, one from the ash, and one from the thorn
and bind them together with a red cord or thread, they are a great protective charm. This charm can then be put into a small bag to wear around

your neck or put into your pocket, or you can hang it over your door or within your ritual space.

Groves of oaks were once the great sacred places of the past, long before the cathedrals were built. Oaks were royal trees, *king trees*, and associated with the sacred Midsummer fires. Which is hardly surprising, since oaks are said to call down the lightning, thus being associated with many old gods of the sky, including Zeus and Jupiter. King oaks of Europe and England were said to grow so large that Robin Hood and his Merry Men could hide out inside a hollow in one of their trunks. Oaks were also where sacred oaths were taken, and the Fey were known to dance beneath oak trees. When an oak tree or grove of oak trees was cut down, and new green sprigs grew up from the stumps, this was especially considered an uncanny place sacred to the Fey and dangerous to trespass on after dark.

Ash trees are associated with fire and the German Yule Log was usually from an ash. One would keep a small bit of the Yule Log from the previous year to use to light the new Yule Log, representing continuity and resurrection. Ash trees are the most common of the sacred trees found growing beside ancient wells. The ash is a tree of rebirth and justice, the most famous of which is Yygdrassil, the Cosmic Tree. The rowan tree is also called the mountain ash and is linked to both witches and the Fey. Rowan berries, in particular, can be used for protection by taking the dried berries and amber beads and stringing them on red thread.

The lone thorn tree or a grouping of three thorn trees out in the middle of a field or growing along a hedgerow is traditionally *the* place that marks a gateway to the realm of Faery. To destroy or steal a branch from one of these thorn trees would draw unwelcome attention from the Fey, from which you risked losing your livelihood or illness or death for those you loved. The whitethorn tree is a member of the *Rosacea* family, which includes the rose, and they have traditionally been used in the creation of hedges throughout the English countryside.

The whitethorn tree's other names include the hawthorn, the hagtree, the May flower or the May blossom because that's when it tends to flower. Its flowers were traditionally used to crown the Queen of the May and also as bridal blossoms. Witches and the Fey would meet under a hawthorn tree and, like any Faery tree, it was dangerous to destroy a hawthorn.

Whitethorn is supposed to protect against negative magick and attract not just the Fey, but all sorts of spirits. May didn't just refer to the time of year, then, but to go "a-maying," before the rise of the sun and collect the flowers of the May. If you gave someone the blossoming branches of the hawthorn, along with rowan, this meant you wished them good fortune—though the wood should not be brought into the house or burnt indoors or it will mean bad luck or a portent of death. These trees also traditionally were found growing near the old sacred wells. In the old days, people would also dance around the well and tree, tearing off bits of their clothing as they went to hang on the branches. Olwen, *She of the White Track*, is said to be the daughter of the whitethorn, Queen of the May and a goddess of love.

Blackthorn's hardwood provides branches for clubs and staffs, as well as blasting or cursing rods. Blackthorn is also called *Straif*, which is related to the word strife. It also gives its name to the term "blackthorn winter," because its flowers might still be blooming in February or March while winter yet lingers. The blackthorn is essentially a wild plum tree and its fruit, known as sloe berries, are said to taste the best after the first frost. But, of course, you shouldn't touch it after All Hallows, for then it belongs to the Fey. You also shouldn't cut a branch from this particular tree without the approval of the Fey.

In some ways, the whitethorn and the blackthorn stand as portals at different times of the year, the two times of the year that the Fey are said to travel from one home to another and when the veil is thin—Beltane and Sovane. The blooming of the whitethorn was an indication of summer, just as the blackthorn berries were a sign of winter. The whitethorn is tied to the Goddess, to the Queen of the Sabbat, and the blackthorn to the Horned One, the Master of the Sabbat. For the Queen of the May is the White Lady, the daughter of the hawthorn and is the reflection in this world of the Queen of Faery. Her consort is the Dark Lord of the Blackthorn Gate who is the wine, the thorn, the crooked rod and the crooked path. Together, they are dark, and light, one at the heart of the other, just as the Fey are at the heart of witches and witches are at the heart of the Fey.

Other trees tied to witches and the Fey include the alder, willow, yew, hazel, walnut, fir, birch, and pine. In Celtic belief, the alder was a Faery Tree of death and rebirth, and springtime and the green dye made from the leaves of the alder tree is the kelly green of Faery. The willow is associated with the Moon, and its name is linked to the word "witch" and "wicker." Willows were said to walk around at night when no one was looking. The yew not only represented mourning, which is why they are planted near graveyards, but the eternal and are said to make powerful wands. The hazel or hazelnut tree has powers of wisdom and fertility, and wands made from its wood could be used to call down rain or dowse for water. The most famous hazelnut tree grows beside a well in Avalon, where the *Salmon of Knowledge* grows wise from eating its fallen nuts.

As for the walnut tree, witches would come together to dance beneath its branches, the most famous example of this being the fabulous walnut tree of Benevento. Walnut trees also were said to be gateways to the Otherworld, especially to the ancestors. The Fey would gather, as well, beneath fir and pine trees, while branches from the birch tree could call the Fey to you and can be used for both protection and fertility. The birch is also considered a Cosmic World Tree, its branches providing protection from evil spirits.

Any of these trees would make for a good Faery tree, especially if they are found near where wild roses are growing or close to a natural spring or near some large stones or a circle of stones. For the stones represent the eternal bones of the earth and the trees the power of change and transformation, which is undoubtedly why they make good wands. The tree and well or spring that gives access to the Otherworld echoes the cosmic tree from which flows the living waters. Even in the story of Eden, the Tree of Life stood over a spring and from that spring came the *Four Rivers of Paradise*, what we see as the four Elements or the four Quarters.

One way of looking for the right Faery tree is to do some research and find out if there is any local lore about a special tree or grove of trees near where you live, one that you might have access to without trespassing on private land. It is, of course, better if the Faery tree is somewhere on your own land as you can more freely decorate and dedicate it to your Fey rites and offerings. If the tree is on public land, you need to be aware of any rules about the times you can be there, especially when you don't want to have your rites observed or interrupted.

For example, I sometimes go to a wooded land that has some walking trails laid out through it. There are many trees off the main tracks that people don't go near and can't see from the trails. I bring a small blanket with me to sit on and leave an offering when I leave again, especially if I've removed any moss or dirt or a fallen branch to use in rituals at home. My best wands are those I've just "found" and have never done anything more to than wrap a ribbon around them or bind a stone to them. You will know right away when you pick one up if it is suitable for your use, the same as with any shaped and carved wand you might find at a store.

Once you've found the place where you intend to create a connection to your Faery tree, close your eyes and take a few deep breathes, grounding yourself in the land. If you have already formed a relationship with the local land spirits, tap into that thread and ask their permission and aid in finding the proper tree. Make your silent appeal then to the Fey to show you the way. If possible, try to get yourself into a light trance state, deep enough to sense the energies and get messages, but not so deep that you can't move around.

Wander through the woods and try not to think, just to observe, as you look at the trees. Try to see the trees as connection points between the *above* and the *below*. One tree, in particular, should stir up your senses or stand out among all of the others. Approach that tree and wait for a feeling of permission from the tree before you touch it. It should feel warm and welcoming. It might even make your hand tingle, or you could feel energy shoot through you and connect you not just to the tree, but to the earth.

If this is the correct tree, you should feel the rightness of it, whether that comes from the tree itself, from the Fey, from the earth spirits, or from all of them. The best course then is to ask the tree if it will accept this charge, to be an intersection between this world and the realm of Faery, a tree where the spirits can reside and build on their relationship with you and this land. If you do not get a clear or positive response, it would be best to keep on looking. It might not be the right tree or it might not be the right area. Some places are not as friendly as others and some energies might not be suitable to work with your own. When it is right, it will feel right.

With public trees and lands, always be respectful of the fact that the land it stands on is not yours, but one that is shared. In which case, any decorations that you place on the tree should be removed before you leave. You can make a small ritual of this, by placing each object mindfully on the tree in a particular order and then removing them again in the same way. You can loosely tie ribbons or cords on the branches, so they are easy to take off again.

Odd numbers of items are better than even numbers of items—such as three mirrors, seven charms, nine pendants, eleven ribbons or thirteen small bells. You might also be able to hide an object in a hollow of the tree, such as a charm bag or carved piece of wood or blessed crystal or other stone so that you can leave it there. You could also choose to place small stones around the roots of the tree where they won't be noticed. These stones can also be charged with energy, and you can paint images on them if you like.

Go with what you feel, but always ask the tree if it will accept each gift and make sure that what you put on the tree will not hurt it. Be mindful not to harm the tree by tying cords or ribbons or wire too tightly on the branches. Make sure that the tree can continue to grow properly. Each object should also mean something to you; you shouldn't just put things on your Faery Tree that are sparkly or pretty or that you like, but things that contain some memory or wish or dream or magick. Under the branches of the tree, you should sense its voice as it blends with the physical objects you've hung upon it

The ribbons and the objects should always be cleansed by incense smoke or consecrated water or both before using them, and it's best if you also bestow some of your own energy into them so that they will also tie you to the tree and the place. Each object on the tree is a song, a prayer, a blessing, a poem. You can also take this literally by writing on the ribbons or pendants, or even rolling up the words on some paper and placing them into a small bag and hang that on a branch.

When you are undertaking a new path or need something, you can invest that into a ribbon and tie it onto a branch of the tree. However, you should not forget that you are also putting ribbons and objects on the tree for well wishes you intend for the Fey, as well as your own wishes or needs. The relationship is a reciprocal one, and this needs to be respected. If you take and take without giving to the Fey, this creates an imbalance, the same as if you give and give and never ask anything of the Fey. In this, always remember:

Don't ask without giving and don't give without asking.

If your Faery Tree is on your private land, you can leave the items on the tree where you have placed them. You can also choose to build a small altar at the base of the tree. Its best to use a flat stone or set of stones, and you can also choose to paint or draw chalk symbols on the stones. In some ways, chalk is the better choice because you will have to re-draw it at times and this will keep the relationship fresh in your mind.

The symbol below can be used because it's a sign of the intersection of this world and Faery:

You can choose to draw symbols equating to the North, East, West, and South, or the Earth, Air, Fire, and Water, or whichever emblem you are using to interact with the Fey. The traditional pentacle is also a good choice. If you have your own set of symbols that you use personally or that your path uses, you can make use of those. The most important aspect is that the symbolism works for you and your path or come from your interaction with the Fey.

When leaving an offering of milk or cream or any sort of Faery drink beneath the Faery tree, its better to use bowls or plates that are made of wood or pottery, especially if you intend to leave them there overnight. If you don't wish to use a bowl or plate, then pour out the milk or cream directly on the ground or on the roots of the tree. Other offerings that can be left are pieces of fruit and cakes or bread, whether ones you have made yourself from the recipes in this book or other recipes. You can use store-bought items, but its best to bless each item before offering it.

Finally, never, ever cut a branch from your Faery tree. That will bring bad luck to you and yours. If, on the other hand, you find a small fallen branch near the tree that's of a size to make into a wand or a staff, this is very good. But be sure to acknowledge the gift by bringing something special for the tree and the Fey for what they have given you freely.

Dedication of Your Faery Tree

We be not dryads.
We be not nymphs.
We be the fey o' the trees...
the great and glorious oaks of king's praise,
the ash of ice and flame
the pillars of thorn
which mark the gate
the elder
from whose flower we drink.

Once you have found a tree for your Faery Tree, you should do a small ritual to dedicate it.

For this purpose, you will need:

- Heavy whipping cream (half and half can be used if no cream is available) or one of the Faery Drinks in this book
- Red wine
- Four Faery Cakes
- Four white ribbons
- Offering for the tree such as wine, honey, tobacco, some food, or even a poem that regals the beauty of trees and nature, preferably one you've written yourself if possible

The four white ribbons should be charged up ahead of time with your feelings for the Fey, what you will bring to the relationship and what you desire in the relationship. You can also write on the ribbons if you want. For example, you can charge up the ribbons with ideals such as *Truth, Faith, Honor, and Love* or use *Protection, Guidance, Respect, and Necessity.* You might want to ask the Fey or use divination to figure out what four feelings/words to use on the ribbons. Of course, as your relationship with the Fey deepens and grows, you can add more ribbons to the first ones that reflect this greater knowledge and communion.

If the branches of the tree are too high to reach easily, you can also choose to use four small white stones instead of ribbons and charge them in the same way.

This rite is best suited for dawn or twilight, but can also be performed after dark if there is a full moon with enough light to see by.

You will need to know the directions surrounding that tree—North, South, East, and West, so if you aren't sure, bring along a compass.

Go to the tree and place your hands on it and ask, one more time, if it agrees to accept this charge, to be an intersection point between you and the Fey. Make an offering at this time to the tree.

Take the cream or Faery drink and walk to the North and carefully pour out the liquid in a line until you reach the tree.

Go to the South and do the same, then the East and the West.

Take the red wine and pour it out in a circle with the tree at the center. This need not be a large circle, but large enough to allow you to move around the tree, so it should be at least 4-5 feet out from the trunk.

Hold up your hands facing the tree and say:

> *At the center of the crossroads*
> *Beyond the river of blood*
> *Stands the great tree*
> *Of life, death, and memory*
> *Be thou for me*
> *That tree*
> *To bear my wishes gladly*
> *To honor my offerings willingly*
> *To witness my promises honestly*
> *To accept my gifts freely*

Tie one of the white ribbons on a tree branch along the line of the North, then follow with one at the South, the East, and the West.

As you tie each ribbon, concentrate on what you have put into it and state that out loud, or you can say:

> *Root, trunk, branch, bud, and leaf*
> *Between the earth and the sky*
> *Between this world and Faery*

If you are using stones instead of ribbons, dig a small hole at the start of the line you drew with cream or other Faery drink or wine and bury the stone there, again concentrating on what you have put into it and stating your intention out loud.

If your Faery tree has a natural hollow or flat spot at the base somewhere, then pour out the rest of the cream or Faery drink and wine there. This will be your primary offering spot in the future, and you can set a flat stone there, build a small Faery altar over it, or even dig a small hole in the ground and line it with stones.

Place three of the four Faery Cakes where you have poured out the liquid offering and slowly eat the fourth Faery Cake while contemplating the connection you are building.

When you are done, you can sit down and meditate and attempt to speak with the Fey or your Fey-other. If the tree is on your private land, you could place a stump or large stone there to sit on in the future or even a rustic chair.

Once you are done, back away from the tree, continuing to face it, until you have gone beyond the circle and crossroads, then bow and leave.

If you have a Faery tree that belongs to an entire coven or group, each person should take part in dedicating and decorating the tree, each placing at least one ribbon or stone. When a new person joins the group, they should be introduced to the tree and make an offering there and also tie on a new ribbon or place a small stone.

If the group has a wish or need that they want to bring to the Fey and the Faery tree, then everyone should put their energy into the item and stand touching the tree as it is placed on the branches or at the roots of the tree.

If your chosen Faery tree is an apple tree, then it can be wassailed in the winter, at Midwinter Eve, so that it will be whole and healthy and bear good fruit. In this particular case, the offering should be of apple cider. Walk around the tree three times and drink from the cider three times, each time saying:

> *So well thee might bloom*
> *So well thee might bare*
> *That we may have apples*
> *And cider this year*
> *Blessings to thee*

Our Faery tree
Good tidings this eve
To all a good year

Pour out the rest of the cider onto the ground or around the roots of the apple tree.

At Beltane, this Faery tree can serve as your gate for ritual. At that time, bring an offering for the Faery tree, placing a small cup or bowl of wine, juice, mead, or ale at the foot of the tree to be blessed by the Fey for you. Drink the liquid and dance around the tree, allowing yourself to grow "drunk" by the blessings of Faery.

You can wear your Faery braid for this "journey" to the Otherworld. You may then be given a glimpse of Faery, a vision, a message or revelation— sometimes something just for yourself or for your group and, sometimes, something that is meant to be shared with the larger community.

Offerings should *always* be made to the tree at All Hallows Eve, in addition to libating your gifts to the Fey and the beloved dead there if that is your practice. Heavy cream of some kind or cream mixed with red wine are suitable, and a plate of Faery cakes that have been consecrated with good wishes and affection. If possible, leave the offering after nightfall, as close to midnight as possible.

If you are doing your All Hallows ritual there, you can also choose to decorate the tree with lanterns hung from the larger branches or placed around the trunk of the tree. If you have concerns about using live flame, you can use solar or battery powered lights.

A fallen branch from your Faery tree is a good choice for a wand, especially for your Faery rituals. When you pick up such a branch, it should feel right to the touch, and you might even sense the wild energy within it. If so, do not cleanse the wand with blessed water or incense before using it because it already had the proper blessing. You can decorate the wand, however, including attaching red thread with a holed stone or with feathers.

If you own the land your Faery tree resides on and intend to move away;
you should un-dedicate your Faery tree. Speak to the Fey and to the tree
first and gain their acceptance and approval before beginning to remove
any of the objects. It's also a good idea to make one final offering at the
foot of the tree as thanks for all it has been and done for you.

Fey Ancestor Rituals

Light the candles.
Sing the songs.
The old songs tell the stories.
You all know the stories,
but to remember their meaning,
you must go deeper.

This ritual is to tap into the hidden knowledge of your Fey ancestors,
your Fey-clan and is best done at the full moon.

For this ritual you will need:

- Eight or four candle holders as desired
- Red and white candles (two of each or four of each)
- Mirror or small cauldron or black bowl
- Silver (or white) candle and holder
- Gold (or yellow) candle and holder
- Wand
- Incense
- Consecrated water
- Skull or skull emblem
- Wreath of red and white roses
- One single red rose
- One single white rose
- Faery Cakes
- Red wine, juice, or one of the rose-flavored Faery Drinks
- Plate large enough for the Faery Cakes
- Bowl or cup

- Small dark cloth
- Bowl or container for libations
- Broom (optional)

You can either set out eight candle holders, one at each cardinal point of North, South, East, and West and at the Cross Quarters, or just set out a candle holder at each of the cardinal points. If you are using eight candles, use a red candle to the West, North-West, North-East, and the South. Place a white candle at the East, South-East, South-West, and to the North. If you are using just four candle holders, then place a red candle to the South and the West and a white candle to the East and the North.

Decorate the altar with apples and roses. In regards to the roses, the wreath and single roses should be real if you can manage it, but otherwise, you can use artificial ones in a pinch. If any of the roses should be real, it's best if the single roses are.

Place the mirror in the center of the altar. This can be a mirror with a stand or a mirror laid flat on the top of the altar. You can also use a small cauldron or bowl with water. If using a bowl, it is preferable that the interior be black.

Green is a good color choice if using an altar cloth.

The silver/white and gold/yellow candle should be placed on the altar as well as the skull or a skull emblem, covered with a dark cloth. It can be put in front of the mirror if on a stand or placed above the flat mirror or the cauldron or bowl of water.

If desired, sweep the ritual space with the broom, then stand and concentrate on your breathing. You can use wordless toning, chant or song to get into a light trance state.

Light the candles on the altar, saying:

> *Between the sun and the moon*
> *Between the earth and the sky*

Let the family gather
Let the feast be laid
Ancestors past and future
Hear the call
Kindred quick and dead
Hear the call
Beneath the great lamp
Where shadows fall
By heart and spirit
In body and blood
Hear the call

Light the candles at the directions, repeating at each:

Hear the call

Draw the circle with the wand.

Light incense and sprinkle the circle with the consecrated moon or rainwater.

Bless everyone in the circle with the water and the incense smoke.

Place the plate and cup or bowl on the altar and put the Faery cakes on the plate and fill the goblet with red wine or juice.

Take the wand and dip it into the consecrated water and use it to draw a spiral pattern on the mirror's surface or a spiral in the water.

Point the wand at each person in the circle, one after the other, dipping the wand back into the water for each person. You can either touch the wand to their heart or simply point at their heart.

All hold up their hands toward the altar and say:

Mother Fate
The clan awaits
The unveiled mystery

Beyond the dread gate
Show us the secrets
Show us the destiny
Of the family

Uncover the skull and place the rose wreath on it and/or place the red rose and the white rose before it, crossed like a pair of crossed bones.

All should sit or kneel down and lay their hands flat on the altar, closing their eyes and concentrating on their breathing, or a chant can be used.

All then say:

Old Ones hear us
Old Ones hear us
Old Ones hear us

Concentrate on sensing your Fey-other standing over you. Feel their hands settle on your head and focus on being one with them and opening yourself up to the Fey-clan to which you both belong.

Say or chant together:

Old Ones
Ancestors
Guardians
Mothers and Fathers of the Beginning

If you have a particular question or need for protection or an insight, you should ask for it at this point silently or out loud.

Keep this in your mind as you pour out a small libation of the red wine, juice, or other Faery drink into the libation bowl and place three of the Faery cakes into it. Set it on the altar in front of the skull.

All put their hands back on the altar and say:

Together we are

One kin
One blood
One spirit
Through the Veil
and Beyond

Pass around the bowl or cup of wine or juice for everyone to take a sip, saying:

Love and mystery be mine
I shall set my will
To the work

Pass around the rest of the Faery cakes on the plate, each person taking a cake and saying before eating it:

Love and mystery be mine
I shall set my will
To the work

If you have a person who is skilled in channeling, they can stand to the East of the circle at this point. Take the rose wreath from the skull and place it on their head.

Hand them the single red and single white rose if being used. They should cross their hands over their chest, one rose in each hand. (If you are practicing alone, you can do this yourself and open yourself up to messages from the ancestors, the Fey and witch kindred.)

Point the wand at the person holding the roses and have everyone concentrate on seeing them as an open gate, a channel for the voice of the Fey, of the ancestors, or the God or goddess of Faery.

People can hum at this point, or a soft chant or song can be used.

Once the message (if any) has been given, remove the wreath and take away the roses and return them to the altar.

At this point, each person should take some of the water or the remainder of the red wine or juice or Faery drink and touch their forehead with it, above their heart, the palms of their hands and their feet.

Stand in a circle and say together, or have one person read and the rest repeat:

> *Bless me Old Ones*
> *Let me walk the path of the ancestors*
> *Freely and unafraid*
> *Between light and dark*
> *Life and death*
> *Earth and sky*
> *Let me see and know and act in honest accord*
> *Of mind, body, heart and spirit*
> *To choose*
> *Freely and unafraid*
> *Divine beauty and strength*
> *Joy, love, passion, and justice*
> *To be a servant of the Gods*
> *A keeper of secrets*
> *A guardian of the land and of the people*
> *A healer of wrongs*
> *A seeker of truth*
> *And a bright flame for the future*
> *Or you can simply say:*
> *Bless me Old Ones*
> *Let me be a bright flame*
> *For the future*

Blow out the candles around the circle, leaving the ones on the altar for last. If desired, all can blow out the altar candles together.

Immediately after closing the circle, write down any messages or insights you received, especially if it included any actions that you are meant to take or symbols or rituals or words you are meant to use.

The libation can be given near your Faery tree.

If desired, this final pledge can also be added to your normal ritual work or circles.

Once you have done the above ritual, you can add in the ritual below during the Solstices and Equinoxes.

For this ritual you will need:

- Altar
- Skull or skull emblem
- Candle holder with candle
- Cauldron, large bowl, or another container of consecrated water
- Red rose (real is best, but artificial if not possible)
- White rose (again, same as the red rose)
- Red ribbon or cord
- Mirror
- Plate filled with cakes
- Goblet or bowl filled with a drink to share

Create a circle as usual.

Clear space on the altar and lay down a mirror. Place the skull or skull emblem on the mirror and set a candle above it.

Place the one red rose, and the one white rose crossed before the skull.

Light the candle, saying:

> *Ancestors*
> *Old Ones*
> *Mothers and Fathers of the Beginning*
> *We who are your children*
> *Brothers and sisters of Air and Fire*
> *Be welcome*

Place the bowl or cauldron filled with water before the altar.

Take the two roses and bind them together, saying:

In the field of roses
Below the great tree
Lies the Well of Memory
The source of all we are
And all we may be

Have someone dip the roses into the water as all begin to slowly circle around, gently using the roses to sprinkle each person with water.

This can be done silently, or all can say:

Dance to remember
Dance to join as one
With our beloved others
To be as one
With the great family

A song or chant can be used as everyone continues to circle until each person has been sprinkled with the water three, seven, or eleven times. You can also choose to hand off who is doing the sprinkling of the blessed water during the course of the dancing.

Set the bound roses above the skull, with the blossoms on the head of the skull.

Place the plate of cakes and the goblet or bowl of drink before the skull.

All touch the altar, saying:

Love and mystery be ours
For we have set our will
To the great work

Make a libation of cakes and drink, either on the ground if outside or into a libation bowl.

Share the rest around with each other, passing the plate and goblet as you say:

I am not afraid
For I walk the path of the ancestors
A blessed child
Of Mother Fate

Continue with any ritual or magical working as desired.

Afterward, place the bound roses into a vase on your Fey or ancestor altar.

If working in a group, each person can take their turn at the different rituals to take the roses home for their altar.

Faery Wreaths

Where fairies often did their measures tread,
Which in the meadows made such circles greene,
As if with garlands it had crowned beene.

--William Browne

Traditionally, wreaths were made to celebrate special occasions and holy days. They were created to honor a good harvest, to express grief, to bestow blessings and love, and to mark out the passage of the seasons. Wreaths were also made and hung up for the purpose of protection.

These wreaths can be made and placed above your door or hearth. In making a wreath for divination purposes, you can place them around a scrying bowl or mirror. They can also be hung from a stang or placed to lean against the altar during ritual work.

When not in use, such a wreath should be covered up with a piece of black silk.

You can either make a wreath yourself or buy a basic one from a craft store. If buying it from a store, be sure to cleanse the wreath with incense smoke before using it.

If making a wreath, take small branches supple enough to bend or lengths of ivy and form them into a circle. They can then be bound together by twine or floral tape or a combination of the two.

Another way to make a wreath is by buying a length of wire—both black and green and copper are readily available—bending it into a circle, and then fixing the greenery and other items to it with floral tape and ribbons. More small branches can then be woven in and around the basic circle until its wide enough. More ribbons can also be intertwined with the branches as you are building it.

You can also create a wreath by taking a piece of heavy-duty cardboard and cutting it out in a ring pattern for the framework. Twigs or sprigs of dried flowers or wheat or real or artificial greenery can then be glued to the outer ring of the cardboard until it is all hidden and more greenery or flowers can be added in the middle portion as desired. Ribbons can also be tied in with the twigs and leaves. A hole can be cut into the top and ribbon or cord tied through it to hang the finished wreath.

What you want to express through your wreath will lend itself to what you intend to put on it. For example, various herbs and plants can be used for protection or against evil wishes, including small green branches from the elder tree. Flowers are generally used for love; the Victorians were masters of this as they had a whole language devoted to what flower meant what and those meanings can be accessed via an internet search. Wheat and seeds are good for harvest wreaths, and we all know that winter means the boughs of the evergreen trees.

A wreath particular to Faery can be made with green leaves and decorated with red and white ribbons, images of the *amanita muscaria*, the red and white-spotted Faery mushroom. When it comes to herbs, sweet woodruff is a good addition, as well as dried yarrow flowers or rowan berries. The rowan berries can even be strung first and then looped around the wreath or placed to hang from the bottom of it. Roses or rosebuds can be attached to the wreath, small mirrors, or the tiny jeweled sprigs found at craft stores in the bridal section.

Feathers can also be attached, small bells, beads, or lengths of ribbon or cords with holed stones at the end. Good choices for stones include crystals, amethyst, aquamarine, moldavite, azurite, aventurine, apatite, lapis lazuli, moonstone, selenite, verdelite, fluorite, celestite, low-grade emeralds or sapphires, and amber. If you can't find stones with holes drilled in them, wire can be wrapped around the stones to hang them.

As ever, found objects for your Faery wreath are best or gifts from friends or family.

Once the wreath is complete, cense it with well with incense smoke. Hold it up as you concentrate on the purpose it was created for. If desired, you can tie in the last three ribbons or charms as you do this, saying:

Circle in
Weave and spin
Never ending
Magick begin

∾ *To Twist and Twine* ∾

White Thorn, flowers bright
Twisted crowns the May Queen
Sacred glory set alight
Sacrifice to life a right

Black Thorn, staff of might
Rise in death the secret rite
Cursed twists to prick the sight
Within on Hallow's Even

White Thorn, Black Thorn
Branches hung with spirits' sighs
Gates to equal realms
Look into each other's eyes

Black Thorn, White Thorn
Eternity to measure
Winter, summer so entwined
In purpose and in pleasure

White, black, grows the Thorn
To twist and twine forever...

White Thorn, Pale Lady knows
Mind you heed Her calling
Love will in promise kept
Set the blood to blooming

Black Thorn, Dark Lord knows
Mind you heed His warning
Strike the sweetest sharpest blows
To keep the truth abiding

Black Thorn, White Thorn
At the season's turning
Pure beauty, quiet strength
Met in magick yearning

White Thorn, Black Thorn
Stem and blossom burning
Bound to dance the sword's edge down
To dance the round reborning

White, black, grows the Thorn
To twist and twine forever...

Chapter 8

Children of the Starry Heavens

We give. You give.
The giving is the gift.
We see. You see.
The seeing is the gift.
What you name the Veil is only in your minds.
Your hearts have the key.
Open your hearts.
Open the door.
Invite in those who have never left you.
Set the table.
Give of your hearts.
Give out of the joy of giving.
What you see is all that is never forgotten
Seen through the Veil of the Heart
Gathered close
The flame feeds upon the love
Of the family.

One All Hallow's Eve, we spoke with the Queen of Faery. She attempted to impart to us various aspects of Sovane and how our world and Faery, how witches and the Fey, interact. She crossed Her arms, inner wrist to inner wrist, and implied to us that this is how we connect across the veil, across the mirror. Obviously, we saw in this image the crossroads but knew it meant more than that. We puzzled and puzzled over it, even as we explored our relationship with Faery and connected to our Fey-others.

It was many years later that we realized that this image had just as much to do with what was created at that meeting point. That it wasn't just where two worlds met, where witch and Fey met, but it was the actual bridge between worlds, a point of eternity outside of time.

This point of eternity outside time is the otherworldly sabbat, the true sabbat, the heart of Faery. When witches and the Fey form a circle there, that circle is the real circle in a time that is not a time and in a place that is not a place, between the worlds and beyond.

This point also exists within the cauldron of rebirth, within the cup of ritual wine we share, within the heart of every witch. What best binds us to the Fey lies not in particular words or actions or even in rituals or spell-work. Sure, we can use those things, and they are powerful, but they remain tools. If we do them without opening our hearts to our brothers and sisters, our kindred of old, and to our eternal spark, then they will not have the effect that we desire.

We have to be naked to Faery for they and our Fey-others know if we are not truly open, what we are trying to hide, even from ourselves. Faery is not fooled. Faery cannot be fooled for Faery knows us...deep down, our deepest self, our deepest desires, and our deepest fears.

So we really need to know ourselves to commune with the Fey. Otherwise, despite the love of our Fey-others for us, Faery can raise our shadows, our terrors, and make them all too real. These dangerous shadows create what is called the *Guardian at the Gate*, the dragon or beast or monster who guards the treasure within the depths, our abilities, and power. Time and again, I have seen those on this path come to face that gate, face that guardian...and either defeat the beast and claim the treasure that was theirs all along or turn and run away.

Those who run, risk not only losing their powers but themselves. For the gold the dragon guards is our light, our own inner divine spark. One lady I know of went on an internal quest once to claim that spark, only to be scared off at the last moment by what she saw as giant white spiders.

These spiders did not mean that her greatest fear was of arachnids, for the spiders represented her fear of mental illness, of the seizures that she had as a child, of being alone and abandoned, of feeling betrayed by others. Sadly, though, instead of facing those fears in both her mundane life and her spiritual quest, she abandoned the effort and so abandoned her power and light.

As a result, she turned away not only from her own light, but all light, and demanded that those around her do the same—to accompany her on her dark path. She imagined and talked about this as though it was an act of love she was asking, but it wasn't. It was fear and shame and anger grown into a monster, consuming from within. Not only did this endanger her, but also all those around her; family and coven alike.

This is one of the dangers of Faery for it can take the shape of what you bring to it, good or bad. This is magnified when you work in a coven or group. A coven working with Faery can create a great darkness as much as a great light. When we create a coven spirit or join a clan spirit, we bring aspects of ourselves to that and effect it. It also affects us, so a group spirit that has become tainted can taint those who belong to it. This feeds and shapes the Guardian at the Gate for the coven, for a coven faces its own quest, its own monsters, as much as an individual in the journey to connect to the knowledge and power of the ancestors, of the Hidden Company.

In this instance, the taint in the coven spirit caused those in the group to feel and do and say things that they regretted once they left the group and cleansed themselves of that influence. Those who left but did not go through the pain and efforts of getting rid of that influence, remained tainted and carried this into their covens, thus continuing the bad blood. They then failed their testing by the Guardian at the Gate, failed to attain the heart of Faery.

The rewards and dangers of working with Faery are great. Each witch, every coven, endures trials and must undergo a transformation; one that strips away what is extraneous and leaves what is essential. Power and magick are double-edged, like a ritual blade, like Faery. You get what you pay for, for magick is never free. If any witch denies this, Faery is quite happy to strip bare their illusions.

In the process of facing the Guardian of the Gate, our illusions are stripped away—often forcefully and painfully—and we are left bare to ourselves and the greater reality. Some people can't cope with this and will seek to go back to "normal," or as normal as they can ever be again for this willful denial never really works well and you can never really go back. Those who try, often become off-balance and end up troubled in mind and body. Or they can start down that dark path that turns them into a shadow of themselves, eaten up from within.

Instead, we must brave the challenge and take hold of our light and power so that we use them for good purposes. For our quest is not for ourselves per se, but is for the community. Witches are here for a reason—to serve evolution, spiritual transformation, and Mother Earth. A witch who does not serve is not really a witch. When we serve the land and the community, we will eventually benefit ourselves, but that is not why a witch seeks out knowledge and power. We seek it out for the community, for the land, for the gods, for what is needful.

The Fey know this, for that is why they choose to be born here; to be witches. Any witch who forgets and decides to start only serving themselves has forgotten why they are here. Not that there's a problem with seeking deeper knowledge and greater power, but it can't be for self-aggrandizement or to try to shore up secret doubts and a lack of self-esteem. A witch who goes around boasting about how powerful they are is not really a witch at all. A witch who does magick solely to serve their own desires is not really a witch at all. Witches are equals, as all of the Fey are equals—each with different skills and talents, but all to serve the Earth and to serve Faery as a reflection of the other.

In undertaking any spiritual quest—you simply can't get there without pain, without struggle, without the courage to face and embrace transformation. It's often true that the greater the struggle, the greater the power and light that results. We all know those whose lives are sharp and bright and wonderful, who have influenced those around them, if not the world itself. Yet, all too often, these people do not endure. It's like there was a choice...to burn brightly, to burn out quickly, or to burn dimmer, softer, not reaching those great heights, but remaining longer.

Witches and covens face these same choices. To risk and to strive to attain power and knowledge, to be a very bright light, to risk going deep into Faery, and even, in some cases, *beyond* Faery, but then to fall and sometimes fall hard, a shooting star. Or we can choose to be a gentler light, an enduring light, protecting the local land, the community, but not achieving great change, great magicks.

Both are legitimate choices, both are necessary.

For small magicks are as vital as great magicks. For instance, healing someone or helping them get a better job or have a healthy child is important. We need to protect the local sacred sites as much as the great wide world. Promoting the well-being of the community, fertile fields, bountiful orchards, clean waters, are all traditional goals of the local witch. For some covens, this is their bread and butter, participating in and enhancing the best and brightest qualities of their communities, materially and spiritually.

However, some witches and covens are called to do magick that extends beyond promoting and providing for the good of the local land and people. This magick can focus on the transformations, the beginnings, and endings, related to the *Procession of the Ages*. On the evolution of an entire nation or country, on summoning up or awakening ancient powers that go beyond the ones associated with the Elements of the Earth, essentially pushing the boundaries of what is known.

Our Fey-others, our Fey-clan, the *Great Family*, will help show us which is our proper path. It is then our choice whether or not to walk that path, to participate in the processes of transformation. That first step is often the most important, for no matter the magick, the changes might start out small, but if they start in the right place and time, they can snowball, riding upon the free flow of energies and powers. This can happen within each of us, within our world, and within the interaction between worlds.

We now know that all that we experience as material is actually formed of energy. Faery is even more aware of that and works directly with the energies behind the scenes, as it were. We might not always be able to see and understand these energies, even with our second sight, but together with the Fey, we can see the invisible currents within all things.

Another traditional aspect of the interaction between witch and Faery is related to the idea of a reversal between worlds so that what is one way here is opposite there, a mirror-reflection. It's true that changes that happen here cause change in Faery and changes in Faery cause change here...but it's not precisely an equal or opposite exchange. Instead, it's much more complex, much more organic. A small change here might affect Faery in great measure, and a great change here might be a small thing in Faery. It's no good doing some huge dramatic sort of spell work that you aim to effect Faery in a big way...the end result might well be just a flicker, a cobweb easily cast aside. Equally, one small word, one small spell, one small song at just the right time and place might work marvels beyond wonder in Faery. It might start a spark that grows into a great conflagration.

The Fey can also aid us in purifying ourselves and opening to our power by how they know things. What the Fey see when they look at us is our energy, our light, our spark. They see *us*, the real us. This can be a wonderful feeling, to be known in this way, but it can also be frightening. We get used to the safety of our minds, to having privacy and being individual, but the Fey can push right past that. They can know us, even as we sometimes do not. They can see into our unconscious minds, which is useful, but scary.

For example, I was having a difficult time with an emotional reaction to an issue once but couldn't articulate just why. Yet my spirit contacts— Fey and familiar—looked deeply into me and were able to point out the source of the problem. It was a rather odd feeling, to have the entity possessing me talking about me in the third person, let alone explaining feelings I wasn't even consciously aware of, but it worked. Once the reason was brought out, I could deal with it, and my reaction made sense. This can be especially helpful in figuring out issues that arise in coven work or on a magickal path, whether you get the insight from the Fey or a familiar spirit via a dream, divination, or possession.

We've also experienced the Fey doing much the same for others. We would be wrestling with trying to understand someone, why they did what they did, and the Fey could provide insights that would bring it all into focus and help it make sense. They can also do this with greater circumstances, helping us to see what is *really* going on, when all that we see is the outer expression. When events take place in our community, our country, in the world, they can provide knowledge that brings it into focus. This is especially true when events seem to echo each other, so you're aware something more is going on, but are missing the key to understanding it. Faery can provide that key.

In this, our Fey-others can help us by allowing us to see ourselves through their eyes. If we can connect deeply enough with them, we can get impressions from them not only about where we are in the moment, but how our whole life has unfolded to that moment. This can be a wonderful insight, but it can also be disturbing. For not just the good experiences shape us, but the bad, and the honest truth is that we need both. We need to face and overcome adversity to make us stronger. It's not pleasant, and no one really wants to go through pain or hardship, but we see it in all stories. There really is no story without it.

With our Fey, we can look at our story with impartial, though sympathetic, eyes. We will not be indifferent to the pain, just as they are not indifferent to our pain, but will see in the larger context—what we have learned from it, how it has changed us, what we will do because of it. Of course, this also holds true for our successes, our achievements, experiences that have awed and existed us. All of this is part of what makes us who we are. As we are normally too close to our stories, too wrapped up in them, to see clearly, we can use this Fey vision to glimpse our story in its greater context.

We also came to see as the Fey see, expanding our view of this world and our place in it. This requires the vision granted not by the eyes, but by the heart, the source of the sight. To do this, we must open our hearts to the vision that the blood can provide for it contains the secrets of the past, the knowledge of both witch and Fey. Our heart pumps our blood, and as the heart is the seat of our spirits, the gateway to who we are, when our hearts are pure, when that gate lies open, then it informs our blood. Our blood awakens, not just to who we are, but to the knowledge of the ancestors, to the great family of witch and Fey, and to the Old Ones. When we close our hearts then, we not only cut ourselves off from others but also from ourselves.

We need to find a means of keeping our hearts open and the key we can use to open them when they become closed. For this will happen, and the greater and deeper the pain and sorrowful experiences that cause our hearts to close, the harder it can be to take that risk again. Accordingly, we may have to start with opening to the one who can never and would never betray us—our Fey-other. Then, once we've established a good, strong connection to them, we can open to other spirits, to people, to the gods, as well as re-connect to other spirits.

This strong sense and knowledge of self are vital to working great magick and allowing the Fey and other spirits to speak and work through us in the world. If we don't have a good foundation, we risk being swept away by the spells we work and the spirits and forces we interact with. We need to know who we are as best we can, what our purpose is, where our will lies, understanding ourselves as one of the powers in the Web of Wyrd.

We serve Wyrd by serving need, by which our own needs will also be served. If we serve our own needs first and foremost, then we might not be serving the greater need, and all we have done will be for naught. We will no longer be working for Mother Fate, but for ourselves. And we all know what happens in the old fairytales when someone serves them-selves over others. They are the ones who fail to gain the helpful guides and guardians, who get lost, who fail in their quest.

One risk we have in forming deep intimate relationships with the Fey and other spirits is that we can be pulled out of balance. We can get too deeply involved with the beauty and power of Faery, become glamoured by what we see and experience there, and lose our grounding in this world. Faery is notoriously enchanting and fascinating, and it can be ever so tempting to wrap ourselves up in that and step away from this place. This can result in a difficulty, even an inability, to deal with ordinary things such as jobs, taking care of our health and watching over others we are responsible for, even being able to understand how others around us who don't interact with Faery might see what we say and do.

I have seen people lose the ability to handle the demands of the ordinary world, who have abandoned interest in anything other than their other-worldly experiences, and who have even turned away from family and friends by focusing on their spirit connections instead. Certainly, most of us know of at least one person who has gone off the deep end on this path. There's no gentle way of putting it, but there is always a fine line between being very spiritual and psychic and having mental or emotional problems.

If we fixate primarily on Faery and disdain this world, we fail to understand that we, as witches, have come here for a reason, to be half of here and half of there. Also, despite the temptation, we shouldn't subsume ourselves in our Fey-others, in our spirit familiars or even in the gods, but hold fast to our strength and purpose. We can only do that if we not only know who we are but work to embrace and enhance that.

How our true self manifests itself in each of our incarnations is different, as we are born to take up the different purposes at different times. The light within shines the same, being eternal, but the patterns and shapes and hue of color that light casts vary from lifetime to lifetime. In each life, we must seek it out and find a means of expressing it best. We must figure out how to act in accord with our inner nature, our inner light, and walk that path.

I have encountered my own true self and the true selves of others a few times. They are neither male nor female, but can be either—much like the Fey—and are truly great spirits, powerful yet humble, compassionate, serious but good-humored, basically embodying the best anyone could aspire to be. They are what we can and should aspire to, and they are the inner star, the self that the Fey can see in each of us.

Even though our Fey-others and familiar spirits can lend their aid to see ourselves, but we still provide the focus. This focus is our will and that is one of the four key components of the *Powers of the Magus—to Know, to Will, to Dare, and to Be Silent.* "To know" is primarily associated with the Fey of the Air, the Seelie, and "to dare" with the Fey of Water, the Unseelie, while "to be silent" is linked to the Fey of the Earth, the ancient, unknowable ones. Some say that silence is the power to keep secret—from which we get the word "occult," or *hidden*—but that silence is also the silence of sheer being. We have each of these within us, of course, in order to be able to work magick, but the lens of our power is that of Fire, of will. Which doesn't mean that we shouldn't pursue knowledge and push past our limitations, to learn, to grow, to create, for that is an important aspect of who and what we are. This is also part of why Faery is so drawn to us, for we push and push and try and try and attempt and even do what is considered impossible...or, at least, highly improbable. We all have within us the flame of creation, and of destruction, and the gift of choice, the gift of the Firestealer, of the Lightbearer.

We have the power to alter even the strands of the Web of Wyrd, to persuade Mother Fate. Our Fey-others stand with us, but we must also always seek to stand on our own feet and be honorable and just and do what is meantt for us to do. In all this, we experience and celebrate both of these aspects, what is known and what is unknown. You can't have one without the other, for even as we push the boundaries of what is known—which is part of our work—the universe continues to evolve and yet more that is unknown is born. We shall *never* know all, for the all is beyond understanding. Neither science nor the sight can render us that, nor all the striving of art, philosophy, psychology, mythology or spirituality in the world. They can all serve to point out pieces of it, but none can claim the whole for that remains beyond.

That remains, Mystery.

Unlocking the Inner Gate

"Bright and sharp, we enter in. How can you not remember us? We walk with you, no matter how far or how dark the road. You know us. We live within the bright part of you. Only if you turn away from the light do you turn away from us. Those who exist in the dark are less merciful than we. They do not breathe with you. Many of you have forgotten us, yet we have not forgotten you. You are our light. We cannot turn away. Though a thousand years may pass, we cannot turn away.

We are the kingly part of you. How else would you make such a shining court? A king may be made king upon the hill, yet the fire and the light are yours as much as his.

Remember the crown, the making, the song, the secret, and all shall be made true."

-The Fey

This exercise can be done either within or without a circle. You can draw a simple protective circle, or you can do it in a place that you normally feel secure and won't be disturbed. It might be a ritual space or room or even your bedroom—basically, anywhere you can tune out distractions and feel comfortable and safe.

Sit or lie down; whichever is possible or convenient.

Close your eyes and take as many deep breaths as you need to relax as fully as possible.

With each breath, let the muscles in your body relax and let tension drain out of you.

If desired, you can hum a tune softly. You can also make use of a visual image in your mind, preferably one you have used before to aid in getting you into a light trance state or an image that makes you feel safe and calm.

Once relaxed, place your hands crossed over your heart, palms downwards. You might feel your heart beating through your hands.

Take more deep and relaxing breaths, trying not to think about anything. Concentrate on your breathing and the pulse of your heart.

Picture a spark of light beneath your hands, pure and perfect. This is your flame, your spark, your connection to the eternal divine. Concentrate on feeling that spark as deeply as possible.

When ready, slowly raise your hands or slide them away from your heart. As you do, feel that flame, that spark, growing and expanding.

Feel your heart opening. It might seem like a spiral unwinding, or a bud unfurling, or simply a door opening. The sensation might feel very good, warming and calming, or it might make you feel vulnerable and uncomfortable.

Keep that inner gate open for as long as you are comfortable. There's nothing wrong with feeling too vulnerable at first and wanting to shut it down after just a few moments or a few minutes. You can always try again.

When you wish to close the gate, slowly put your hands back, crossed over your heart and let the spark shrink down again.

Gently, withdraw your awareness from it until you are just concentrating on your heartbeat and your breath once more.

Begin to quicken your breathing.

Stretch the muscles in your body, tensing and then releasing them again.

Finally, open your eyes and let yourself come back to normal awareness.

If you've done this in a protective circle, take down the circle. If you're doing this in the context of a ritual, you can continue with the ritual at this point.

Doing this exercise alone at first is a good idea, and then, if you work in a coven or group, you can make it a regular part of your practice. This way, you will not only learn how to open up to your powers and your Fey-other but to each other—a necessary stepping-stone if you're going to create a group or coven spirit.

In the case of doing this together, its best to do any group work while each person still has their inner gate open. You can practice this ahead of time by drawing a protective circle and having each person undertake the exercise while someone else reads it out loud. The person should then try to remain as open as possible for as long as it is comfortably possible. Eventually, with practice, that length of time will increase, and you will feel more and more open, both with yourself and with others.

You can also create or use a symbol, or phrase, or mantra, or chant to concentrate on, one that will become a trigger to open the inner gate. A rhyming phrase is best, especially if used in a group setting. For example, we use deep breathing and free-form toning, not just relax and open up, but to tune into each other. When we're done, we're not just in the proper ritual mindset but our normal shields are down, and we have grounded and centered in our inner selves.

In one coven I was in, we had a song we used at the beginning of every ritual. By singing it together, we were brought closer to each other, emotionally and spiritually. I have seen other groups use a set of phrases, the familiar words triggering the same feeling of closeness and openness to each other.

Morning and Evening Prayers

Staring at the mountain
The moon hides
The stars a crown
We stand just one more time
Waiting for the future
One foot in the past
One foot in other
Overlapped by our Faery selves
Each a crossing road
One that even Fate may not deny

These prayers are to be said upon rising in the morning and before going to bed at night. This is not just a prayer of willful blessing, but of mindfulness. The house is not just your home, but your body. The all who have come before are not just your ancestors, but your past lives, your spirit contacts—both the Fey and others—and the all who come after are not just the descendants of yourself and your family, but spirit contacts yet to be known and lives yet to be lived.

The family is your own blood that you have been born into, but also the greater family of the heart and the spirit that death can never divide—your Fey-clan, your magickal brothers, and sisters of the Craft, your fathers and mothers and sons, and daughters, your loves and lovers.

For this blessing, start by facing the North with your hand to your heart.

Bow and raise your hand before you, palm up and say:

> *Blessings be upon this house*
> *And upon all who dwell within*

Return your hand to your heart and turn to the East. Bow and raise your hand before you say:

> *Blessings be upon all who came before*
> *And upon all who are yet to be known*

Again, return your hand to your heart and face the South.

Bow and raise your hand and say:

> *Blessings be upon the family*
> *Both the quick and the dead*
> *My kindred all*

Return your hand to your heart and turn to the West.

Bow and raise your hand and say:

> *Blessings be upon all that I love*
> *For that is the greatest blessing of all*

Return your hand to your heart and turn one last time to face the North.

Take a few deep breaths and feel yourself at the center of the Four Directions, the Four Quarters. Feel yourself part of the family, both quick and dead. Let yourself be aware of this precise moment and, through time, the eternal spark that is your true self.

This blessing can also be said without turning to face the directions, but while lying in bed before getting up. In the evening, you can say it after you get into bed, before falling asleep.

Faery Mirror

*The realm of Faery is a strange shadow land,
lying just beyond the fields we know.*

-Unknown

You can use the Faery mirror for divination, and you can use it to peer into other worlds. The Faery mirror is an eye, a gate to be opened, a portal. You can use it not just for seeing into the Otherworld or other worlds, but to see more clearly your own life and where you need to go, what you need to do.

A round mirror is best, though you can also use an oval mirror. Before decorating or using the mirror, you should cleanse it with consecrated water and incense smoke.

If the mirror has a frame, the frame can be painted red and white, with red on the outer edge and white on the inner. It can also be painted with images of the red and white spotted mushroom or with twigs from the elder tree. Small pine cones can also be attached to the mirror as they represent the whirling, generative powers.

You can lay the mirror on the floor or on a low altar or table to gaze down into it, but you can also rest it on a small easel.

To use the mirror for divination, have ready a bowl with red wine and one of consecrated water.

Dip a finger in the red wine and use it to mark out the four sides of the mirror, beginning at the top, then to the left, to the right, and finally at the bottom.

Dip a finger into the consecrated water and use it to trace out a spiral pattern, starting at the top and moving first to the left, spiraling inwards until you reach the center.

Lay this spiral pattern three times and when creating the first spiral say:

>*Between here and there*
>*Between now and then*

For the second spiral say:

>*Between what is*
>*What was*
>*And what will be*

For the final spiral say:

>*Let me see*
>*Let me see*
>*Let me see*

Breathe on the mirror three times.

Stare deeply into the mirror.

Sometimes you will see things in the mirror, but sometimes you will find your eyes growing heavy instead. If so, let your eyes naturally go shut and the vision may come that way.

To use the mirror to see into other worlds, have ready a bowl of consecrated water and one of honey. Take the honey on a fingertip and touch the top, the right side, the left side, and the bottom of the mirror.

Dip your fingers into the consecrated water and run them three times from the top to the bottom of the mirror, saying:

By rushing winds and shining thread
Of storms and stars
The eternal web

Run the side of your hand or fingers three times from left to right on the mirror, saying:

The mirrored gate that lies within
The whirling light
The dark between

Finally, place the tips of your fingers to the center of the mirror and concentrate on seeing the crossroads you have drawn as part of a larger web of crossing strands, the Web of Wyrd.

Spiral wide and there reveal
Worlds far away
Within and near
Show me
Show me
What I must see
Far away
Within and near

Again, you might see something in the depths of the mirror, or you might find your eyes growing heavy and see things once you close them.

To use the mirror to gain insight into your own life and self, have ready a bowl with red wine, one with honey, one with ashes and one with milk.

Take some of the ash on your fingers and touch the left side of the mirror.

Take the wine and touch the bottom of the mirror.

Take the honey and touch the top of the mirror.

Take the milk and touch the right side of the mirror.

Finally, put your fingers to your mouth and then draw a line down the center of the mirror, saying:

> *By blood and bone*
> *Breath and flame*
> *Within the heart of truth*
> *The pearl of Fate*

Finally, touch your fingers to your forehead, mouth, and heart, saying:

> *The hall of mirrored doors*
> *Of gates*
> *Where the cup of life*
> *And death awaits*
> *To drink*
> *To know*
> *To see*
> *To be*

Repeat:

> *To drink*
> *To know*
> *To see*
> *To be*

When the Faery mirror is not in use, it should remain covered, preferably with a piece of black silk.

To un-dedicate, the Faery mirror, wash it thoroughly with salt water and bury it in the earth or salt for a while. When the mirror feels inert to the touch, without any buzz of energy, you can then give it away or sell it or donate it.

If the Faery mirror breaks while you own it, take the pieces and bury them in salt until they feel inert, then you can take them and put them in a safe place in the earth. An offering should be made, and knowledge sought from the Fey if your mirror breaks, for it may be a sign of either a problem or that you were attempting something for which you did not yet have the skill or a proper foundation.

⁂

∼ *Dead Time and Hallows Call* ∼

Snow falls
The trees gather their veils
White and pale
They huddle against the dark
The sleepless and those who dream
The deathless and the dead.

He walks among them
Darker still than most
The king of frost and horn
Of black and bone
And silent chase
A stirring in the dark
All around him
Eyes where there can be no eyes
Silence deeper
Than sound.

Most have known him before
His nature
If not his voice
For he is what they fear
When the falling ends
When the stillness starts
And the whole world hangs
Between one land
And another
When time itself is unsure

If there will be any other.

No footprints leave
A trace behind
No scant record of his passing
As though he walks not
Upon the land itself
Not upon the snows
But remains a part of the air itself
As though borne up by night
Unseen
Unknown
Spirits of rushing madness and fear
From deep pools
Of cold and breathless water
Grey death
The touch of tiny hands
Ever after.

Hard as he is to see
Those who follow
Are more spectral still
Born of blood and desire
With rough fur white as snow
Ears tipped red
As though marked by their nature
And with eyes as black
As his own might well be
If you could but bear them
If you could but see him
Standing there
His hands held up and out
Caressing bony backs
Knowing their hunger
His own.

Walking here and there
And gone again

As though a shadow called home
As though a ghost
Made once more unknown
No sound
No breath
Remaining
Though the snow still falls
Drifting always towards Midwinter
A king in all but name
A walking shadow
Of a king
The lonely lord of the hollow time
Of the lost
And dreaming days.

Chapter 9

The River of Blood

To be a witch is to traverse the veil in spirit, to cross the river of blood, passing from life to death and returning again to life, but without forgetting. Most who journey to Faery in their dreams come back without memory of it, or with only a few lingering flashes of memory. When we cross in truth from death to life, we also forget.

But a witch needs to remember and so to seek to be a witch in communion with Faery is to court the means of memory.

Life and death are transition points, gates between one world, one state of being, and another. Of old, the Fey are intimately involved with such transformations. They were invited—or came without being invited when it came to that—to the birth of a child or to their naming. They also were said to appear to warn of impending death, either that of the person who saw them or the death of a member of the family they were affiliated with.

Many today equate the Fey with nature and the Elements, but far less attention is paid regarding their traditional roles relative to birth and death. Yet folklore and fairy tales tell us the part they played in these powerful changes in human life that we all must go through, points that also involve many ritual elements that mark out their importance not just to the individual in question, but to the whole community.

At death, our loved ones pass to the Otherworld and join the ranks of the ancestors, spirits who watch over, guard and guide those who remain in the world of the living. Obviously, they have a vested interest in protecting the family line. They rejoin that line as they choose to be born again, returning to the same blood, to the same familial relationship, the same kindred. So, just as there is a coven spirit, a clan spirit, there is a family spirit of each bloodline, and this family spirit can also take on a consciousness of its own over time. This consciousness resides over the destiny of the family, guides and protects it.

As a death here is a birth in the Otherworld, so each one who passes away is welcomed by the family on the other side. We "come home," joining with our loved ones in the realm of death, just as we are born back to those same loved ones once we come back to the world of life. Accordingly, a birth in the material realm marks a "death" in the spirit realm. Thus, we are our own ancestors, our own descendants. We return again and again to those we love and who love us.

When a witch dies, we become one of the Fey. It's as simple as that. We go to reside in the realm of Faery, there to continue the work of the Great Family in a different plane and state of being. As the Great Family exists on both sides of the veil, the Fey are called to attend to the gates of birth and of death as they, as we, pass from one side to the other.

Despite the natural fear of death, those who pass beyond the veil while in life, who jump the Hedge and return from the Otherworld, who know Faery, can overcome this fear through that knowledge. You do not have to hope that there is a life after death, for you know that there is. Belief is not needed when you have direct and intimate knowledge of what happens once the last breath fades and is lost, when the spark fades out from someone's eyes.

While, in the old days, your birth family was the same as your spirit family, your witch family, now, we are often born to those who have little or no knowledge of the power in the blood. We are born to those who often would deny it or condemn it if they did know. So, we seek out our spirit kindred as they are born to other families, other lines. We seek to awaken the knowledge in our blood, and so reclaim our Fey family, our witch clan. We know them when we meet them—the people who we feel an immediate kinship with, who we feel we have known them forever.

What this means is that, when we die, our ancestors are two-fold—
our blood family and our family of the blood. This makes it more
complicated for we can be met by both, so long as there is love and
understanding.

For example, I fully expect my grandparents to be there for me, yet they
were not witches and would have looked askance, or worse, at such an
idea. My one grandmother was a very devout Catholic who believed
in evil and the Devil and would put witches and the Craft in the same
category. How can I expect her to welcome me on the other side? Yet
love overcomes and enlightens and so long as she loves me and I love her,
once in the realm of the dead, restrictive beliefs fall away as our understanding of the universe and of ourselves is deepened and expanded. She
will remain her true self, but all of the dogma she learned and adhered
to out of fear will have gone, for the closed-mindedness of her strict, religious upbringing often clashed with her kindness and her love of nature
and growing things.

It's quite possible, though, that it will turn out that one of my distant rel-
atives may have been a witch, despite not calling themselves that, as there
are family stories of ancestors seeing spirits and even one great-grand-
mother claiming that the other one was a witch. Or they might have
been a witch in a past life, just as I know I have been. We aren't always
awakened to the potential in our blood in each life. It might also be that I
will discover that a relation was a witch, but never knew it themselves or
never really talked about it.

I can very well believe that my grandfather could have been a witch
either in this life or a past one. There was just something about him, in
how he viewed the world, a hint of the tricksy nature of Fey. I believe he
certainly had the potential to be a witch and may even have practiced
certain magicks in secret, but didn't call what he did magick or think to
talk about it. Certainly, now that he has passed, I feel that he is watching
over me with a wicked twinkle in his eye and I can feel his power around
me when I need it and call on him; power that I only occasionally sensed
while he was alive.

What this means is that, just because our family of birth doesn't seem
to have witches popping out all over, doesn't mean that they aren't there

or that the potential isn't in their blood. It doesn't mean that they are waiting on the other side to chastise us for practicing witchcraft or for worshiping Pagan gods. When we pass through the veil, the greater story is revealed, and we know not just ourselves, but our loved ones. We can even find out that those we choose as family, those of our circles, of our covens, our magical associates, are also part of the same family, having been born elsewhere than within the same bloodline.

Through all this, the Fey are intimately involved with us, with our dying, our birth, our lives as we pass back and forth through each gate. Many cultures have stories of Fey who attend the birth of a child or, in some cases, the ceremony where they are named, names being a very important part of who someone is and will become. Magickally, knowing someone's true name, even the true name of a god or goddess, gives you power over them. If you are named in the Christian faith, then you belong to that faith, while if you are named in the Craft, then you belong to the Craft which is why, if you were raised to be one and then became a witch, you were given a new name. You became a new person.

To have the Fey at a birth or naming is not only an acknowledgment of them for the new life, but they can grant blessings or divine the future of the child. In fact, the Fey association with the birth and naming of a child is so important and ancient that, in later times, it became linked to the idea of the Fey being invited to the Christening of a new child. It's an odd idea to think of the Fey being invited to what is, essentially, a Christian ceremony where your parents and godparents declare they will raise you to be a good Christian and disavow the Devil on your behalf. It's very likely that this shows how old ideas and new ones became interwoven so that both Pagan and Christian rituals would both be honored at the same time, something that was actually fairly common.

Hand in hand with that, we also get the famous *Fairy Godmother*, a figure we find in many fairy tales and in books and movies today. The image of the Fairy Godmother—beautiful, glittering, often with wings and bearing a sparkling starry wand—is actually fairly recent, owing much to the works of the French fairytale writer, Charles Perrault. He gave us one of the versions of "Cinderella" in 1697 that included a Fairy Godmother, and it was also Perrault who added the Fairy Godmothers to the "Sleeping Beauty" story.

We can see clues as to where this idea came from in the Brothers Grimm version of "Cinderella," called "Ashenputtel," for it wasn't a Fairy God-mother in their story that helped the girl but the tree that had been planted over her mother's grave. As the ancestors are said to reside in trees, it was her mother's spirit who was now helping her. In this way, it *was* a Fairy Godmother who was helping Cinderella, but in the aspect of a familial spirit. We can also see reflections of this in the Christian belief in a guardian angel, who looks after you from birth to death.

In the "Sleeping Beauty" fairytale, the king and queen invite the local Fey to the christening of their lovely baby daughter and, clearly, these are the traditional birth Fey. There are different versions of the story of how many Fey are invited, but generally, it is 3 or 7 or 13. The point is that one of the Fey is overlooked or insulted in some fashion by a lack of courtesy or gifts and rather than giving good blessings to the child such as grace or beauty, she curses the child to one day prick herself on a spindle and die. In another version, she is meant to prick herself on a sharp piece of flax, also related to spinning.

In folklore, these birth Fey were said to show up on the third night after a child had been born, there to bestow what they would. Of course, the family of the child would prefer if this consisted of all good things and useful gifts. Attempts were made to court and please them by welcom-ing them and offerings were set out on a special table. Clearly, "Sleeping Beauty," tells us what might result if these offerings are not pleasing to the Fey.

Baltic folklore gives us Fey called the *Fati* or *Fatit* who appear three days after a child has been born to bestow their destiny. All of these stories about the Fey showing up to bestow gifts, to bless, or to dictate the destiny of a newborn child show us how closely they are tied to the idea of Fate. Unsurprisingly, the Fey who appear at the birth of a child as representatives of Dame Fate are also sometimes called Fates or *Fata*. After all, it's from the word *fata* or *fatum* that we get the word for Fey via the French word *fee*.

Other Baltic folklore gives us Fey called the *Laimos* who are tied to the birth of children. Akin to the Fates, they are also related to spinning and weaving and appear in threes. Unsurprisingly, the Laimos are followers of a goddess of Fate named Laima. Like most Fate goddesses, Laima can bless or curse, provide prosperity and fertility or sorrow and misfortune. She's deeply involved with new babies, from how they will be born, to their eventual death, to the life they will have between the two. Offerings were made to honor Her and to try to persuade Her to bestow a good outcome for the birth for both mother and child. Lithuanian folklore has a similar spirit entity called the *Laima* or *Laime*, also related to fate and the destiny of a new child.

In addition, we also have the Greek Moirae and the Norse Norns, other goddesses or powerful spirits of Fate. The Fates are said to weave our lives, and when they appear in threes, one is often said to spin it, one to measure it, and one to cut it or one is said to wrap the thread around the spindle, one to spin it, and one to snip it off in the end. The Fates traditionally have power over all, even over the Gods, and it's hardly coincidental that there are so many witch and Faery goddesses tied to spinning and spinning magick.

Such goddesses include Mother Holle and the Basque great goddess, Mari. The ancient Romans had a Fate goddess by the name Necessitas because the idea of Fate is that which is unchangeable, what is necessary to happen. The Greeks had the goddess, Ananke, who represented destiny, depicted as holding a starry spindle. She could also be seen as the *Serpent of Eternity* intertwining with the *Serpent of Time*, thus forming the familiar symbol of the caduceus, an image attached to healing down through the centuries. This is akin to the symbol of the serpent and the rainbow that is intertwined on the *poteau mitan* of Voudoun, the bridge between worlds along which the spirits travel.

The Fey attend the birth or naming of a child due to their interest in the family, as one of the family, or in their role as a messenger of Dame Fate. We honor all these aspects when we ask them to grant their blessings and protection for a child or to bestow boons for the child's life such as abilities to heal and to do magick, give good fortune, prosperity, charm, beauty, powers of vision, and even actual physical gifts. They can also divine the life purpose of the child and lend guidance to achieve those ends.

Not that the Fey have the power to control that fate, but they can sometimes mitigate aspects of destiny and give foresight into problems or questions that a child may face. Even Fairy Godmothers in the stories, despite all their magickal powers, could not fix everything. They relied on the godchild making their own choices and taking risks as needed. Cinderella was given the ability to get to the ball, but what she did there was on her. So the Fey can offer gifts and lend insight but do not take away our inherent right of choice. Of course, the best choices are made when we have the knowledge to make them, and here our Fey-others and our own ancestral wisdom, once awakened, become vital.

In modern times, it can be more problematic to lay out offerings to the Fey as it used to be done. Of course, the Fey can be invited to the birth of a child to help protect both mother and baby as, even today, a birth can be difficult and even result in death. Certainly, if the mother has a strong link to her Fey-other, they should be called upon to attend, as well as the Fey who is meant for the child about to be born. We might not be able to set up a large offering table to the Fey and perform a ritual to invite them to attend as was done in the past, at least in most situations that involve a hospital—though some of that is changing—but, certainly, a small plate and cup can be set out with small gifts of food, flowers, along with a small glass of milk or cream.

If this is simply not possible, the Fey can still be invited to the naming of a child and the traditional offering table laid out for them there. You can choose to name the child legally, hold a non-pagan gathering for friends or family who aren't in the Craft and wouldn't understand, and then present the child in a ritual context and give them their name when they are presented to the guides and guardians of the group and of the family. That way, everyone can be involved and join with you in welcoming the new baby.

For a ritual naming, a special plate and cup should be chosen, preferably one that has been used before in a sacred family context. If you don't have such a plate and cup, then this will be the first time it should be used, and you can then keep it, either for the child to use when they are older for offerings, or it can be kept and re-used to welcome each new child to the family. This then can become your coven or family offering cup and plate, one that each member has been welcomed with.

Another aspect of welcoming a child to the Craft is the choice by the parents of those who can be spiritual guardians and teachers and guides. In a Christian context, this is, of course, members of the family or close friends who the parents choose to be the baby's godparents and who stand with the parents as the child is baptized. In this case, however, the two people are to be the child's "Fairy Godparents" in a way.

A set of Fairy Godparents can be called upon to help guide the child in the unfolding of their destiny. At least, this is what they should strive for when they take up the task. This requires a combination of the ability to be deeply involved with the child and yet to be able to "step aside" in those affections in order to see best what it is they need. They also should be able to tap into their own Fey-other to have that vision at hand in order to see, as much as is possible, what Mother Fate has laid out for the child in question. If the child later decides to join the Craft, one or both of these Fairy Godparents can then serve to sponsor them.

It's also not a coincidence that witches and the Fey are traditionally linked to the practice of midwifery, to the birth of new life and to the passage beyond. For in the past, midwives weren't there just to aid in the birth of a child, but also to mediate and ease in death.

Midwives of old were said to be able to bestow blessings of fertility, to protect against unwanted pregnancy, and interact with the spirits on behalf of mother and child and to protect them during this dangerous and often deadly transition. This goes back to the classical world where midwives and witches were said to be able to cause abortions via herbs or spells. These same abilities are part of what brought midwives under accusation in the past as being witches for their gift of being able to grant fertility or take it away. Midwives and witches of the past were blamed for the death of children, specifically of killing the baby after they were born or even before they were born as an offering to "Satan" and this has continued into today in stories that revolve around Satanism and the accusation of the stealing of and sacrificing of—even the eating of—innocent babies.

Visitations or sightings of some kinds of Fey are also seen as a foreshadowing of death. The most famous example of this is the Banshee, or *Bean Sidhe*, the *Washer at the Ford*, the *White Lady*. The Banshee could appear as lovely or terrifying, as a young woman or an old hag. She often appears near a river, representing the boundary line between one side and another, at the very place where people go to cross over. Often, she is seen washing the clothes of the person who is about to die.

Fey, like the Banshee are not evil of course, but are simply attached to certain families and come to warn that one of their own is about to leave this world for the other. The wailing of the Banshee is one of mourning or *keening*, the shrill vibrating cry that can be found in many cultures as an expression of grief. The Banshee or White Lady is often seen as wearing white or shimmering white, the traditional color associated with death. White has come to symbolize purity and chastity today in the West, echoing the color of the modern wedding dress, but this is a rather recent invention. Whereas, black as the color of death was because of its protective powers against the spirits of the deceased or other spirits who might be attracted to a funeral or grave.

Other death spirits include the Slavic house spirit called a *Kikimara*—a small female figure that could fly and had chicken feet. If you saw her spinning it could mean that someone was about to die. Clearly, this chicken-footed Fey has some kind of link to the goddess of the infamous chicken-footed or goat-footed hut made of bones, Baba Yaga. Baba Yaga is a goddess who also has the power of life and death and fertility and flies around in a mortar and pestle, wearing a necklace of skulls.

There are also death omens in seeing the Faery Dogs or, in Welsh, the *Cyn Annwn*. These Faery dogs belong to the King of Faery and travel with the Wild Hunt along the ghost roads. They are also called the Gabriel Ratchets or the Wish Hounds and are said to be shining white with red-tipped ears. The sound that they make is sorrowful, terrifying, and oddly sounds louder the further away they are and softer as they approach.

Visions of so-called corpse candles or goblin funerals and other pro-cessing spectral funerals were also signs of impending death. The corpse candle has a blue flame and is held by a ghostly figure or merely hangs in the air before you by some invisible means. The goblin funeral would appear as real funeral procession, sometimes with figures in white or black carrying a coffin that contains the spirit of the person about to die.

The procession could also remain invisible and only be heard as it passes. In either case, it might be accompanied or presaged by the sound of a beating drum, and if it passes over a stream or river, clearly emblematic of the boundary of veil, the person can no longer be saved from certain death.

In Ireland, they have the *Black Coach* or *Death Coach*, another spectral death omen. If this supernatural coach is seen to stop by your door, then someone within that house was certainly doomed to die. Some say that the coach is pulled by a team of black, sometimes headless, horses and that the Banshee might even be seen riding within it.

Unfortunately, Western society generally has driven a wedge between the worlds of life and death by adhering to a rather dualistic viewpoint and a modern scientific-rationalistic mentality that refuses to acknowledge for the most part anything that cannot be studied, defined, and hence "proven." Yet as the ages change, so the paradigms are altered to be more holistic, to have a more inclusive perspective and perception. This new paradigm actually hearkens back to the beliefs of the past as much as to the future as it acknowledges that life and death, light and dark, past and future, this world and the Otherworld are part of a unified whole.

We who exist in time flip back and forth from the realm of life and the realm of death, continuing our connection to our loved ones, our family of spirit, our Fey-clan, on both sides of the veil. When we are born to this world, we tend to forget what we knew as one of the Fey, especially as we grow older and society trains us to not believe in such things...but we can seek to tap back into that knowledge as it never really goes away. It exists within us no matter that we might forget it and can always be awakened if we have the will and desire and the courage.

We become aware of the consciousness of the blood, and it becomes aware of us. Many of us carry this potential within us, but it remains just potential unless it is awakened. We may be of the same family as the Fey, part of a Fey-clan, but if we remain unaware of that, we haven't really taken steps to become an active member of that bloodline, of our kindred. But once we have done so, it's like the old stories about people having journeyed into Faery and returned again—once you return, if you return, you are never the same again.

The *River of Blood* is something we need to dare to cross, yet it's also a choice, and once we've made that choice, we can never go back. Still, cross it we must, connect to it, be as one with this, for this is a true initiation. We die to our old lives, our old awareness, and worldview, and are born to a new one. Because it's a transition point into our Fey-clan, into the blood, the Fey are always there, always part of it. Sometimes, they watch and witness and welcome. Sometimes, they take an active role, either through others or in our dreams or mediations, calling us to the Craft, teaching us beneath sacred Faery trees or below the hollow hills of old.

Ritual to Welcome a Child to the Earth

Fairies black, grey, green and white,
You moonshine revelers and shades of night,
You orphan heirs of fixed destiny,
Attend your office and your quality.

-William Shakespeare

This ritual is to acknowledge the birth of a child to the family and to ask the blessings of the Fey.

If family or friends are invited to the ritual who are not understanding of the Craft, then you can do as much of the ritual as they might be comfortable with.

Set up a ritual space in the house where the child will be living. This can be the ritual space that might normally be used, or the living or dining room, whichever is best. Place the altar or table on one side of the room, covered with a cloth, and decorate it with flowers and bright colors. This is the time to get out your good china and silver, especially if there are any that are family heirlooms or have been used for special family occasions down through the years. It's best if the plates and bowls and cups are brightly colored, or they can also be decorated with buds, flowers, ribbons, and bows and so on. Colors and items usually used for baby showers are readily available and more than appropriate.

The cloth for the table or altar should be a new one and can be given to the parents of the child afterward for any rituals that the child will take place in for the future or can even be kept for that child should they decide they wish to practice the art when they are older. The altar can also be decorated with baby items such as rattles and baby spoons, preferably ones that were used in the past by members of the child's family.

Any food or drink offering to be placed on the plates, in the bowls and cups, doesn't need to be too large, for the focus is less actual physical portion size than the good feelings and thoughts behind the offerings.

The food can include cookies, cake, bread, fruit, flowers, eggs, cream, honey, basically all manner of sweet, good things. It's best if the food and drink have been made by the person involved and it is better still if the parents or children's godparents had a hand in preparing it.

No one should eat or drink from the offerings laid out on the table or altar—this food and drink is for the unseen guests, and once the event or ritual is concluded it all should be libated. A feast for the rest of the attendees can take place later.

For this ritual you will need:

- Altar or table for offerings
- Plates, bowls, cups for offerings
- Buds, flowers or ribbons
- New altar cloth
- Food/drink for offering
- Bowl or cauldron of water
- Three candles in candle holders
- Broom or feather fan
- Incense or a sage or ritual spray
- Consecrated water
- Plate and cup/goblet
- Faery cakes

- Heavy whipping cream

No circle is drawn for this ritual

Set three candles on the altar or offering table. Place an empty plate and an empty cup to either side of the three candles.

Set a bowl or cauldron of consecrated water before the candles.

Sweep the space with a small broom or fan.

Have someone sprinkle the space with the consecrated water and take around lit incense or spray the space with incense or sage spray, saying:

> *Spirits of Air be welcome*
> *Spirits of Fire be welcome*
> *Spirits of Water be welcome*
> *Spirits of Earth be welcome*
> *Bless this place*
> *Bless this time*
> *Ancestors*
> *Old Ones*
> *Kindred spirits all*
> *Mother and child make safe*
> *Make well*
> *Make whole*

Have the mother and/or the father light the main candle, or they can do this together.

The child's promised spiritual guardians, the Fey Godparents, each can light the other two candles.

One parent holds the child, and the other holds their hand, palm downwards, over the child's heart, and one or both says:

> *Dear ones*
> *Kindly folk*

> *Here is my (our) child*
> *I (we) ask your blessings*
> *On her (him)*
> *A long life*
> *A happy one*
> *Love and joy*
> *Health and prosperity*
> *In good measure*

Have the godparents lay a hand on the parent's or each of the parent's shoulder and say:

> *We ask your blessings*
> *On this child*
> *As we swear to guide and to guide*
> *To love him (her)*
> *As our own*

Have the parent(s) and the godparents each place a cake on the empty offering plate and pour some cream into the empty offering cup. At this time, each can also promise to make or give or perform some act as an additional offering for the Fey on behalf of the child.

Set the additional offerings on the offering table.

You can, at this point, proceed to a celebration and feast, giving gifts to the child as you would at a regular baby shower.

Guests are welcome to put money into the bowl or cauldron of water during the rest of the celebration, along with a best-wish blessing for the child. The coins should be kept for the child and placed on any altar that they set up when they are older.

Antique or bright shiny coins minted in the same birth year as the child would be a good choice. For example, pretty foreign coins, English shillings, American silver dollars or silver dimes, and so on. The best old coins would be one from a collection that an ancestor might have kept. The coins I inherited from my great uncle mean so much more to me than any actual financial worth they might have because he valued them and I valued him. The focus is not on the monetary value of the actual coins, but on the prosperity and luck that they are meant to represent.

All of the food and drink offerings should be libated later at your Faery tree or altar or in your normal offering spot.

Faery Naming Ritual

Good luck betide thee, son, for at thy birth
The Faery ladies danced upon the hearth
Thy drowsing nurse hath sworn she did them spy
Come tripping to the room where thou didst lie
And, sweetly singing about thy bed,
Strew all their blessings on thy sleeping head.

-"L'Allegro," John Milton

This ritual can be used when the child is a few months older, and you wish to introduce them to the Craft and your guardian spirits and gods. This not only acknowledges the child's connection to your own coven or working group or path, via their parents, other relative or Faery Godparents but recognizes that it is a return from Faery to this world, a return to those who have known and loved this spirit before. It places them under the guardianship of that family, informing the hidden spirits of the child's name in this new life.

For this ritual you will need:

- Normal altar and any ritual tools
- Magickal blade or wand
- Consecrated water
- Small table for offerings
- Coins, ribbons, crystals, charms to be offered
- White cloth for offering table

- Candles for each person
- Red altar candle
- White altar candle
- Black altar candle

Create a circle as usual.

Place the offering table to the North-East of the circle and put the white cloth on it.

Starting in the North, raise your blade or wand, and say:

> *Spirits of the North*
> *Spirits of Earth*
> *Come ye*
> *To this presentation*
> *Of the child of the Art*
> *Be welcome*

All can repeat:

> *Be welcome*

Go to the East and do the same, saying:

> *Spirits of the East*
> *Spirits of Air*
> *Come ye*
> *To this presentation*
> *Of the child of the Art*
> *Be welcome*

All repeat:

> *Be welcome*

Proceed to the South and repeat, saying:

Spirits of the South
Spirits of Fire
Come ye
To this presentation
Of the child of the Art
Be welcome

All say:

Be welcome

Finally, go the West, raise your wand or blade and say:

Spirits of the West
Spirits of Water
Come ye
To this presentation
Of the child of the Art
Be welcome

All repeat:

Be welcome

All stand in the circle while the priest or priestess or chosen person says:

We gather together to bid welcome
To one whom we have known before
To one whom we have loved before
And who has known and loved us in turn
We welcome our (brother) (sister) in spirit
Who dared traverse the Veil
All to be reborn to flesh

The parents and chosen Faery Godparents then should each lay their hands on the child at the same time, and each say:

I (circle name or real name)

> *Swear to witness and guard*
> *This child of the Craft*
> *Beloved of the Gods*
> *And of the Great Family*
> *All then say:*
> *Spirits of Earth*
> *Spirits of Air*
> *Spirits of Fire*
> *Spirits of Water*
> *Shining Ones of the Blessed Realm*
> *Ancestors*
> *Old Ones*
> *We present (child's name) (or child's ritual name-to-be)*
> *Bless and protect (him) (her)*
> *By and for and in Love*
> *Which is the greatest power of all*

A drop of the consecrated water should be touched to the baby's forehead and the symbol of an equal-armed cross made.

One of the parents or Faery Godparents says:

> *For life*
> *For luck*
> *For health*
> *For wealth*

The other parent or Faery Godparent takes a drop of the consecrated water and draws a circle around where the cross was traced.

The other parent or Faery Godparent says:

> *To keep thee*
> *To shield thee*
> *To surround thee*
> *And sain thee*

Light the red candle on the altar, saying:

To keep thee

Light the black candle on the altar, saying:

To shield thee

Light the white candle on the altar, saying:

To surround and sain thee

All should then light their own candles from the white candle, taking turns to give words of welcome for the child.

All in the circle stand around the child and raise up their candles, saying:

> *We welcome thee with love*
> *The greatest power and gift of all*
> *Be thou filled*
> *With the virtue of the Old Ones*
> *There be grief*
> *And here rejoicing*
> *A new star rises*
> *In the earthly realm*
> *We welcome our loved one*
> *For they are our own (brother)(sister)*

The parents and others who have agreed to the honor of raising the child and who will pledge guardianship of them should put their good wishes and energy into coins, ribbons, stones, charms and place these offerings on the altar. The items can later be put into a small bag for the child and can be hung up in their room and given to them when they are older to be used for their own altar if desired.

With the parent's approval, all in the circle can pass the child sunwise while each one who holds the child briefly and bestows a good wish for them or one of the parents can carry the child around the circle. Traditionally, any good wishes are best done in rhyme and should be written by the person in question.

All can then share food and drink in circle or close the circle and feast together afterward.

Ritual of Remembrance of One Who Has Passed Beyond

"We sing. They spin. What is magick if not this? You, you dance. That is your magick. When you sing, when you spin, when you dance, you call upon great powers, old powers, so old they have no name. Powers older than those you call Gods. That, that is the secret. The pattern is older than the Gods. Follow the pattern..."

-The Fey

These days it's difficult, if not impossible, to stand a death vigil. Our modern wake isn't quite the same thing as we generally can't stay up all night with the body of our loved one. In the past, a wake was held in the home so friends and family could remain with them, a true wake. However, that doesn't mean that we can't honor and celebrate the remembrance of those who have passed beyond in our own way. Thus, even as we grieve, which is perfectly natural, we can acknowledge that he or she we have loved can never be lost from that love, from us, especially since they have gone to be with our own kind. They leave us, yet they don't leave us.

If your family or the family of the person who has died won't understand or approve, you can still attend the normal wake and funeral and then hold your own ritual later.

For this ritual, choose a taper candle to represent the person. If they were part of your coven or working group and had a symbol related to them, or a token that was theirs, you can use this. The symbol may be drawn or carved into the candle, or a small charm can be tied to it with a piece of red thread. For example, if the loved one's totem is a wolf, then a small wolf token or wolf charm can be attached to the candle. The person's name can also be carved or drawn on the candle or on a piece of ribbon to be wound around the bottom of the candle.

As for the color of the candle, some might automatically reach for a black candle—the color black, of course, being associated with grief and death in much of the Western world—but despite our grief, this is also a recognition of their passage to the Otherworld, to Faery, to the *Land of Youth*. A white candle, then, is actually a good choice as the old color of death and of the spirit, or a green candle for the color of Faery. But if the person in question had a favorite color, one that makes you think of them, then this might be the best choice.

The altar can be decorated with objects and images that represent the person who has died, including their interests and contributions to the world. For example, if the loved one enjoyed painting or knitting or cave-exploring, paintbrushes or knitting needles or a flashlight can be placed on or around the altar. In addition, any gifts that the person gave you that meant a lot to you can be brought and either placed on the altar or around it, as gifts create and represent bonds. Of course, a photo of the person is a good choice to add to the altar.

For this ritual you will need:

- Representative candle
- Consecrated water
- Mirror
- Six votive or tea light candles
- Candleholder
- Flowers enough for all participants
- Food and drink for a shared feast

Create the circle as usual.

Clear the altar of everything and lay the mirror in the center.

Place the votive candles or tea lights around the mirror and set any token items or images on the altar around it.

Take the candle meant to represent the person and consecrated water
and draw an equal-armed cross on it, then draw a circle around that.

Have one person or all say:

> *In joy*
> *In peace*
> *In truth*
> *In love*
> *By all that is good*
> *Be thou freed*
> *Be thou found*
> *Be thou blessed and sained*
> *Surrounded by the grace and beauty*
> *Of the Old Ones*

Take the candle and light it.

Pass the lit candle around the circle widdershins. As each person holds it,
they should express a memory of the person, if possible in rhyme or song,
or they can simply remember them silently.

Place the candle in a candle holder and set the candle holder in the center
of the mirror.

Hand around the flowers so that everyone can take one or three blooms.

A chosen person says:

> *(Loved One's Name)*
> *Sleep this night*
> *In the arms of the Mother*
> *Be thee consoled*
> *In the arms of the Father*
> *Away with sorrow*
> *Away with pain*
> *Joy and grace and comfort*
> *Be thine*

The peace of the land beyond
The home of autumn
Of spring and of summer
Where the stars shine eternal
There to remain
Till light and dawn
Shall come again

Light the votive candles or tea lights. One person can do this or people can share in lighting them.

All then say:

Here be grief
And there rejoicing
A new star rises in the realm of Faery
The ever-young
Make welcome our loved one
For they are your own (brother)(sister)

Each person can step forward to lay their flowers on the altar, saying:

Make welcome

All then sit down to feast together.

During this time, its good to share memories and stories of the person who has passed beyond the veil, especially if that person helped or guided you in any way if they had an impact on your life or the lives of others that you know about. You can speak about their accomplishments, what they leave behind, what you loved and appreciated about them. This is a time of sadness, of grief, but it can also be a time of shared love, of thankfulness, of acknowledgment of what that person meant to you and how you know that you will be with them again in Faery and in another life.

~ *Twilight's Call* ~

When day is past, shadows they laugh
From sacred lake and mound and grove
Harlequin called, ruthless and bold
The world they will fly, they who know

Beneath the horns of crown and moon
The two lands stand close, still and lone
Til through the Veil the ancient wail
Yearning for life, for blood and bone

Will 'o the wisp and horn resounding
Hallow the night on a milk-white steed
Will you flee or will you follow
This restless dream
The Wild Hunt

Truth and terror spring from the barrow
Course the hounds of howling night
Dread Queen of Air, the winds Her hair
With He who rides the edge of sight

Pale, thin, dark-eyed, the rushing tide
Pass betwixt the earth and sky
Few dare perceive this blackest eve
Who may live, who's doomed to die

Those who shudder oh build your pyre
And pray for the return of light
Hard on the scent, they'll not relent
In twilight's call, the furious flight

But those who dare the maddening fare

Through field and wood to chase the beast
Will break their fast, gather home at last
Wine and bread, the changeling feast

Will 'o the wisp and horn resounding
Hallow the night on a soot-black steed
Will you flee or will you follow
This restless dream
The Wild Hunt

Conclusion

"You ask—who are we? Why not ask instead—who are you? To know us is to know yourselves. We are as you, of you, yet not. You are of us, of us, yet not. To know this, truly, within the depths of your heart is what binds us as one. The same holds true for those you name Ancestors. They are as you, of you, yet not, for their time is not now. You are as them, of them, yet not, for your time is not their time. Yet, within, the oneness of the heart, their time and your time be only illusion.

What is this oneness? It is that which binds all together, and only forgetfulness of this can render separation, loneliness, loss, grief, and fear...you cannot hold these sorrows in your heart if your heart is full. That it can ever truly be empty is also illusion, is forgetful, is the willful delusion fostered by those who desire power over the things of the heart, who promise they and only they can fill such an emptiness.

Do not believe them. They lie. Do not fill the cup of your heart with false cheer. Open to the everlasting oneness and it will never empty."

-The Fey

At this time, we are in the midst of a great transformation, one that some resist and that some embrace. Witches and the Fey play an intrinsic and powerful role in this transformation; just as we have played our part in many transformations over the ages. In this, we must both participate in and remain separate from it at the same time, for we must remain true to the bones that are the foundation for each age, even as it rises like a phoenix, like a winged serpent, from the ashes of the old. Thus, it is equally important for us to join in fully in order to remain relevant, even ahead of the curve, to be torchbearers for what is coming, yet not lose the connection to the ancient beliefs, to the ancestral thread, to the light that casts the shadows of passing ages.

The current transformation finds expression in many ways, including the fantasy stories that talk about the return of Faery, the return of magick. This can be a bit misleading as it's not so much a return per se, but a remembrance of something that the beliefs of the last 2000 years or so have driven underground. Our ancestors knew that the world we see with our eyes is not the only world that exists, and that we are not alone in it. This ancestral understanding is returning to us, and so we begin to see as they saw, including sensing conscious powers and spirits around us, how all things, all creatures, are part of a living greater whole, and that our western concepts of time, healing, even reality itself, are limited.

It's not a surprise that witchcraft is coming further and further out of the broom closet or that there is such a renewed fascination with the super-natural, even in certain Christian churches. It's no coincidence that there is also a rise in fundamentalist, even extremist, groups who continue to adhere to the Piscean paradigm, clinging to the past tooth and nail and refusing to move on. In fact, they would rather, in some cases, see the world come to an end than accept the changes we are undergoing.

What form will the Craft and Faery appear in as the Aquarian paradigm takes hold? Well, that remains to be seen as we are only in the beginning stages of the transition. But it will certainly not be the dualism of the Piscean Age—a good versus evil mentality that expresses itself in a heaven (for the good) and a hell (for the evil) and an ultimate battle between the two that will end time. For one thing, time is not about to end, for the Progression of the Equinoxes continues and, thousands of years from now, Aquarius will give way to another paradigm, another age.

As witches, as the Fey, as members of the Great Family that spans life and death and all of time, we have passed through many such changes and know it is as much a beginning as an ending. We have served those changes, just as we must serve this one, whether alive or dead. In fact, some of us return to the world of the living at just such times in order to facilitate the change of the ages. We become a force to end the old or to lay the foundation for the new, each according to need and to our own disposition.

Accordingly, those of us who are here now are either protecting and planting the seeds of the future of the coming time, or we are engaged in tearing up the old, burning it down to soot and ashes and fertile earth.

Whether we are a solitary witch or the member of a coven, we share this destiny with our Fey kindred and walk this path with them, close and closer than any human companion could ever really be. They are our true "soul mates," our spirits intertwined with their spirits as we tap into Truth and work needful magick. We have been on this journey with them since the beginning, through countless challenges, and we will continue on with them through countless more. Our covenant is eternal, bridging across worlds, life, and death no hindrance, only lack of remembrance.

The Fey have not forgotten us, nor could they. Forgetfulness is not part of their nature. It is part of our nature to forget, part of the bargain we make in order to be born to this world, to the realm of physical reality. When we remember the Fey, we remember being one with the Fey, becoming one again with our own spirits and with the greater spirit that we are all a part of. With remembrance comes knowledge and power, the better to act in the material world that we choose to come to. But where some simply seek knowledge and power for themselves, Faery knowledge is for those who want to guide, to guard, to heal, and to rejoice.

For a true mystery cannot truly be told, but only known. All that the Fey know they cannot impart, even if they would desire to do so. The knowledge of the Fey, just as the knowledge that lies in the fire, the blood of the witch, must be imparted in its proper time, its proper place, and to the one to whom need requires it be made known. The Fey can impart knowledge directly, pouring it into your mind and heart and body through the pathway of your spirit linked to theirs, but you still must be open to receiving it. After which, you must then find a means to understand that knowledge, that *gnosis,* to the best of your ability and make good and true use of it.

The Fey are here to help guide our destiny, the unfolding of our spiritual and physical evolution. We are not alone. We don't have to do this alone. We need Faery and Faery needs us.

Together, we gather and we dance at the crossroads of forever, casting shadows, casting light, making patterns. Each circle we cast is a piece of Faery, and the more we know that, the more we know them, and how what is between can reflect in many ways, many places, many times. The *Elder Children* have much to teach us, yet we have something they do not. We have the flame of the stars within us. We bear the fire of creation, a beautiful and terrible gift. Faery is ever drawn to that flame.

As witches, we are equally drawn to Faery. Some part of us knows our own, and we return to them again and again. It is our heritage. Life after life, death after death, we are drawn together, as a coven, as a family, as a clan, and we join in the consciousness of that, the destiny. We evolve together, as one and as many, part of the on-going story of the Earth. For we and our Fey kindred have been through this time and again. We are intimates of trial and tribulation and transmutation, with the ancient Fey-witch powers over life, death, and rebirth that we are not only able to bring to bear but are compelled to.

We face it with one foot here and one foot there, awakening memory and, with it, power and understanding. The closer we can grow to our Fey-other, the more we can take a conscious and active role in the charge of our Fey-clan. For we are the physical representations of that clan in the material world and we not only need to know that deep down, bone-deep but act out of it, with honor and truth and passion and compassion.

In joy and with purpose, we dance and sing, and spin and magick is the result, witch magick, and Fey magick. We work upon the threads of the tapestry, with the very strands of the Web of Wyrd.

The realm of Faery is all around us if only we have eyes to see it. On occasion, we do see it, and we always seek to know it more deeply. We yearn to journey there in our rituals, in our magicks, in our dreams. On rare occasion, we physically wander into Faery. For most people, this is a strange place that they quickly seek to forget. We seek to know it more deeply.

Together, we are part of the evolving story, the spiritual undertaking of this world. We have our other with us, the one who knows us best... and loves us supremely just for who we are. Our Faery-wives, our

Faery-husbands, they stand with us, no matter where we go and what we do. They are our shadow, just as we are theirs. We are their light, just as they are ours. Together, we make up a greater whole.

We don't have to do it alone.
We don't do it alone.
We face it with those who we love and who love us.
For we are all children of Elfhame.

Basic Faery Ritual

"When you wear green, you honor us. You remember us, we who are the green wood, the Faery tree, the thorn and the hedge, the mossy stone of promise. Not all that falls from the sky is black. Green has always been promise. Blue is Witchfire and green is ours. Together, they make the blue-green star, the peacock boon, the lord of dawn and day, the crown, the halo, the brightest of all lights visible within the world."

-The Fey

This ritual can be done as part of your normal rituals or on special occasions. Certainly, the two best times to do it are on May Eve and All Hallow's Eve.

For the ritual you will need:

- Mirror
- Skull or skull emblem
- Red wine or other Faery drink
- White rose
- Red rose
- Red cord or ribbon
- Cauldron or bowl to hold water
- Consecrated water
- Cup or goblet
- Plate
- Faery cakes, enough for all, plus one extra
- Green altar cloth if desired

If this is the first time you are doing this ritual, also have on hand for each person a red cord or thread or ribbon with an amber bead or set of three amber beads knotted on it. It can be long enough to wear around the neck or to be tied on an ankle or wrist, depending on what is desired by each person. The amber beads should be cleansed before use.

Create a circle as usual.

Clear space on the center of the altar and place the mirror in the center.

Set the skull or skull emblem on the mirror and set the candle behind the skull.

Place the red rose and the white rose, stems crossed, before the skull.

Light the candle, saying:

> *Ancestors*
> *Old Ones*
> *Mothers and Fathers of the Beginning*
> *We who are your children*
> *Brothers and sisters*
> *Of wind and fire*
> *Be welcome*

Bind the roses together with red cord or ribbon.

Place the bowl or cauldron before the altar and pour in the water, saying:

> *In the field of roses*
> *Beyond the Veil*
> *Beneath the great tree*
> *That joins all worlds*
> *Lies the well of memory*
> *The source of all we are*
> *And all we may be*

Priest or priestess or chosen person can go up to each person with the amber and tie on their ankle or wrist or place it around their neck. If this is not the first time you are doing this ritual, each person can put on their amber at this time.

> *So dance to remember*
> *Dance to join together*
> *With our beloved*
> *To be as one*
> *With the Great Family*
> *As of old*

Take turns holding the roses and dipping them in the water to sprinkle all as they dance past. Use a song or chant as desired. Otherwise, sharing in laughter is more than appropriate.

At the proper time, all should drop down and touch the altar, concentrating on the mirror and the skull, emblem of the gate to Faery and of the ancestors.

Place the roses back on the altar and place the plate with Faery cakes before the skull. Put the goblet or cup of wine in the center of or by the plate.

All stand and hold out their hands, saying:

> *What we share*
> *Can never be lost*
> *Only forgotten*

Libate some of the wine and a cake, then pass the plate and cup around to all. Feasting can be done at this time when people can choose to share any visions or insights granted by the Fey or ancestors.

When done, all stand and join hands. Hold joined hands out to the altar, saying:

> *To not forget*

Close the circle as usual.

The Faery Oath

Old Ones
I swear to thee
Kindred
I swear to thee
Brethren
I swear to thee
I shall ever heed the call
From first breath unto last
From the heart of the bone
Wherein blooms the flame of love
Beneath the sign of the rose
I swear to thee
To be to know to do to dare
One among four that are one
In Fate

"*A Witch is never a Witch alone, even if they aren't in a coven. Together, with our spirits, we can seek the dream that beckons us to go into the darkness of the unknown. To undertake the journey in the company of our loved ones and in so doing, raise up an ever-greater inner flame. This very flame then calls to us even greater spirits, even greater gods. You need not see yourself as a solitary Witch so long as you have your familiars, no matter what form they take.*"

-Excerpt from Sorgitzak II: Dancing the Blood -Pendraig Publishing, 2013

About the Author

Veronica has been practicing magick since before she had even heard of paganism. Even as a young child she set up a stone altar with a pig's skull and used one of its teeth as a protective amulet. She also wrote poems to the moon as her mother and practiced calling the wind. She felt spirits around her, though she did not know until many years later that it was the Fey who had always been with her. The Gods and Goddesses of the Sorgitzak path showed up during a ritual on All Hallow's Eve a good 25 years ago, including the Goddess of the Fey. Veronica has been dedicated to both Her and to the Fey ever since.

Besides non-fiction, she also writes fantasy and erotic fiction, poetry, and does pen-and-ink drawings. She would love to publish a book of art and poetry someday, as well as take a trip to the Black Forest region of Germany.

Other Books by Veronica Cummer

Sorgitak: Old Forest Craft. *2008 Pendraig Publishing*

Sorgitak II: Dancing the Blood. *2013 Pendraig Publishing*

Masks of the Muse. *2009 Pendraig Publishing*

To Fly by Night: The Craft of the Hedgewitch. *2010 Pendraig Publishing.*

HELGA HEDGEWALKER

Cover artist, Helga Hedgewalker, is a visionary artist, Gardnerian High Priestess and Witch with decades of professional experience in print design, illustration, book design, package design, web graphics and advertising. She is a founding member of the *Minneapolis Collective of Pagan Artists*, and co-owner of *The Spirit Parlour*: a shop and blog of Magic, Mysticism and Spirituality, which can be found at **SpiritParlour.com**

In her spare time, Helga works in large-scale painting, digital collage, costuming and designing coloring books, including her most recent: **"Color a Magick Spell: 26 Picture Spells to Color & Manifest"**, co-created with Estelle Daniels. It is available from **SpiritParlour.com** or your favorite book vendor.

She also loves creating ritual tools, making seasonal crafts, and swimming. Someday she plans to become a mermaid and swim far away...

You can see more of her art at **HelgaHedgewalker.com**